TRANSACTION COST ECONOMICS

Transaction Cost Economics

Recent Developments

Edited by

Claude Menard

Professor of Economics,
University of Paris (Panthéon–Sorbonne)
and Director of ATOM (Centre for
Analytical Theory of Organizations and Markets),
University of Paris (Panthéon–Sorbonne)

Edward Elgar
Cheltenham, UK • Brookfield, US

© Claude Menard 1997

Published by
Edward Elgar Publishing Limited
8 Lansdown Place
Cheltenham
Glos GL50 2HU
UK

Edward Elgar Publishing Company
Old Post Road
Brookfield
Vermont 05036
US

A catalogue record for this book is available from the British Library

Library of Congress Cataloging-in-Publication Data
Transaction cost economics: recent developments/edited by Claude Menard.
    Includes bibliographical references.
    1. Transaction costs—Congresses.   I. Menard, Claude, 1944–   .
HB846.3.T73   1996
338.5'1—dc20   96–26476
                                                                         CIP

ISBN 1 85898 483 1

Printed and bound in Great Britain by Biddles Limited, Guildford and King's Lynn

Contents

List of figures vii
List of tables ix
List of contributors xi
Preface xiii

1 Hierarchies, markets and power in the economy: an economic
   perspective 1
   Oliver E. Williamson
2 Internal characteristics of formal organizations 30
   Claude Menard
3 Contractual relationships within the firm 59
   Jean-Paul Bouttes and Pascal Hamamdjian
4 Privatization in Russia: what should be a firm? 86
   Paul L. Joskow and Richard Schmalensee
5 Illegal markets and new institutional economics 127
   Margherita Turvani
6 Transaction costs through time 149
   Douglass C. North

Index 161

Figures

1.1   A layer schema   8
2.1   Modalities of internal relationships   38
2.2   Organizational forms in relation to asset specificity   47
4.1   Soviet industrial hierarchy, early 1980s   91

Tables

3.1   Main features of three elementary contracts   72
3.2   Examples of coordination failures   78

Contributors

Jean-Paul Bouttes is lecturer in Economics, Ecole Polytechnique (Paris), and Head of Methodology Department, General Economic Studies, Electricité de France.

Pascal Hamamdjian is Senior Economist at the International Division, Electricité de France.

Paul L. Joskow is Mitsui Professor of Economics and Management, and Head of the Department of Economics, at the Massachusetts Institute of Technology.

Claude Menard is Professor of Economics at the University of Paris (Panthéon–Sorbonne) and Director of ATOM (Centre for Analytical Theory of Organizations and Markets).

Douglass C. North is Professor of Economics at Washington University in St Louis, and the Nobel Prize winner for 1993.

Richard Schmalensee is Professor of Economics at the Massachusetts Institute of Technology.

Margherita Turvani is Professor of Economics at the Dipartimento di Analisi Economia e Sociale del Territorio, at the Istituto Universitario di Architettura di Venezia.

Oliver E. Williamson is Edgar F. Kaiser Professor of Business Administration, Professor of Economics and Professor of Law, at the University of California in Berkeley.

Preface

This book results from a public conference, followed by a workshop, held at the Sorbonne in 1994.* The idea behind both meetings was to explore some important questions on the research agenda of transaction cost economics (TCE). As it should appear by reading the chapters below, two major issues clearly emerged, shared by all the participants: the use of transaction costs to analyse internal properties of large organizations; and the subtle interactions between institutional environment and governance arrangements.

It has long been recognized that transaction costs do matter for understanding the internal nature and characteristics of formal organizations, and particularly of large firms. However, this dimension of the research programme of TCE is much less developed than other aspects. But several avenues have been or can be explored, as shown in some of the following contributions.

Williamson comes back to key concepts of TCE and relates them to the analysis of formal organizations (or 'hierarchies'). Studies of the attributes of transactions in a world of positive transaction costs suggest the existence of discriminating alignments: some transactions will align – for the purpose of efficiency – with one set of governance structures (or 'institutional arrangements', in North's terminology) while other transactions will align with other arrangements. One major consequence of this analysis is the fundamental statement that organizations have 'a life of their own', not that obvious a statement in modern economics. As such, organizations require investigation with adequate economic tools. The argument developed in Williamson's chapter is that TCE already provides us with a set of powerful concepts and instruments, but that they need to be 'dimensionalized', in order to become fully operational.

This is precisely the direction adopted by Menard, and by Bouttes and Hamamdjian, in their respective chapters, both of which investigate some internal characteristics of large organizations, mainly firms.

Menard focuses on the diversity of human assets involved in such organizations: their degree of specificity is viewed as crucial in explaining the nature of the employment relationship, where the variety in the specificity of relevant assets requires diversity of contractual arrangements as well as diversity of hierarchical arrangements. He also argues that the analysis of the specificity of human assets involved can substantially contribute to our understanding of: (i) the configuration of corporations, that is, organizational forms such as U-forms, M-forms, or J-forms; (ii) the trade-off among these configurations; and (iii) their mode of governance, namely, the role of their constituents in their internal government.

Bouttes and Hamamdjian largely complement and substantiate these arguments. Their analysis focuses on contractual arrangements that can be identified within large firms. Using a classification introduced by Williamson in 1985 (and also referred to by Menard), and reexamining the standard literature on contracts, they explore the nature of the firm as a hierarchical system of three different types of contracts, and they show how these contractual arrangements are intertwined. Based on their experience in the management of one large organization, they also argue that an efficient organization is one that implements a hierarchy of these contracts in such a way as to preserve the differentiation of these contracts, in relation to the diversity of human assets, while maintaining the advantages of an integrated structure. Conclusions are drawn about the structure of a firm, the characteristics of its corporate governance, and the role of its constituents. These conclusions are similar to the properties emphasized by Menard.

The second type of problem addressed in the book concerns the subtle interactions between institutional environment and governance arrangements, of which large firms are only a part, in addition to markets and 'hybrid organizational forms'. The chapters by Joskow and Schmalensee, and from Turvani show that the research programme sketched by North is already in progress.

Joskow and Schmalensee propose a detailed analysis of the Russian privatization programme implemented after 1992, in a context where privatization was, and still is, confronted with problems related to inadequate or nonexistent rules of the game. Much of their argument involves links between microanalytic factors and the institutional environment. The microanalytics relates to the structure of Russian industries prior to privatization, with 'enterprises' often identified with monoproduction plants, and with coordination by a central plan that made site specificity a major component of the industrial structure of the country. As a consequence, privatization involved high risks of opportunism and hold-up strategies, two main problems that TCE has emphasized as particularly crucial in a context without appropriate institutional arrangements to implement and enforce adequate contractual arrangements. Their chapter also analyses how these problems were addressed.

Turvani explores a somewhat similar difficulty, although in a very different context. Her analysis focuses on a sector of activity, the narcotic markets, where institutional order is of a very specific type. Because this activity is illegal, the usual institutional environment of a developed market economy cannot provide a positive framework for monitoring transactions. As a result, private ordering prevails. Two major characteristics of this ordering are of particular interest in a TCE perspective: (a) complicity develops as a form of internal control, implementing a de facto hostage relationship, with the ambiguous figure of the customer-dealer at the centre of retail distribution; (b) there is very limited vertical integration, in order to break up the transaction chain so as to circumvent the risks related to the illegal dimension of these markets. Her conclusion is that there is a multiplicity of institutional orders, and that black markets enter into the category of private orders that develop when there is a very small amount of institutionalization that could protect agents and their transactions.

These problems of institutional ordering are at the core of the concluding chapter, by North. The distinction between private and public ordering is substantiated, with examples of the Law Merchant for the former, and of nation states for the latter. North emphasizes the key role of protection and enforcement of property rights in the development of such institutions, a problem at the forefront of Joskow's and Schmalensee's, and Turvani's chapters, but also present in all other contributions. He also examines problems of measurement, particularly when highly specific and interdependent assets are involved, and of enforcement when opportunistic behaviour can develop: these problems find many illustrations in the previous chapters. Last, he provides important indications of the 'marriage' of science and technology, and of its significant consequences for transaction activities as well as for production circumstances, consequences that are too often neglected in transaction cost literature.

Hence, this book deals with some of the most fundamental problems raised by recent literature on transaction costs. All chapters are also strongly oriented towards increasing the operationality of the concepts. They all point to important aspects of the ongoing and rapidly expanding research programme in transaction cost economics.

Note

*   The generous support of the University of Paris I (Panthéon–Sorbonne), through its Scientific Council, is gratefully acknowledged: it made possible the organization of both the conference and the workshop. I would also like to thank for their comments and participation: Marina Bianchi (University of Rome), Olivier Favereau (University of Paris–Nanterre), Jean Michel Glachant (Centre ATOM, University of Paris Panthéon–Sorbonne), Irena Grosfeld (Delta, Ecole Normale Supérieure), Pierre-

Yves Hénin (Scientific Council, University of Paris Panthéon–Sorbonne), Frederic Jenny (Conseil de la Concurrence et des Prix, Ministère des Finances), Maurice Levy-Leboyer (University of Paris–Nanterre), Rudolf Richter (University of Sarrebrucken), and Daniel Vitry (Vice-Chancellor, Universities of Paris). Researchers from ATOM (Centre for the Analytical Theory of Organizations and Markets) generously provided their time and energy and contributed greatly to the success of the two meetings.

Acknowledgements
Permission to reprint the following papers is gratefully acknowledged:

'Privatization in Russia: What Should Be a Firm?', by Paul L. Joskow and Richard Schmalensee was initially published in *International Journal of the Economics of Business*, **2** (2), 1995, pp. 297–327. Reprinted by permission of Carfax Publishing Co., PO Box 25, Abingdon, Oxfordshire OX14 3UE, and 'Hierarchies, Markets and Power in the Economy', by Oliver E. Williamson was initially published in a slightly different version in *Industrial and Corporate Change*, **4** (1), 1995, pp. 21–50. Reprinted by permission of *ICC*, Oxford University Press.

1 Hierarchies, markets and power in the economy: an economic perspective

Oliver E. Williamson

1 Introduction

I address the study of hierarchies, markets and power in the economy from *an* economic perspective – which is different from *the* economic perspective. As matters stand presently, there is not one economic perspective that is pertinent to these issues but many – neoclassical, behavioural, evolutionary, technological, agency theory, transaction cost economics and strategic/game theoretic perspectives being among them. Of these, I appeal mainly to transaction cost economics.

Real differences among these several perspectives notwithstanding, most of these adopt a 'rational spirit' and employ a 'systems approach' to the issues. That, I submit, is *the* economic perspective and is where I begin the discussion. I thereafter shift to the more focused lens of transaction cost economics – which is, by construction, an interdisciplinary approach to economic organization in which law, economics and organization are joined.

The nature and role of hierarchies are briefly discussed in Section 3. Power is the subject of Section 4 and authority is treated in Section 5. Concluding remarks follow in Section 6.

2 The economic perspective

General

As described by Kenneth Arrow, 'An economist by training thinks of himself as the guardian of rationality, the ascriber of rationality to others, and the prescriber of rationality to the social world' (1974, p. 16). Taken in conjunction with the systems approach out of which economics works, this is a very powerful prescription.

To be sure, all of the social sciences have a stake in rationality analysis (Homans, 1958; Simon, 1978). What distinguishes economists is that they push the approach further and more persistently. As it turns out, that has been a productive exercise. Rationality is a deep and pervasive condition that manifests itself in many subtle ways (recall Adam Smith's reference to the 'invisible hand'). It has application to spontaneous

1

and intentional governance alike, which is to say that it applies to organizations of all kinds – markets, hybrids, public and private bureaux. Yet rationality excesses – of which four kinds can be distinguished: oversimplification, maximization, natural selection and hyperrationality – are a chronic hazard.

It is elementary that what may be a fruitful simplification for some purposes can be an egregious oversimplification for others. Thus, although the theory of the firm-as-production-function is a useful construction for examining a wide variety of price and output issues, it is not an all-purpose theory of the firm for purposes of ascertaining firm boundaries (the make-or-buy decision), the nature of the employment relation, the appropriate choice of financial instrument, corporate governance mechanisms, divisionalization and the like. To insist that the production function conception of the firm has universal application is to miss and/or misconstrue much of the relevant organizational action.

The general rational spirit approach is not, however, coterminous with orthodoxy. The response to those who would oversimplify is to insist that problems be addressed on whatever terms are most instructive. Theories of the firm (plural) rather than one, all-purpose theory of the firm (singular) is the appropriate way to proceed. The rational spirit approach does not preclude that there be several side-by-side alternatives out of which to work.

A second criticism of rationality analysis in economics is that many economists and fellow travellers assume that economic agents – consumers, investors, traders – are continuously engaged in maximization. Sometimes that is a poorly defined concept (Simon, 1978; Furubotn and Richter, 1991, pp. 26–8), in which event the exercise loses content; and sometimes maximization is justified not because it is realistic but because it is tractable.[1]

Relevant to this last is Herbert Simon's argument that 'Parsimony recommends that we prefer the postulate that men are reasonable to the postulate that they are supremely rational when either of the two assumptions will do our work of inference as well as the other' (Simon, 1978, p. 8). But while it is easy to agree that satisficing is a less demanding postulate than maximizing, the analytical toolbox out of which satisficing works is, as compared with maximizing apparatus, incomplete and very cumbersome. Thus if one reaches the same outcome through the satisficing postulate as through maximizing, and if the latter is much easier to implement, then economists can be thought of as analytical satisficers: they use a short-cut form of analysis that is simple to implement.[2] Albeit at the expense of realism in assumptions, and at the risk of overapplication, maximization often gets the job done.

The argument, moreover, that human agents lack the wits to maximize can sometimes be salvaged by invoking natural selection (Alchian, 1950; Friedman, 1953). That, however, is subject to the precaution that if selection 'is the basis for our belief in profit maximization, then we should postulate that basis itself and not the profit maximization which it implies in certain circumstances' (Koopmans, 1957, p. 141). Accordingly, we should 'expect profit maximization to be most clearly exhibited in industries where entry is easiest and where the struggle for survival is keenest' (Koopmans, 1957, p. 141).

The efficacy of selection remains controversial (Nelson and Winter, 1982; Barnett and Carroll, 1993) and early resolution does not appear to be in prospect. The following are none the less pertinent:

1. selection pressures are manifold and subtle, especially within the economic domain, where selection operates at and through every contractual interface whatsoever – the most obvious being competition in final product markets and capital markets, but includes intermediate product markets and labour markets as well;
2. real differences between politics and economics notwithstanding, selection on efficiency operates within the political arena as well (Moe, 1990a,b; Stigler, 1992);
3. weak-form rather than strong-form selection often suffices, the distinction being that 'in a relative sense, the *fitter* survive, but there is no reason to suppose that they are *fittest* in any absolute sense' (Simon, 1983, p. 69; emphasis in original); and
4. selection reasoning is widespread throughout the social sciences (Simon, 1962; Hannan and Freeman, 1977, pp. 939–40;[3] Eccles and White, 1988, S24), which is to say that economics is not uniquely culpable.

The outer limits of hyperrationality reasoning are reached by the Arrow–Debreu model of comprehensive contracting, according to which contracts for all goods and services across all future contingencies are made between all agents at the outset. Although the Coase theorem, according to which the assignment of liability one way rather than another has no allocative efficiency consequences, is a partial rather than general equilibrium construction, it similarly assumes zero transaction costs (Coase, 1960). Analyses of both kinds make patently unrealistic assumptions about the cognitive ability of human actors to receive, store, retrieve and process information.

Counterfactuals are often illuminating, however, and there is no disputing that the fictions of comprehensive contracting/zero transaction costs have been productive. One instructive way to proceed is to use the counterfactual to display what an 'ideal' system would accomplish, thereafter to inquire into what factors are responsible for missing markets, in response to which nonmarket forms of organization often arise (Arrow, 1963), and where and why positive transaction costs arise, whereupon assignments of property rights one way rather than another do have efficiency consequences. Note, moreover, that the practice of looking ahead, discerning consequences, and factoring these back into the original organizational design does not require hyperrationality. 'Plausible farsightedness' (Williamson, 1993a, pp. 128–31) will often do – which invites economists and other social scientists to adopt a systems approach in their studies of economic organization.

Systems conception   One of the advantages that Coase ascribes to economics, as compared with the other social sciences, is that economics works out of a systems conception of the issues (Coase, 1978, pp. 209–10):

> The success of economists in moving into the other social sciences is a sign that they possess certain advantages in handling the problems of those disciplines. One is, I believe, that they study the economic system as a unified interdependent system and, therefore, are more likely to uncover the basic interrelationships within a social system than is someone less accustomed to looking at the working of a system as a whole. . . . [The] study of economics makes it difficult to ignore factors which are clearly important and which play a role in all social systems. . . . An economist will not debate whether increased punishment will reduce crime; he will merely try to answer the question, by how much?

Thus even though such an approach may fail to relate to all of the pertinent issues and may even deflect attention from some, a systems conception of the issues often has a good deal to recommend it (Coase, 1978, p. 210).

Pertinent to this last is the question of what are the lessons for the other social sciences? One possibility is that, once the merits are displayed, other social scientists will undergo a conversion and adopt the farsighted contracting/systems approach out of which economics works. Were that to obtain, Coase projects that the advantage of economists in relation to practitioners of the 'contiguous disciplines' will accrue to those with deeper knowledge of the phenomena (Coase, 1978, p. 210; emphasis added):

> [I]f the main advantage which an economist brings to the other social sciences is *simply* a way of looking at the world, it is hard to believe, once

the value of such economic wisdom is recognized, that it will not be acquired by some practitioners in other fields. . . . [In that event] economists who try to work in the other social sciences will have lost their main advantage and will face competitors who know more about the subject matter than they do.

That, however, assumes that those social scientists who are persuaded of the merits of the systems conception out of which economics works will be able easily to internalize it.[4] Thomas Kuhn's remarks are pertinent (1970, p. 204):

> To translate a theory or world view into one's own language is not to make it one's own. For that one must go native, discover that one is thinking and working in, not simply translating out of, a language that was previously foreign . . . [Otherwise] like many who first encountered, say, relativity or quantum mechanics in their middle years, [a scholar] finds himself fully persuaded of the new view . . . [yet is] unable to internalize it. . . . Intellectually such a [person] . . . lacks the constellation of mental sets which future members of the community will acquire through education.

In the event that the systems approach out of which economics works is alien to many purveyors of the other social sciences, then economists and other social scientists will need to learn how to coexist with and complement one another.

Plainly, however, some noneconomists have accomplished the transition – March (1978), Coleman (1990), and the positive political theory movement being examples. Furthermore, some economists have invested heavily in the other social sciences – George Akerlof (1984), Jean Tirole (1986), and many of those associated with the new institutional economics movement being examples. Not everyone, moreover, needs to commit to research of a thoroughly interdisciplinary kind. Provided that specialists are respectful of what each side has to offer, fruitful exchange and collaboration are in prospect (Kreps, 1992).

Transaction cost economics
Transaction cost economics frequently invokes the fiction of zero transaction costs as a device by which to engage a systems view of a problem, thereby better to expose core issues. It immediately thereafter asks, however, wherein do positive transaction costs arise and why? Even more pertinent is to establish when and why differential transaction costs arise between alternative modes of organization. The fiction of zero transaction costs is used thus as an entering wedge and is always and everywhere followed by an insistence on studying the world of positive transaction costs (Coase, 1984, 1992). The latter relieves

excesses of hyperrationality and focuses attention on feasible organizational alternatives.

Note that whereas the fiction of zero transaction costs is thought mainly to apply to the study of property rights, the same fiction can be and has been used to examine organization. The result in both cases, moreover, is similar.

Within the property rights arena, the argument is this: the assignment of property rights has no allocative efficiency consequences because, in a world of zero transaction costs, the parties will bargain costlessly to an efficient solution whichever way property rights are assigned. The corresponding proposition in the organization's arena is that choice of governance structure is of no account – since any advantages that are ascribed to one form can be replicated costlessly by another (Williamson, 1979, p. 233; Hart, 1990, p. 156).

The 'real world', however, is beset by positive transaction costs on which account the assignment of property rights and choice of governance structures do matter. Assuming that positive transaction costs are not so great as to block the assignment of property rights altogether (Demsetz, 1967; Arrow, 1969), then differential transaction costs will warrant the assignment of property rights one way rather than another. Similarly with respect to organization: except where positive transaction costs block the organization of some activities altogether, differential transaction costs will give rise to discriminating alignment – according to which some transactions will (for efficiency purposes) align with one set of governance structures and other transactions will align with others. Without more, however, this last is tautological. It needs to be operationalized, which describes the transaction cost economics project.

The general strategy out of which transaction cost economics works is set out elsewhere (Williamson, 1985, 1991a, 1993a). Crucial features include the following:

1. the transaction is the basic unit of analysis;
2. the critical dimensions with respect to which transactions differ (for transaction cost purposes) are frequency, uncertainty and, especially, asset specificity (this last being a measure of asset redeployability);
3. each generic mode of governance (market, hybrid, private bureau, public bureau) is defined by a syndrome of attributes, whereupon each displays discrete structural differences of both cost and competence;
4. each generic mode of governance is supported by a distinctive form of contract law;
5. predictive content turns on the argument that transactions, which

differ in their attributes, are aligned with governance structures, which differ in their costs and competence, in a discriminating – mainly, transaction cost economizing – way;

6. additional predictive content obtains by treating the institutional environment (political and legal institutions, laws, customs, norms (North, 1991)) as the locus of shift parameters, changes in which induce changes in the costs (and, especially, in the comparative costs) of governance; and

7. transaction cost economics, always and everywhere, is an exercise in comparative institutional analysis – where the relevant comparisons are between feasible alternatives, whence hypothetical ideals are operationally irrelevant and the test for inefficiency is one of remediableness.

Transaction cost economics invites and has been the subject of considerable empirical testing (Joskow, 1988, 1991; Shelanski, 1991; Masten, 1993). Furthermore, it invites comparison with rival and complementary theories of organization in explanatory, predictive and empirical respects.

The three-level schema out of which transaction cost economics works is set out in Figure 1.1. As shown, the institutions of governance (interfirm contracts, corporations, bureaux, nonprofits, and so on) are bracketed by the institutional environment from above and the individual from below. The main effects in this schema are shown by the solid arrows. Secondary effects are drawn as dashed arrows.

The institutional environment   The first of these main effects runs from the institutional environment of governance. Changes in the institutional environment (or, if making international comparisons, differences between institutional environments) are treated as shift parameters, changes (or differences) in which shift the comparative costs of markets, hybrids and hierarchies. Linking the institutional environment to the institutions of governance in this way is the source of numerous refutable implications (Williamson, 1991a). It furthermore permits transaction cost economics to relate more productively to recent research on comparative economic organization in which differences in the institutional environment are featured (Hamilton and Biggart, 1988).

Behavioural assumptions   The behavioural assumptions out of which transaction cost economics works are bounded rationality – behaviour that is intendedly rational, but only limitedly so – and opportunism –

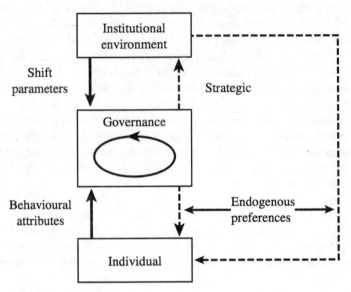

Figure 1.1   A layer schema

which goes beyond simple self-interest seeking to make provision for self-interest seeking with guile. The import of this last is that the potentially adverse effects of simple self-interest seeking could be eliminated costlessly by asking the parties to make self-enforcing promises to behave 'responsibly' (in a joint-profit-maximizing way). That stratagem will not work if parties will renege on promises when it suits their purposes, in which event promises need to be buttressed with credible commitments.

Opportunism is a relatively unflattering behavioural assumption and many understandably prefer to describe self-interestedness in a more benign way – as, for example, 'frailties of motive and reason' (Simon, 1985, p. 303). Experience with the benign tradition in economics reveals, however, that this is fraught with hazard (Coase, 1964; Krueger, 1990; Williamson, 1991b). Robert Michels's concluding remarks about oligarchy are pertinent: 'nothing but a serene and frank examination of the oligarchical dangers of democracy will enable us to minimize these dangers' (1962, p. 370). If a serene and frank reference to opportunism alerts us to avoidable dangers which the more benign reference to frailties of motive and reason would not, then there are real hazards in adopting the more benevolent construction.

Ex post hazards of opportunism arise in a world of long-term, incomplete contracts implemented under uncertainty. Farsighted responses of several kinds can be distinguished. One would be to refuse to engage in such transactions (in favour of shorter and simpler transactions). A second would be to adjudge the price of the complex transaction to reflect the added hazards. A third and deeper response would be to create *ex ante* safeguards (credible commitments), the effects of which are to mitigate opportunism. This last is to be contrasted with Machiavelli, who also subscribed to opportunism but viewed contracting myopically. Thus, whereas Machiavelli advised his Prince to breach contracts with impunity – get them before they get us – transaction cost economics advises the Prince to devise (give and receive) credible commitments. Not only will the latter deter inefficient breach but it encourages investment in productive but otherwise risky assets and supports greater reliance on contract (as against no trade or vertical integration). Farsighted agents who give and receive credible commitments will thus outperform myopic agents who are grasping.

Organization has a life of its own   Organization theorists have long been alert to the existence of the subtle, unintended consequences that attend efforts to exercise control and have scolded economists and others who work out of a 'machine model' in which such effects are ignored (March and Simon, 1958, pp. 34–47). The arrow that turns back on itself in Figure 1.1 is intended to capture the proposition that organizations, like the law, have a life of their own. That is an important proposition and is ignored only at peril.

The existence of such effects demonstrates the need for deep knowledge about organizations, but it does not imply that the economic approach to organization (which easily misses such effects) is fatally flawed. On the contrary, the systems approach out of which economics works can and should make provision for all regularities whatsoever. Once apprised of predictable, recurring, unintended consequences, the informed economist will thereafter factor such effects into the *ex ante* design calculus. Unwanted costs will then be mitigated and unanticipated benefits will be enhanced – which approach exactly tracks the earlier argument on dealing with opportunism.

Because transaction cost economics is a more microanalytic contracting exercise and is more respectful of the discrete structural differences that define and distinguish alternative modes of organization than is economic orthodoxy, transaction cost economics has helped to discern and explicate hitherto neglected contractual regularities. Among the more important of these are fundamental transformation and the impossibility of selective intervention.

The first of these explains when and why a large-numbers bidding competition at the outset is transformed into a small-numbers supply relation during contract execution and at contract renewal intervals. Such a transformation obtains for transactions that are supported by nontrivial durable investments in transaction-specific assets – which investments give rise to a condition of bilateral dependency (on which account identity matters and continuity of the exchange relation is the source of productive value). Classical market contracting – 'sharp in by clear agreement; sharp out by clear performance' (Macneil, 1974, p. 738) – breaks down in these circumstances. The legal rules approach to contract thus gives way to the more elastic concept of contract as framework (Llewellyn, 1931; Macneil, 1978; Speidel, 1993).

The impossibility of selective intervention is the transaction cost economics answer to the query 'Why can't a large firm do everything that a collection of small firms can do and more?'. Were it that a large firm could replicate small-firm performance in all circumstances where small firms do well and intervene always but only where expected net gains from added coordination can be projected, then the large firm can always do as well as the collection of small firms (through replication) and will sometimes do better (through selective intervention). As it turns out, that is an impossible prescription because 'promises' to exercise discretion only with good cause are not self-enforcing. That has several consequences, not the least of which is that incentives are unavoidably degraded when transactions are taken out of markets and organized internally. The upshot is that incentives and controls in firms and markets differ in discrete structural ways.

Other subtle (many of them intertemporal) consequences to which organization theorists have been alerted and that can be subsumed within the systems approach are:

1.   the Iron Law of Oligarchy;[5]
2.   the successive build-up of identity/capability (codes, routines, culture/reputation);[6]
3.   the benefits (such as information disclosure) that sometimes accrue to conflict;[7] and
4.   the intertemporal burdens of bureaucracy.[8]

The issues are discussed elsewhere (Williamson, 1993a, pp. 117–19). Suffice it to observe here that each of these effects takes on added significance when it is examined in a farsighted way – whereupon the ramifications of once unanticipated consequences are expressly introduced into the *ex ante* design calculus. Organization theory thus both informs and is informed by economics.

3   The nature and role of hierarchies
The nature and role of hierarchies have been featured in transaction cost economics from the outset (Coase, 1937; Williamson, 1971, 1975; Alchian and Demsetz, 1972) and is an issue to which I return in Section 5. My purpose here is to examine the alternative forms of hierarchy to which Masahiko Aoki (1990) has recently called to our attention.

Aoki distinguishes between the Western form of hierarchy (what he refers to as the H-form) and the Japanese form of hierarchy (the J-form). He also describes disturbances of three kinds: those that arise in stable, oligopolistic markets that produce standardized products; those that arise in markets where tastes change and/or demands shift rapidly; and those that involve novel technologies in which 'highly uncertain innovations involving new conceptualizations of market potential and highly specialized scientific approaches' are needed (Aoki, 1990, p. 9). Letting C_H and C_J be the cost of H-form and J-form respectively and letting $\Delta = C_J - C_H$, Aoki argues that Δ is positive for disturbances of types one and three, whereupon the H-form enjoys the advantage, but is negative for disturbances of type two, which is where the J-form excels (Aoki, 1990, pp. 3–9).

Aoki makes a plausible case for these assignments, but I would point out that (i) the comparisons refer strictly to equilibrium forms of organization; (ii) the comparison is strictly two-way (J-form versus H-form), which does not exhaust the possibilities; and (iii) type three disturbances are often associated with newly developing markets for which equilibrium concepts of organization are poorly suited. In consideration of all three, I suggest that a third form of organization, the T-form, where T denotes temporary or transitional, be considered.

T also denotes timeliness, which plays a huge role in the success and failure of firms that are operating in newly developing markets where technology and rivalry are undergoing rapid change. Change – being in the right place at the right time – is important in these circumstances, but it bears remark that firms that are flexibly positioned and quickly responsive have the edge. Large, mature and diffusely owned firms are at a disadvantage to smaller, younger and more entrepreneurial (concentrated ownership) firms in these circumstances (Williamson, 1975, pp. 196–207). Also, what may be thought of as 'disequilibrium' forms of organization can be important in real-time responsiveness respects.

Joint ventures and alliances should sometimes be thought of as T-forms of organization that permit the parties to remain players in a fast-moving environment. Each party being unable, by itself, to assemble and deploy the requisite resources in a timely way, the requisite resources are instead assembled by pooling. Thus construed, both successful and unsuccessful joint ventures will commonly be terminated when contracts expire. Successful joint ventures will be terminated because the combined effort has permitted each to remain viable and learn enough and/or buy time to go it alone. Unsuccessful joint ventures will be terminated because the opportunity to participate will have passed them by.

Our understanding of T-forms of organization is not good but is steadily improving (Nelson and Winter, 1982; Dosi, 1988; Teece, 1992; Barnett and Carroll, 1993; Teece et al., 1993). Type three markets and T-form firms and associations require concerted study.

4   Power

Because B is bigger than A, B enjoys a power advantage in the exchange relation between them. Or because A is dependent on B, B has a power advantage over A. Or if A and B were initially on a parity, but a disturbance has occurred that works in B's favour, then parity is upset and B now has more power.

Power is routinely invoked in these and other ways. Being a familiar condition, power is believed to be intuitively obvious and does not require explanation: 'Power may be tricky to define, but it is not that difficult to recognize' (Pfeffer, 1981, p. 3). I submit that there is less to power than meets the eye.

One of the problems with power is that it is a diffuse and vaguely defined concept. Within the commercial arena, the most ambitious effort to define power comes out of the 'barriers to entry' literature (Bain, 1956). That, however, is a deeply flawed exercise because differential efficiency and power are confused (Stigler, 1968). Recasting the issues in terms of strategic behaviour discloses that power is a much narrower concept (Dixit, 1980; Williamson, 1983).

Most discussions of power never identify the critical dimensions on which power differentials work. Instead, they become an exercise in *ex post* rationalization: power is ascribed to that party which, after the fact, appears to enjoy the advantage. Related to this last is the propensity to examine power myopically. If A enjoys the advantage now and B enjoys the advantage then, and if A and B are in a continuing relation with each other, is it really useful to switch power assignments back and forth?

I argue that power has little to contribute to the study of contract and organization in circumstances where the parties to an exchange can and do contract in a relatively farsighted way. Since that varies with the circumstances, the argument is that power has relatively less to offer to the study of capital and intermediate product markets, has more bearing on labour and final product markets and is especially relevant to politics. Even with respect to this last, however, power plays a much more limited role than is widely believed.

The problem of tautology
Ronald Coase has defined a tautology as a concept that is 'clearly right' (1988, p. 19). In a world where confusion is the rule rather than the exception, important insights that help to unpack deep puzzles ought to be celebrated rather than disdained. There is none the less a grave problem with broad, elastic and plausible concepts – of which 'transaction cost' is one and 'power' is another – in that they lend themselves to *ex post* rationalization. Concepts that explain everything explain nothing.

The tautological status of transaction costs in the mid-1970s was described by Stanley Fischer as follows: 'Transaction costs have a well-deserved bad name as a theoretical device . . . [partly] because there is a suspicion that almost anything can be rationalized by invoking suitably specified transaction costs' (1977, p. 322, n. 5). There being too many degrees of freedom after the fact, the pressing need was to delimit the concept of transaction costs, thereby to give it operational (predictive) content before the fact.

John R. Commons (1934) took the first step by proposing that the transaction be made the basic unit of analysis. The question that then needed to be asked and answered was, 'What are the crucial dimensions with respect to which transactions differ?'. Transaction cost economics began to overcome its tautological reputation only on asking and answering that question.

Power will not shed its tautological reputation[9] until a unit of analysis has been named and dimensionalized. Conceivably the transaction is the basic unit of analysis in the power arena as well. If so, that needs to be stated. Whatever the declared unit of analysis, the critical dimensions with respect to which that unit differs in power respects need to be identified. In addition, the analysis of power would benefit by adopting the farsighted systems view described above. Finally, power needs to develop the refutable implications that accrue to this perspective and demonstrate that the data line up.

Power and efficiency
Efficiency plays a larger role in the degree to which parties are assumed to engage in contracting in a voluntary, relatively knowledgeable, and farsighted way. Voluntarism is widely disputed by sociologists (Baron and Hannan, 1994, p. 1116) and biases in decision processes – in dealing, for example, with low-probability events (Kunreuther et al., 1978), but to include probabilistic choice more generally (Tversky and Kahneman, 1974) – raise grave doubts about the competence of human actors to deal with complex events.

The opposites of voluntary, knowledgeable, farsighted contracting – namely, involuntary, uninformed and myopic contracting – are associated with power. Which description applies where and when? As developed below, power has less to contribute to the study of intermediate product markets and capital markets than it has to contribute to labour and final goods markets and to the study of politics.

Intermediate product markets   Resource dependency is one of the two dominant theories of organization (Friedland and Alford, 1991, p. 235), the other being population ecology. Resource dependency is very much a power perspective, the argument being that 'power accrues to those social actors who provided critical resource for the organisation and who cannot be readily replaced in that function' (Pfeffer, 1981, pp. 112–13).

Dependency, of course, is precisely the condition to which asset specificity refers. Given that all complex contracts are incomplete and that promises to behave continuously in a fully cooperative way are not self-enforcing, investments in transaction-specific assets pose hazards. Resource dependency theory holds that the dependent party – which varies with the circumstances[10] – is at the mercy of the other. Working, as it does, out of a myopic perspective, the theory holds that dependency is an unwanted and usually unanticipated condition. The recommended response to a condition of resource dependency is for unwitting victims to attempt, *ex post*, to reduce it.

Transaction cost economics regards dependency very differently because it works out of a farsighted rather than a myopic contracting perspective. Not only is dependency a foreseeable condition but, in the degree to which asset specificity is cost-effective, dependency is (i) deliberately incurred and (ii) supported with safeguards. Thus, although less dependency is always better than more, *ceteris paribus*, deliberate recourse to asset specificity will be undertaken in the degree to which net benefits (due allowance having been made for safeguards) can be projected.

Pertinent to a net benefit assessment is whether the attendant hazards can be mitigated by crafting *ex ante* credible commitments (penalties, adaptive governance structures), the effect of which is to infuse confidence into trade. More generally, contract, under the transaction cost economics setup, is a triple in which price, asset specificity and contractual safeguards are all determined simultaneously. Safeguards, under this conception of contract, will progressively build up as asset specificity increases. In the limit, interfirm contracting will be supplanted by unified ownership (vertical integration). The evidence from the intermediate product markets is corroborative (Joskow, 1988; Shelanski, 1991).[11]

An interesting case in which the power versus efficiency perspectives collide is provided by contracting practices for gem-quality uncut diamonds. De Beers dominates this market (with an 80–85 per cent market share) and is generally conceded to enjoy monopoly power. Such a condition would be expected to give rise to muscular contracting under a power perspective, and that appears to be borne out in practice. Thus Roy Kenney and Benjamin Klein describe contracting between the Central Selling Organization (CSO) of De Beers and 300 'invited' diamond traders and cutters as follows (1983, p. 502):

> Each of the CSO's customers periodically informs the CSO of the kinds and quantities of diamonds it wishes to purchase. The CSO then assembles a single box (or 'sight') of diamonds for the customer. Each box contains a number of folded, envelope-like packets called papers. The gems within each paper are similar and correspond to one of the CSO's classifications. The composition of any sight may differ slightly from that specified by the buyer because the supply of diamonds in each category is limited.
>
> Once every five weeks, primarily at the CSO's offices in London, the diamond buyers are invited to inspect their sights. Each box is marked with the buyer's name and a price. A single box may carry a price of up to several million pounds. Each buyer examines his sight before deciding whether to buy. Each buyer may spend as long as he wishes examining his sight to see that each stone is graded correctly (that is, fits the description marked on each parcel). There is no negotiation over the price or composition of the sight. In rare cases where a buyer claims that a stone has been miscategorized by the CSO, and the sales staff agrees, the sight will be adjusted. If a buyer rejects the sight, he is offered no alternative box. Rejection is extremely rare, however, because buyers who reject the diamonds offered them are deleted from the list of invited customers.
>
> Thus stones (a) are sorted by De Beers into imperfectly homogeneous categories, (b) to be sold in preselected blocks, (c) to preselected buyers, (d) at nonnegotiable prices, with (e) buyers' rejection of the sales offer leading to the withdrawal by De Beers of future invitations to purchase stones.

If this isn't muscle, what is?

Kenney and Klein, however, offer an efficiency interpretation. They observe (1983, p. 501) that gem-quality diamonds vary greatly in value, even after being sorted into more than 2,000 categories (by shape, quality, colour and weight). That being the case, there are private returns to searching through each diamond category to select the best stones. As this proceeds, the average value of the remaining stones will drop below the listed price. Picking-and-choosing thus has two costly consequences: oversearching and successive repricing. De Beers could respond by incurring added classification costs (for example, sorting into 4,000 categories), but it has responded instead by imposing a set of trading regularities. It assembles sights and offers these to invited buyers under an all-or-none purchase rule and an in-or-out trading rule.

The all-or-none purchase rule precludes buyers from picking-and-choosing individual diamonds. Being constrained to purchase the entire sight, it now makes sense to take a sample and ascertain whether the average value exceeds the asking price. The all-or-none purchase rule thus economizes on oversearching.

But what purposes are served by the in-or-out trading rule? Surely that smacks of muscle? Not necessarily. Although the all-or-none purchase rule reduces oversearching, picking-and-choosing has merely been moved from the level of individual stones to the level of sights. The purchase criterion becomes: accept the sight if the estimated average value of the sample exceeds the per unit asking price, otherwise reject. De Beers is still, therefore, confronted with cherry-picking.

What the in-or-out trading rules does is introduce an intertemporal dimension that further reduces search costs and brings reputation effects more effectively to bear. Given the in-or-out trading rule, a dealer who plans to be in business for a long time has an incentive to accept sights as presented, thereafter to ascertain in the marketplace whether he or she has received adequate value. The true valuation of a sight need not, therefore, be carefully determined through an *ex ante* assessment (oversearching) but is the automatic byproduct of allowing the market to disclose value *ex post*. If sometimes De Beers is high and sometimes low, that will all work out.

If, however, a dealer is confronted with a series of sights in which the asking price exceeds realized value, then the presumption that De Beers is presenting fairly valued sights is placed in doubt. The next sight will therefore be carefully scrutinized and if it is refused sends a powerful signal that De Beers is not to be trusted. In a market where other dealers are knowledgeable and communication is good, that has powerful reputation-effect ramifications (Kreps, 1990).

The combination of the all-or-none purchase rule with an in-or-out trading rule thus infuses greater credibility into a market that is otherwise fraught with high transaction costs. It is in the interests of the system that these costs be reduced.

Note that this efficiency interpretation takes initial conditions – namely, the De Beers monopoly – as given. Conceivably that is too passive, in that, as a matter of good public policy, the De Beers monopoly should be broken up. That, however, is another story (and may or may not be feasible). The confusion to be avoided is to assume that nonstandard practices at the contracting stage invariably magnify power disparities at the initial stage. That needs to be shown rather than assumed.[12] The details are where the action resides. These need to be explained in a coherent way.

Capital markets   Samuel Bowles and Herbert Gintis contend that 'capital markets tend to penalize non-hierarchical enterprise structures' (1993, p. 93) and aver that 'Capital markets concentrate power because rational lenders prefer to transact with organizations with undemocratic political structures quite independently of their administrative structure' (1993, p. 94). By contrast, I argue that the only preference to which capital reliably relates is that of seeking high (risk-adjusted) returns. According to the latter view, undemocratic political structures are relevant only as these have a bearing on contractual hazards. Holding the investment project constant, capital will be priced on better terms for those political structures to which lower hazards are projected, *ceteris paribus*. The Bowles and Gintis argument is akin to one advanced earlier by John Bonin and Louis Putterman, who define a worker-managed enterprise by the single proviso that 'ultimate decision-making rights are vested in the workers, and only in the workers' (1987, p. 2). Because Bonin and Putterman contend that this proviso is innocuous, they declare that there is no objective reason why capital should ask for a risk premium in dealing with such enterprises.

I submit that different forms of finance need to be distinguished and that equity capital incurs added risk when it is excluded from decision-making, which is what the worker-management proviso demands.[13] My argument is an application of the proposition that debt and equity are not merely financial instruments but are also governance instruments. Contrary to the Modigliani and Miller (1958) theorem, transaction cost economics maintains that debt and equity need to be matched to the attributes of a project for which finance is needed.

The argument, in brief, is this (Williamson, 1988):

1. easily redeployable assets are appropriately financed by debt;

2. highly nonredeployable assets are ones for which equity finance is better suited;
3. the governance structure associated with debt is more legalistic and works out of rules while that associated with equity is more hierarchical and allows greater discretion;
4. the board of directors is a discretionary control instrument that is efficiently awarded to residual claimants – namely, to equity in firms in which investments in durable, nonredeployable physical assets are significant;
5. refusal to award control over the board of directors in such firms to equity finance poses an investment hazard, the effect of which is to raise the effective price of finance; and
6. some firms – mainly professional firms (law firms, accounting firms, investment banking, consulting) – involve negligible investment in firm-specific physical assets and are appropriately organized as worker-controlled partnerships.

According to the 'power' view of capital in which 'political preferences' are featured, the scarcity of worker-managed enterprises is explained by the hostility of capital to democratic decision-making. The efficiency view, by contrast, is that equity capital must have access to (is virtually defined as) discretionary control, whence democratic decision-making is poorly suited to organize firms for which significant investments in specific capital are required. The efficiency view is borne out by the data (Hansmann, 1988).

Labour and final product markets It is more plausible to assume that parties to a transaction are knowledgeable for transactions between two firms than it is for transactions between firms and workers or, especially, between firms and consumers. That is because of information asymmetries in which firms often enjoy an information advantage in relation to both workers and consumers.

Thus, many final consumer and some labour market transactions are characterized by (comparatively) shallow knowledge, confusion, inability to craft a specialized governance structure, weak reputation effects and costly legal processes. Although groups of consumers could and sometimes do create their own specialized agents to contract on their behalf, there are serious collective action problems in forming such groups and in excluding free-riders (Arrow, 1969). Unlike firms, moreover, consumers are rarely able to integrate backward – thereby to relieve the troublesome transaction by placing it under unified ownership. (Backward integration into day care by parents who organize

nonprofit day-care facilities is an exception (Ben-Ner and Van Hoomissen, 1991).)

To be sure, the producers and distributors of hard-to-measure goods
and services sometimes can and do create added safeguards through
branding, warranties, authorized service and the like. Whether best
private efforts of buyers and suppliers to concentrate the costs and
benefits can be further improved on with net gains (remediableness) is
then the question. Public ordering may be warranted if best private
efforts are severely wanting. Consumer protection regulation – information disclosure, standards, legal aid – often has these origins.

Similar arguments apply to labour, although here the possibility of
private collective action is often more feasible. Transaction cost economics observes in this connection that the efficiency benefits of
collective action, including associated governance structure supports,
will vary with the degree of human asset specificity. Accordingly, labour
unions ought to arise earlier and governance ought to be more fully
elaborated in firms where human asset specificity is great (Williamson
et al., 1975; Williamson, 1985, Chapter 10).

Differences between the 'industrial pluralists' – Harry Schulman,
Archibald Cox, Arthur Goldberg, Justice Douglas – and Katherine
Stone over the interpretation of the Wagner Act are pertinent. The
former adopted what, in effect, was an efficiency view: the purpose of
the Act was to harmonize labour relations, promote cooperation and
please the parties. By contrast, Stone (1981) advanced an adversarial
interpretation, according to which the purpose of the Act was to equa-
lize power. Thus, whereas the pluralists viewed arbitration as a means
by which to resolve disputes in favour of the idiosyncratic needs of the
parties, Stone recommended a legalistic approach in which the National
Labor Relations Board is directed to 'interpret the language of the
written agreement, *not please the parties*' (Stone, 1981, p. 1552, n. 238,
emphasis in original).

Although a legalistic approach to contract is understandably recommended by those who prefer confrontation, that can be a costly way to
organize society. For better or worse (depending on one's preferences),
the efficiency view has prevailed. Interestingly, Japanese economic
organization can be interpreted as an effort to move to a higher degree
of contracting perfection (Aoki, 1990; Williamson, 1991c).

Politics   The idea that politics is the product of knowledgeable and
farsighted contracting is surely preposterous. 'Everyone knows' that
voting is irrational and that to expend efforts to vote knowledgeably is
especially irrational. Robert Ellickson (1993) responds that politics is a

consumption good, whence participation has a rational basis. Still, political choices are often complex and ignorance is widespread.

Terry Moe (1990a,b) has reframed the issues in terms of interest groups. He maintains that while voters in general are poorly informed, interest groups not only have extensive knowledge of the issues but also understand a great deal about the consequences of structural choice. Thus, whereas bureau design is a matter with which voters express concerns only after the fact, when they can observe how a bureau operates, interest groups are actively involved in the *ex ante* design of bureaux and know what they want. As Moe and Caldwell bluntly put it, 'on issues of structure, virtually all pressures come from the groups . . . structural politics is interest group politics' (1994, p. 173) – which is to say that politics is an exercise in power.

There are more and less efficacious ways to exercise power, however, and the economic approach advises that bureaux will be designed with farsighted purposes in mind. In the degree to which the current majority perceives that its hold on political office is insecure, forward-looking politicians will recognize that those very same bureaux through which favours are awarded to a target population could become instruments for reversing earlier actions (perhaps even to reward the opposition) by successor administrations. Therefore, agencies will be designed with reference to both immediate benefits (which favours responsive mechanisms) and possible future losses (which often favours crafting inertia into the system). The creation of a bureau will be attended therefore by some degree of (apparent) design inefficiency – that being the forward-thinking way to protect weak political property rights (Moe, 1990a,b). What is furthermore noteworthy is that such inefficiencies may be irremediable – given the rules of the game.[14]

The issue of remediableness also arises in George Stigler's recent examination of political choice. He queries whether an 'apparently inefficient' political programme should be regarded as inefficient if the programme in question has passed 'the test of time'. Consider the US sugar programme, which Stigler describes as follows (1992, p. 459):

> The United States wastes (in ordinary language) perhaps $3 billion per year producing sugar and sugar substitutes at a price two to three times the cost of importing the sugar. Yet that is the tested way in which the domestic sugar-beet, cane, and high-fructose-corn producers can increase their incomes by perhaps a quarter of the $3 billion – the other three quarters being dead-weight loss. The deadweight loss is the margin by which the domestic costs of sugar production exceed import prices.

How is such a programme to be assessed? A common interpretation is that the deadweight loss represents inefficiency: 'The Posnerian theory would say that the sugar program is grotesquely inefficient because it fails to maximize national income' (Stigler, 1992, p. 459). The fact that the sugar programme has statute-based, rather than common law-based, origins is, purportedly, a contributing factor.

Stigler takes exception to efficiency of law scholarship both in general (the statute-based versus common law-based distinction) and in his interpretation of the sugar programme. The problem with the argument that the common law is efficient while statute law is problematic (Landes and Posner, 1987) is that it rests on an underdeveloped logic (Stigler, 1992, pp. 459–61). More pertinent for my purposes is Stigler's argument that 'Maximum national income ... is not the only goal of our nation as judged by policies adopted by our government – and government's goals as revealed by actual practice are more authoritative than those pronounced by professors of law or economics' (Stigler, 1992, p. 459).

Rather than appeal to deadweight losses in relation to a hypothetical ideal, Stigler proposes that the appropriate criterion is the test of time, according to which criterion he declares that the 'sugar program is efficient. This program is more than fifty years old – it has met the test of time' (Stigler, 1992, p. 459).

In effect, the test of time is a rough-and-ready way to assess remediableness – the assumption being that if there were a cheaper, feasible and implementable alternative then it would be implemented. That test makes no provision for organizational breakdowns, however, and it assumes that the democratic process has been and is working acceptably. I address these issues elsewhere. On making allowance for egregious intertemporal breakdowns of organization and/or politics, the Stiglerian test of time criterion is reformulated as a rebuttable presumption (Williamson, 1993b).

The upshot is that efficiency plays a significant role even in the power arena (politics), especially if the relevant test for inefficiency is that of remediableness.

5 Authority[15]

As discussed in Section 2 under the heading 'transaction cost economics', transaction cost economics maintains that each generic mode of organization is supported by a distinctive form of contract law. That contradicts the view that the firm is no different from the market in contractual respects, as argued by Alchian and Demsetz (1972, p. 777):[16]

The single consumer can assign his grocer to the task of obtaining whatever the customer can induce the grocer to provide at a price acceptable to both parties. That is precisely all that an employer can do to an employee. To speak of managing, directing, or assigning workers to various tasks is a deceptive way of noting that the employer continually is involved in renegotiation of contracts on terms that must be acceptable to both parties. . . . Long-term contracts between employer and employee are not the essence of the organization we call a firm.

That it has been instructive to view the firm as a nexus of contracts is evident from the numerous insights that this literature has generated. But to regard the corporation only as a nexus of contracts misses much of what is truly distinctive about this mode of governance. As developed below, bilateral adaptation effected through fiat is a distinguishing feature of internal organization. But wherein do the fiat differences between market and hierarchy arise?

One explanation is that fiat has its origins in the employment contract (Barnard, 1938; Simon, 1951; Coase, 1952; Masten, 1988). Although there is a good deal to be said for that explanation, I propose a separate and complementary explanation: the implicit contract law of internal organization is that of forbearance. Thus, whereas courts routinely grant standing to interfirm disputes over prices, the damages to be ascribed to delays, failures of quality, and the like, courts will refuse to hear intrafirm disputes – between one internal division and another – over identical technical issues. Access to the courts being denied, the parties must resolve their differences internally. Accordingly, hierarchy is its own court of ultimate appeal.[17]

The underlying rationale for forbearance law is twofold:

1. parties to an internal dispute have deep knowledge – both about the circumstances surrounding a dispute as well as the efficiency properties of alternative solutions – that can be communicated to the court only at great cost; and
2. permitting internal disputes to be appealed to the court would undermine the efficacy and integrity of hierarchy.

If fiat were merely advisory, in that internal disputes over net receipts could be pursued in the courts, the firm would be little more than an 'inside contracting' system (Williamson, 1985, pp. 218–22). The application of forbearance doctrine to internal organization means that parties to an internal exchange can work out their differences themselves or appeal unresolved disputes to the hierarchy for a decision. But this exhausts their alternatives. When push comes to shove, 'legalistic' arguments fail. Greater reliance on instrumental reasoning and mutual accommodation result. The argument that the firm 'has no power of fiat, no authority, no disciplinary action any different in the slightest degree from ordinary market contracting' (Alchian and Demsetz, 1972, p. 777) is exactly wrong: firms can and do exercise fiat that markets cannot.

Viewing fiat and the zone of acceptance through the lens of efficiency leads to different predictions that obtain when these same features are interpreted in terms of power. According to the efficiency perspective, the zone of acceptance will be broad or narrow depending on the nature of the transaction. The idea here is that (holding the nature of the task constant), workers will ask for greater compensation if the zone across which they are expected to be compliant includes a larger set of unpopular jobs, *ceteris paribus*. Accordingly, a zone will be widened to include more potentially adverse assignments only in the degree to which that is perceived to be cost-effective.[18]

Arguments that power manifests itself in the design of jobs go back to Adam Smith and Karl Marx and have been surveyed recently by James Rebitzer (1993, pp. 1401–9). It is beyond the scope of this chapter to assess these issues here, but I merely make four points:

1. persistent inefficiency in the design of jobs in a competitively organized industry reflects either a condition of market failure (private gains with systems losses) or a condition of disequilibrium contracting;
2. inefficiency by design is more apt to be incurred where value or rent dissipation is the concern (and in any event may not be remediable);
3. power-serving purposes that have inefficiency consequences are continuously threatened by credible contracting structures to which the parties attach confidence; and
4. the relevant efficiency criterion for job design is not a hypothetical (but unattainable) ideal but is that of remediableness.

6 Conclusions

As described above, the economic approach to the study of organization works out of a rational spirit perspective in which parties approach contracting in a farsighted way. Transaction cost economics adopts this perspective and moves it to a more microanalytic level of analysis than is customary in economics and develops the microanalytics in a more operational way than has been customary in organization theory or than was attempted by the older type of institutional economics. Kenneth Arrow's remarks are pertinent (1987, p. 734):

Why . . . has the work of Herbert Simon, which has meant so much to all of us, nevertheless had so little direct consequence? Why did the older institutional school fail so miserably, though it contained such able analysts as Thorstein Veblen, J.R. Commons, and W.C. Mitchell? I now think that there are two answers: one is that in fact there are important specific analyses, particularly in the work . . . of the New Institutional Economics movement. But it does not consist primarily of giving answers to the traditional questions of economics – resource allocation and the degree of utilisation. Rather, it consists of answering new questions, why economic institutions have emerged the way they did and not otherwise; it merges with economic history, but brings sharper nanoeconomic . . . reasoning to bear than has been customary.

Thus, whereas transaction cost economics deals with many of the micro-analytic phenomena with which organization theory has long been concerned, it examines these predominantly from an efficiency perspective in which intended but limited rationality manifests itself as 'incomplete contracting in its entirety'. The efficiency perspective out of which transaction cost economics works further eschews Pareto optimality in favour of a remediableness standard – according to which an extant condition is held to be efficient unless a feasible alternative can be described and implemented with net gains.

A huge number of puzzling phenomena are reinterpreted in this way and a large number of predictions (which, as it turns out, are variations on a small number of transaction cost economizing themes) are realized. Such regularities by no means exhaust all of the interesting variety that is out there. The economizing lens is nevertheless a useful place to start.

Notes

1. Milton Friedman describes the relevant trade-off as follows: 'The gains from greater accuracy . . . must be balanced against the costs of achieving it' (1953, p. 17).
2. Indeed, Simon has himself employed this approach (1976, p. 140).
3. Hannan and Freeman take a weaker position in subsequent work (see Hannan, 1989).
4. Although most noneconomists need to live with economics for a while before the approach becomes intuitive and congenial, a few undergo a mystical conversion. The latter are recognized as 'true believers'. They become missionaries and emphasize the endless powers of economics without regard or respect for its limitations.
5. See Michels (1962).
6. See Polanyi (1962); Nelson and Winter (1982); Teece (1992); Kreps (1990).
7. See Eccles and White (1988).
8. See Williamson (1975, Chapter 7; 1985, Chapter 6).
9. James March concludes that 'Power has proven to be a disappointing concept. It tends to become a tautological label for the unexplained variance in a decision situation, or as a somewhat more political way of referring to differences in resources (endowments) in a system of bargaining and exchange' (1988, p. 6). This repeats an assessment that he had reached over 20 years earlier (see March, 1988, pp. 148–9).
10. Consider a buyer who purchases from a supplier who has made specific investments in support of the buyer's special needs. Suppose that demand falls significantly. The buyer says cut your prices or cancel the order. Given that the assets are

nonredeployable, the dependent supplier slashes prices.

But suppose instead that demand increases substantially. The buyer asks the supplier for more products. The supplier responds that this is very costly and that he will comply only if the buyer pays a large premium. The dependent buyer, who cannot obtain equivalent low-cost products from unspecialized alternatives, pays.

Dependency is evidently a variable (contingent) condition.

11. Although resource dependency would also advise that safeguards should be created to get relief from dependency, that is strictly an *ex post* exercise. Because dependency is an unwanted condition, the main lesson is to avoid it in the future. Accordingly, parties will not renew dependent contracts when these expire and generic investments and spot contracts will be much more widespread under this perspective.

12. Yet another example in which power and efficiency explanations collide is over the interpretation of franchising restraints – where size asymmetries between franchisor and franchisees are commonly great. For a discussion, see Klein (1980) and Williamson (1985, pp. 181–2).

13. Bonin and Putterman, joined by Jones, now evidently agree (Bonin et al., 1993, p. 1309).

14. As it turns out, recourse to inefficiency by design is employed – as rent and/or property rights protective measures – in the private sector as well (Teece, 1986; Heide and John, 1988; Helper and Levine, 1992). The apparent disjunction between politics and commerce is therefore not as great as Moe suggests. What we observe in both are variations on a weak property rights theme.

15. This section is based on my treatment in Williamson (1991a, pp. 274–6).

16. Both have since modified their position. See Alchian (1984) and Demsetz (1988).

17. To be sure, not all disputes within firms are technical. For a discussion of personnel disputes, see Williamson (1991a, p. 275).

18. This does not imply that all tasks will be made as narrow and repetitive as possible. If job variety is valued by workers, greater variety will be introduced in the degree to which this is cost-effective. Given, however, any specification of the task, workers will ask for more compensation if the zone of acceptance is expanded to include less-favourable outcomes.

References

Akerlof, G. (1984), *An Economic Theorist's Book of Tales*, New York: Cambridge University Press.

Alchian, A. (1950), 'Uncertainty, Evolution and Economic Theory', *Journal of Political Economy*, **58** (June), 211–21.

Alchian, A. (1984), 'Specificity, Specialization and Coalitions', *Journal of Institutions and Theoretical Economics*, **140** (March), 34–49.

Alchian, A. and H. Demsetz (1972), 'Production, Information Costs, and Economic Organization', *American Economic Review*, **62** (December), 777–95.

Aoki, M. (1990), 'Toward an Economic Model of the Japanese Firm', *Journal of Economic Literature*, **28** (March), 1–27.

Arrow, K.J. (1963), 'Uncertainty and the Welfare Economics of Medical Care', *American Economic Review*, **53** (December), 941–73.

Arrow, K.J. (1969), 'The Organization of Economic Activity: Issues Pertinent to the Choice of Market Versus Nonmarket Allocation', in US Joint Economic Committee, *The Analysis and Evaluation of Public Expenditure: The PPB System*, Vol. 1, 91st Congress, 1st Session, Washington DC: US Government Printing Office, pp. 59–73.

Arrow, K.J. (1974), *The Limits of Organization*, first edition, New York: W.W. Norton.

Arrow, K.J. (1987), 'Reflections on the Essays', in G. Feiwel (ed.), *Arrow and the Foundations of the Theory of Economic Policy*, New York: New York University Press, pp. 727–34.

Bain, J. (1956), *Barriers to New Competition*, Cambridge, MA: Harvard University Press.

Barnard, C. (1938), *The Functions of the Executive*, Cambridge, MA: Harvard University Press (fifteenth printing, 1962).

Barnett, W. and G. Carroll (1993), 'How Institutional Constraints Affected the Organization of the Early American Telephone Industry', *Journal of Law, Economics, and Organization*, 9 (April), 98–126.

Baron, J. and M. Hannan (1994), 'The Impact of Economics on Contemporary Sociology', *Journal of Economic Literature*, 32 (September), 1111–46.

Ben-Ner, A. and T. Van Hoomissen (1991), 'Nonprofit Organizations in the Mixed Economy', *Annals of Public and Cooperative Economics*, 62 (4), 519–50.

Bonin, J. and Putterman, L. (1987), *Economics of Cooperation and Labor Managed Economies*, New York: Cambridge University Press.

Bonin, J., D.C. Jones and L. Putterman (1993), 'Theoretical and Empirical Studies of Producer Cooperatives: Will Ever The Twain Meet?', *Journal of Economic Literature*, 31 (September), 1290–320.

Bowles, S. and H. Gintis (1993), 'The Revenge of Homo Economicus: Contested Exchange and the Revival of Political Economy', *Journal of Economic Perspectives*, 7 (Winter), 83–114.

Coase, R.H. (1952), 'The Nature of the Firm', *Economica* N.S., 4 (1937), 386–405. Reprinted in G.J. Stigler and K.E. Boulding (eds), *Readings in Price Theory*, Homewood, IL: Richard D. Irwin.

Coase, R.H. (1960), 'The Problem of Social Cost', *Journal of Law and Economics*, 3 (October), 1–44.

Coase, R.H. (1964), 'The Regulated Industries: Discussion', *American Economic Review*, 54 (May), 194–7.

Coase, R.H. (1978), 'Economics and Contiguous Disciplines', *Journal of Legal Studies*, 7, 201–11.

Coase, R.H. (1984), 'The New Institutional Economics', *Journal of Institutional and Theoretical Economics*, 140 (March), 229–31.

Coase, R.H. (1988), 'The Nature of the Firm: Influence', *Journal of Law, Economics, and Organization*, 4 (Spring), 33–47.

Coase, R.H. (1992), 'The Institutional Structure of Production', *American Economic Review*, 82 (September), 713–19.

Coleman, J. (1990), *The Foundations of Social Theory*, Cambridge, MA: Harvard University Press.

Commons, J.R. (1934), *Institutional Economics*, Madison, WI: University of Wisconsin Press.

Demsetz, H. (1967), 'Toward a Theory of Property Rights', *American Economic Review*, 57 (May), 347–59.

Demsetz, H. (1988), 'The Theory of the Firm Revisited', *Journal of Law, Economics, and Organization*, 4, 141–62.

Dixit, A. (1980), 'The Role of Investment in Entry Deterrence', *Economic Journal*, 90 (March), 95–106.

Dosi, G. (1988), 'Sources, Procedures, and Microeconomic Effects of Innovation', *Journal of Economic Literature*, 26 (September), 1120–71.

Eccles, R. and H. White (1988), 'Price and Authority in Inter-Profit Center Transactions', *American Journal of Sociology*, 94 (Supplement), S17–S51.

Ellickson, R. (1993), 'Property in Land', *Yale Law Journal*, 102 (April), 1315–400.

Fischer, S. (1977), 'Long-Term Contracting, Sticky Prices, and Monetary Policy: Comment', *Journal of Monetary Economics*, 3, 317–24.

Friedland, R. and R. Alford (1991), 'Bring Society Back In', in Walter Powell and Paul DiMaggio (eds), *The New Institutionalism in Organizational Analysis*, Chicago, IL: University of Chicago Press, pp. 232–66.

Friedman, M. (1953), *Essays in Positive Economics*, Chicago, IL: University of Chicago Press.

Furubotn, E. and R. Richter (1991), 'The New Institutional Economics: An Assessment', in E. Furubotn and R. Richter (eds), *The New Institutional Economics*, College Station, TX: Texas A&M Press, pp. 1–32.

Hamilton, G. and N. Biggart (1988), 'Market, Culture, and Authority', *American Journal of Sociology*, **94** (Supplement), S52–S94.

Hannan, M.T. (1989), *Organizational Ecology*, Cambridge, MA: Harvard University Press.

Hannan, M.T. and J. Freeman (1977), 'The Population Ecology of Organizations', *American Journal of Sociology*, **82** (March), 929–64.

Hansmann, H. (1988), 'The Ownership of the Firm', *Journal of Law, Economics, and Organization*, **4** (Fall), 267–303.

Hart, O. (1990), 'An Economist's Perspective on the Theory of the Firm', in O. Williamson (ed.), *Organization Theory*, New York: Oxford University Press, pp. 154–71.

Heide, J. and G. John (1988), 'The Role of Dependence Balancing in Safeguarding Transaction-Specific Assets in Conventional Channels', *Journal of Marketing*, **52** (January), 20–35.

Helper, S. and D. Levine (1992), 'Long-Term Supplier Relations and Product-Market Structure', *Journal of Law, Economics and Organization*, **8** (October), 561–81.

Homans, G. (1958), 'Social Behavior as Exchange', *American Journal of Sociology*, **62**, 597–606.

Joskow, P.L. (1988), 'Asset Specificity and the Structure of Vertical Relationships: Empirical Evidence', *Journal of Law, Economics, and Organization*, **4** (Spring), 95–117.

Joskow, P.L. (1991), 'The Role of Transaction Cost Economics in Antitrust and Public Utility Regulatory Policies', *Journal of Law, Economics, and Organization*, **7** (Special Issue), 53–83.

Kenney, R. and B. Klein (1983), 'The Economics of Block Booking', *Journal of Law and Economics*, **26** (October), 497–540.

Klein, B. (1980), 'Transaction Cost Determinants of "Unfair" Contractual Arrangements', *American Economic Review*, **70** (May), 356–62.

Koopmans, T. (1957), *Three Essays on the State of Economic Science*, New York: McGraw-Hill Book Company.

Kreps, D. (1990), 'Corporate Culture and Economic Theory', in J. Alt and K. Shepsle (eds), *Perspectives on Positive Political Economy*, New York: Cambridge University Press, pp. 90–143.

Kreps, D. (1992), '(How) Can Game Theory Contribute to a Unified Theory of Organizations?', unpublished manuscript.

Krueger, A. (1990), 'The Political Economy of Controls: American Sugar', in M. Scott and D. Lal (eds), *Public Policy and Economic Development*, Oxford: Clarendon Press, pp. 170–216.

Kuhn, T.S. (1970), *The Structure of Scientific Revolutions*, Chicago, IL: University of Chicago Press.

Kunreuther, H., R. Ginsberg, et al. (1978), *Protecting Against High-Risk Hazards: Public Policy Lessons*, New York: John Wiley & Sons.

Landes, W. and R. Posner (1987), *The Economic Structure of Tort Law*, Cambridge, MA: Harvard University Press.

Llewellyn, K.N. (1931), 'What Price Contract? An Essay in Perspective', *Yale Law Journal*, **40** (May), 704–51.

Macneil, I.R. (1974), 'The Many Futures of Contracts', *Southern California Law Review*, **47** (May), 691–816.

Macneil, I.R. (1978), 'Contracts: Adjustments of Long-term Economic Relations under Classical, Neoclassical, and Relational Contract Law', *Northwestern University Law Review*, **72**, 854–906.

March, J.G. (1978), 'Bounded Rationality, Ambiguity, and the Engineering of Choice', *Bell Journal of Economics*, **9** (Autumn), 587–608.

March, J.G. (1988), *Decisions and Organizations*, Oxford: Basil Blackwell.

March, J.G. and H. Simon (1958), *Organizations*, New York: John Wiley & Sons.

Masten, S. (1988), 'A Legal Basis for the Firm', *Journal of Law, Economics, and Organization*, **4** (Spring), 181–98.

Masten, S. (1993), 'Transaction Costs, Mistakes, and Performance: Assessing the Importance of Governance', *Managerial and Decision Economics*, **14**, 119–29.

Michels, R. (1962), *Political Parties*, Glencoe, IL: Free Press.

Modigliani, F. and M.H. Miller (1958), 'The Cost of Capital, Corporation Finance, and
the Theory of Investment', *American Economic Review*, **48** (June), 261–97.

Moe, T. (1990a), 'The Politics of Structural Choice: Toward a Theory of Public Bureaucracy'. in O. Williamson (ed.), *Organization Theory*, New York: Oxford University Press,
116–53.

Moe, T. (1990b), 'Political Institutions: The Neglected Side of the Story', *Journal of Law,
Economics, and Organization*, **6** (Special Issue), 213–54.

Moe, T. and M. Caldwell (1994), 'The Institutional Foundations of Democratic Governance: A Comparison of Presidential and Parliamentary Systems', *Journal of Institutional
and Theoretical Economics*, **150** (March), 171–95.

Nelson, R.R. and S.G. Winter (1982), *An Evolutionary Theory of Economic Change*,
Cambridge, MA: Harvard University Press.

North, D. (1991), 'Institutions', *Journal of Economic Perspectives*, **5** (Winter), 97–112.

Pfeffer, J. (1981), *Power in Organizations*, Marshfield, MA: Pitman Publishing.

Polanyi, M. (1962), *Personal Knowledge: Towards a Post-Critical Philosophy*, New York:
Harper & Row.

Rebitzer, J. (1993), 'Radical Political Economy and the Economics of Labor Markets',
Journal of Economic Literature, **31** (September), 1394–434.

Shelanski, H. (1991), 'A Survey of Empirical Research in Transaction Cost Economics',
unpublished manuscript, University of California, Berkeley, CA.

Simon, H. (1951), 'A Formal Theory of the Employment Relation', *Econometrica*, **19**
(July), 293–305.

Simon, H. (1962), 'The Architecture of Complexity', *Proceedings of the American Philo-
sophical Society*, **106** (December), 467–82.

Simon, H. (1976), 'From Substantive to Procedural Rationality', in S.J. Latsis (ed.),
Method and Appraisal in Economics, Cambridge: Cambridge University Press,
pp. 29–48.

Simon, H. (1978), 'Rationality as Process and as Product of Thought', *American Economic
Review*, **68** (May), 1–16.

Simon, H. (1983), *Reason in Human Affairs*, Stanford, CA: Stanford University Press.

Simon, H. (1985), 'Human Nature in Politics: The Dialogue of Psychology with Political
Science', *American Political Science Review*, **70**, 293–304.

Speidel, R. (1993), 'Article 2 and Relational Sales Contracts', *Loyola of Los Angeles Law
Review*, **26** (April), 789–810.

Stigler, G.J. (1968), *The Organization of Industry*, Homewood, IL: Richard D. Irwin.

Stigler, G.L. (1992), 'Law or Economics?', *Journal of Law and Economics*, **35** (October),
455–68.

Stone, K. (1981), 'The Postwar Paradigm in American Labor Law', *Yale Law Journal*, **90**
(June), 1509–80.

Teece, D.J. (1986), 'Profiting from Technological Innovation', *Research Policy*, **15**
(December), 285–305.

Teece, D.J. (1992), 'Competition, Cooperation, and Innovation: Organizational Arrangements for Regimes of Rapid Technological Progress', *Journal of Economic Behavior
and Organization*, **18** (June), 1–25.

Teece, D.J., R. Rumelt, G. Dosi and S. Winter (1993), 'Understanding Corporate Coher-
ence: Theory and Evidence', *Journal of Economic Behavior and Organization*, **22**
(January), 1–30.

Tirole, J. (1986), 'Hierarchies and Bureaucracy: On the Role of Collusion in Organizations', *Journal of Law, Economics, and Organization*, **2** (Fall), 181–214.

Tversky, A. and D. Kahneman (1974), 'Judgment under Uncertainty: Heuristics and
Biases', *Science*, **185**, 1124–31.

Williamson, O.E. (1971), 'The Vertical Integration of Production: Market Failure Considerations', *American Economic Review*, **61** (May), 112–23.

Williamson, O.E. (1975), *Markets and Hierarchies: Analysis and Antitrust Implications*, New York: Free Press.

Williamson, O.E. (1979), 'Transaction-cost Economics: The Governance of Contractual Relations', *Journal of Law and Economics*, **22** (October), 233–61.

Williamson, O.E. (1983), 'Credible Commitments: Using Hostages to Support Exchange', *American Economic Review*, **73** (September), 519–40.

Williamson, O.E. (1985), *The Economic Institution of Capitalism*, New York: Free Press.

Williamson, O.E. (1988), 'Corporate Finance and Corporate Governance', *Journal of Finance*, **43** (July), 567–91.

Williamson, O.E. (1991a), 'Comparative Economic Organization: The Analysis of Discrete Structural Alternatives', *Administrative Science Quarterly*, **36** (June), 269–96.

Williamson, O.E. (1991b), 'Economic Institutions: Spontaneous and Intentional Governance', *Journal of Law, Economics, and Organization*, **7** (Special Issue), 159–87.

Williamson, O.E. (1991c), 'Strategizing, Economizing, and Economic Organization', *Strategic Management Journal*, **12**, 75–94.

Williamson, O.E. (1993a), 'Transaction Cost Economics and Organization Theory', *Industrial and Corporate Change*, **2** (2), 107–56.

Williamson, O.E. (1993b), 'Redistribution and Inefficiency: The Remediableness Standard', unpublished manuscript.

Williamson, O.E., M.L. Wachter and J-.E. Harris (1975), 'Understanding the Employment Relation: The analysis of Idiosyncratic Exchange', *Bell Journal of Economics*, **6** (Spring), 250–80.

2   Internal characteristics of formal organizations*
Claude Menard

1   Introduction

Contributions of transaction cost economics to the analysis of the continuous trade-off among decisions of using the price mechanism ('to buy'), relying on administrative coordination ('to make'), or having recourse to 'hybrid' organizational forms, are now widely recognized. Alternative 'governance structures' (Williamson, 1985, 1991, 1996) or 'institutional arrangements' (Davis and North, 1971) have been identified, and attributes of transactions have been explored to explain how and why shifts from one form to another occur. Numerous empirical tests have shown the robustness of these hypotheses.[1]

However, one dimension of transaction cost economics is much less developed. Let us assume that a transaction is 'a good or service transferred across a technologically separable interface' (Williamson, 1985, Prologue); then there are also transactions within formal organizations.[2] This explains the emphasis by both Coase (1937, 1988, 1992) and Williamson (1975, 1985, 1996) that transaction costs do matter for understanding the internal nature and properties of formal organizations such as firms.[3] Despite the potential fecundity of this perspective and notwithstanding several contributions by Williamson, few studies have yet been developed in this direction.

In the following pages, I intend to take these suggestions a step farther and to show how promising the application of transaction cost analysis to the study of organizations can be. My position is straightforward: characteristics of transactions have substantial consequences for how formal organizations are structured, which forms of task interdependence they develop, what incentives and control devices they implement, and what type of internal government they install. I will substantiate these ideas by referring mostly to studies already published, some of which are now standard references in the literature, but also by including examples from ongoing research.

The chapter is organized as follows. Section 2 explores some basic characteristics of work organization and contractualization in a context where hierarchy is the basic mechanism of adaptation. *Testable propo-*

sitions are elaborated, relating properties of organization to characteristics of contracts. Section 3 extends some recent research, particularly from Williamson and Aoki, in order to better understand the internal configuration of organizations as well as the role of constituents in their governance. Here again, my major concern is to *operationalize* available concepts. Section 4 concludes.

2 Organizing human assets

The very idea that formal organizations have characteristics of their own, differentiating them from other institutional arrangements, has been challenged. Following the pathbreaking paper by Alchian and Demsetz (1972), several authors (McManus, 1975; Jensen and Meckling, 1976; Cheung 1983) argued that organizations can be understood as 'a nexus of contracts', and that these contracts do not differ from any other contract that organizes market exchanges. On the other hand, numerous organization theorists, as well as economists, have defended the thesis that something substantially different is at stake in organizations, related to the nature of the 'superior–subordinate relationship' (Williamson, 1975, Introduction, 1991; Simon, 1951, 1991; Demsetz, 1988; March, 1962, 1988; Masten, 1988).

In this section, I would like to summarize arguments developed in the latter direction and to analyse some properties of labour contracts and the related employment relationship (first subsection). I will then proceed further and explore modalities of the 'hierarchical relationship' in relation to attributes of transactions (second subsection). I will conclude the section by relating contractual forms identified in the first subsection to the typology of hierarchies developed in the second subsection.

Employment relationship

Several authors, both in organization theory (for example, Barnard, 1938; Simon, 1951, 1991) and in transaction cost economics (for example, Coase, 1937; Williamson, 1975, Chapter 1; 1985, Chapters 9 and 10; Masten, 1988), have emphasized the role of the employment relationship in characterizing formal organizations.[4] This relationship would be specific because of the radical incompleteness of labour contracts and, therefore, because of the central role of *ex post* adaptations, so that the efficiency of work organization does not solely depend on incentive assignments defined *ex ante*, as in agency theory, but also requires 'forcing instruments' (Williamson, 1993).

Labour and the incompleteness of contracts　Though incompleteness is not restricted to labour contracts, it has *distinctive aspects* in these contracts: within the employment relationship, details of formal agreements will deliberately be left unspecified in order to deal with two aspects particular to human assets. (i) Estimated future gains for workers depend on the posture of coworkers as well as on the posture of employers. Indeed, expected income or rents depend on the combination of discretionary power with cooperative behaviour (Menard, 1994). (ii) Contracts can only obligate employees to perform duties to a set of minimum standards, not according to an (undeterminable) optimum performance, since there are irreducible unobservabilities in work efforts. Hence, labour contracts are typically 'relational' (Williamson, 1985, Chapter 3), and involve hierarchy as 'its own court of ultimate appeal'.

Thus, the efficiency of a formal organization depends largely on its capacity to implement work attitudes to achieve performance superior to that determined by contracts[5] and, therefore, to gain a competitive advantage.

Masten (1988) has substantiated the specificity of employment transactions versus commercial transactions by examining the case law governing the relationship between employers and employees in the US. He identified a set of duties and obligations that are unique to employment transactions, and he showed the existence of specific sanctions and procedures to implement them. The duties and obligations concern *obedience*: the law emphasizes the authority of management, with the employee 'legally obligated to reveal relevant information' to the employer; 'loyalty, respect and faithfulness' are expected. Sanctions and procedures are designed to implement these duties: threat of dismissal, but also 'common law remedies for insider trading as well as a number of practices prohibited to employees but open to outside contractors'; accountability of employees for pecuniary losses resulting from failing to disclose relevant facts; presumption of validity for managerial directives, and so forth. Conversely, the employer is responsible 'for any harms the employee causes to third parties in the course of his employment'. Differences also exist regarding what constitutes breach of contract. Most of these provisions are motivated by the necessity of maintaining some flexibility in the labour contract which, in turn, must be explained by the necessity of combining specific human assets in an environment where uncertain events will require adaptations.

Hence, there are *two faces* to the incompleteness of labour contracts from the point of view of organization: a *negative* side, related to the possibility opened by specificity of human assets to post-contractual opportunistic behaviour (Klein, Alchian and Crawford, 1978); and a *positive* side, which is the capacity it opens, through cooperation and/

or adequate monitoring, of generating performance superior to what can be specified in contracts.

Forms of labour contracts A major challenge to formal organizations is therefore determining the degree of incompleteness that will create favourable conditions for exceeding the standards fixed by contract. An effective labour contract induces members to go beyond what it specifies: *this, typically, does not make sense at all for transactions involving physical assets.* Therefore, the crucial question for labour contracts becomes: which form of contractual arrangement will pair specific human assets with idiosyncratic tasks in such a way as to maximize transactional efficiency?

Two characteristics of labour contracts are of particular importance to deal with this problem. First, there is the question of the optimal duration of labour contracts. Short-term contracts provide flexibility but also involve frequent renegotiations: this creates high transaction costs and a major source of uncertainty for both employers and employees. As a result, 'loyalty' and related incentives for employees to invest in order to specify their asset according to the needs of the organization is unlikely. Conversely, long-term contracts tend to implement rigid rules and routines that make very difficult and costly the required adaptation of human assets to changes within the organization or in the environment. Costs of frequent renegotiations are reduced, but with loss in flexibility. Hence, labour contract duration involves difficult trade-offs: transaction cost economics can help to clarify these trade-offs, as we will see below. Second, there is the question of the degree of completeness of labour contracts. Efficient contracts are open-ended to keep open the possibility of adjusting and adapting human assets. But again there is a trade-off, in relation to the specificity of human assets involved. Transaction cost economics suggest that the more specific these assets are, the more incomplete contracts will be, in order to allow for forms of cooperation to act as incentives to exceed formal standards specified by contracts. Changes in specific human assets, necessary to facilitate adaptation and to reduce transaction costs, require cooperation and credible commitment from both parties to the contract. This suggests the advantages of *a nonconflictual approach to labour relations*, particularly when asset specificity is high.

With these problems in mind, I would like to propose a reinterpretation of a very stimulating paper by Williamson (1985, Chapter 10). Using two criteria, human asset specificity (noted k_0 if specificity is weak, and k_1 if it is high) and separability of work relations (noted S_0 if separable, and S_1 if nonseparable), he identified four modalities of internal arrangements of labour.[6] Through all that follows, it must be remembered that we are within organizations, so that specificity of some assets is necessarily involved.

1. With the combination (k_0, S_0), *the internal spot market* will be the efficient governance structure. Contracts will be of the short-term type, and incentives will be highly individualized. The internal organization of labour is very similar to that of a market (Williamson suggests the example of migrant farm workers), and factors other than human specificity must be examined to explain the existence of the organization.
2. With (k_0, S_1), *primitive teams* will develop. Specificity of human assets is relatively weak, but there are difficulties in identifying individual performance and, therefore, in evaluating individual contributions. Labour contracts become more complex and, therefore, more difficult to implement: monitoring develops and renegotiations of contracts become more costly. Duration of contracts is longer than in spot markets, but remains of the relatively short-term type, since low specificity facilitates replacement of workers.
3. The pair (k_1, S_0) implies an *obligational market*, characterized by highly specific human assets and requiring significant investments in human capital, but with observable individual performance. Therefore, specificity will generate contracts of longer duration, while separability will facilitate their implementation through well-designed incentives and 'obligation', so that relatively detailed contracts can be expected. The 'professional bureaucracy' described by Mintzberg (1983) provides an example.[7]
4. Last, the combination (k_1, S_1) requires a complex organization of work in order to deal efficiently and simultaneously with high degrees of specificity and nonseparability: *relational teams* will develop, with cooperation based on shared values that reduce opportunism, and discretionary rules that can take full advantage of specificities. Contracts can be expected to be of relatively long term, to capitalize the costs of building team capabilities, while hierarchical monitoring will require expertise, thus reducing the number of levels and increasing the role of organizational incentives over monetary incentives ('social conditioning', extension of the domain of decisions, and 'egalitarian practices' tend to develop) so that the contract operates essentially as a very broad framework. Firms working at the forefront of new and complex technologies illustrate this arrangement (see also 'adhocracies', as defined in Mintzberg, 1983[8]).

Thus, transaction cost economics strongly supports the idea of a diversity in labour contracts related to differences in human assets involved. For similar reasons, one can expect modalities of the hierarchical relationship to be diversified. Moreover, it is very likely that forms of labour organization identified above will be related to these modalities of hierarchy.

Organizations as hierarchies[9]

The analysis of hierarchical relationships must be understood on the basis of the fundamental question raised by Coase (1937): which institutional arrangement is best suited to govern a specific transaction? Indeed, an answer to this question requires the determination of how alternative governance structures proceed and what can make them more or less efficient. When it comes to the comparative advantages of formal organizations, the presence of a 'discretionary power', with the capacity of some members to 'give orders' so that the organization largely operates as 'its own court of ultimate appeal' (Williamson, 1991) is a central tenet of transaction cost economics.[10]

'Fiat': at the core of organizations   Although the idea that 'authority' characterizes firms has been challenged (Alchian and Demsetz, 1972), there is an increasing consensus among new institutional economists[11] that what distinguishes formal organizations from markets or from 'hybrid forms' in coordinating resources and monitoring transactions is the central role of some agents, the 'entrepreneurs' or managers, in *directing* decisions, while other agents give up the *prerogative* to decide (Coase, 1937; Cheung, 1983). The presence of 'administrative decisions' involves a right of 'superiors' to impose choices upon their 'subordinates' and thereby to change substantially what would otherwise be a perfectly decentralized market economy (Simon, 1945; Demsetz, 1988; Coase, 1991; Williamson, 1991).

I have explored elsewhere (Menard, 1995b) the nature of this capacity *to impose* adaptation through 'fiat' and the conditions required for such a mechanism to operate. This asymmetry among participants, formally represented by asymmetric rights, constitutes the bedrock of formal organizations (Dow, 1987), and it has some major consequences on how resources are allocated and how transactions are governed. First, formal contracts are usually not sufficient for piloting transactions within organizations. Effective labour contracts can be designed when 'routines' can be implemented; but as soon as the human assets involved become more specific, routinization becomes unlikely and detailed contracts lose their effectiveness (see above; and Bouttes and Hamamdjian, this book, Chapter 3). Contract failures develop, and the hierarchical relationship responds. To overcome these failures necessitates discrete assignment capabilities, giving some agents the 'power' to fill in the blanks left by contracts. This role is explicitly *recognized and implemented* by the legal system (Williamson, 1985, Chapter 10, pp. 249 seq.; Masten, 1988). Second, the origin of these failures explains the nature of hierarchy. The conjunction of uncertainties and of limited capacity of boundedly rational agents to predict and react supports the role of 'discrete assignment': some 'must *obey first* then seek recourse' (Williamson, 1985, p. 249; his emphasis). 'Fiat' exists because it provides the capacity to adapt when decision-making is submitted to time constraints and to incomplete specification of tasks to be done. Hierarchy develops its own capacity *to arbitrate and to constrain*. Major attributes of a superior over subordinates are: the *assignment principle*, that is, the capacity to assign tasks discretionarily; the *nomination principle*, that is, the capacity to designate the position of a member in relation to others; and the *constraining principle*, that is, the ability to make one's decision systematically prevail over those made by subordinates.

Forms of discretionary power   This capacity *to command* requires *a formal status*[12] based on rights and rules defined at the level of the 'institutional environment': supervisory functions indicate the presence of organizations as specific 'governance structures' for processing transactions. But the exercise of this discretionary power and the related modalities of control vary significantly from one organization to another. There are substantial differences among *hierarchies*.

Transaction cost economics suggests a strong relationship between the characteristics of transactions at stake and the governance structure adopted. It seems quite natural to extend this explanation to the internal analysis of organizations: attributes of transactions on human assets *within an organization* should considerably influence the way command will be structured.

In order to develop this idea, *let us assume a well-defined set of transactions*, so that I will proceed within a *static framework*. Following Williamson (1985, 1991, 1993), I will describe transactions according to their attributes: the uncertainty affecting them; their frequency; and the specificity of assets involved. *Uncertainty* can be *exogenous*, when it depends on characteristics of the suppliers, changes in demand, or modifications of the institutional environment; or *endogenous* when it results from technical difficulties, maintenance and other coordination problems, or opportunistic behaviour of members and the related difficulties of implementing orders. In order to focus attention strictly on the internal properties of organizations, I will assume exogenous uncertainty as fixed. As for endogenous uncertainty, transaction cost economics suggests that: *(H1) the more uncertainty there is, the more complex internal transactions are to organize, requiring tighter coordination and, therefore, more centralization of strategic decisions.*[13]

Frequency has more ambiguous effects. On one hand, frequent internal transactions facilitate routinization and, therefore, the implementation of complete contracts, thus diminishing the necessity of discrete intervention. On the other hand, repeated transactions make high-ranked managers more familiar with their properties, thus inviting centralized controls. Information illustrates well this ambiguity: higher frequency of transactions generates more reliable information, which in turn reduces endogenous uncertainty, allowing more efficient contracts, but also more effective controls. Because of advantages of market incentives over administrative decisions, I hypothesize that the first effect will predominate: *(H2) the more frequent internal transactions are, the more routinized tasks will be, thus reducing the need for discretionary decisions.*

Finally, *asset specificity* has so far been the most useful variable for explaining the trade-off among alternative governance structures (Joskow, 1988; Williamson, 1991). I suggest that this variable also provides a powerful explanation of the modalities of hierarchical relationships. Because of the very nature of hierarchy, we are concerned here with *human assets.*[14] Human assets become very specific when agents develop, through their operations within an organization, qualifications that are not easily redeployable on the market.[15] When specificity is high, *bilateral dependency* becomes a crucial factor. The fundamental proposition of transaction cost economics is that the more specific assets are, the more likely it is that integration will occur in order to coordinate efficiently. Applied to the hierarchical relationship, this prediction can be formulated as: *(H3) the more specific human assets are, the more incomplete are contracts and the more monitoring requires discrete interventions from the hierarchy.*[16]

I now want to raise the following question: can we combine these three hypotheses in order to better understand the types of hierarchies that we find in organizations? I suggest that we can, though we may need initially to simplify some assumptions. In a companion paper (Menard, 1995b), I explored the links between endogenous uncertainty, specific assets and frequency, showing that the uncertainty is positively correlated with specificity and negatively correlated with frequency.[17] I therefore defined the *intensity of a hierarchical relationship*, measured by, for example, the immediacy of discrete intervention, as a function

HUMAN ASSET SPECIFICITY

		Low	High
FREQUENCY	Low	Quasi market (I)	Simple hierarchy (III)
	High	Autonomous group (II)	Complex hierarchy (IV)

Figure 2.1   Modalities of internal relationships

of asset specificity and of frequency, endogenous uncertainty being subsumed by these two variables. We have:

$$HI = HI\ (AS,\ F)$$
$$+\ \ -$$

with *HI* for 'hierarchical intensity' and signs for the direction of variation. This suggests an explanation and a reconceptualization of the classification of hierarchies sketched by Williamson (1975, Chapters 3 and 5; also 1986, Chapter 9).

(P1)   Specific combinations of asset specificity and of frequency will determine different *modalities* of hierarchical relationships.

To simplify, let us assume that asset specificity and frequency can take two values, low and high, respectively.[18] This produces the following combinations (See Figure 2.1):

a.   With relatively low specificity of human assets and low frequency of internal transactions (see I), monitoring tasks is easy, notwithstanding that these tasks involve some variability. Contracts of the 'internal spot market' type can be defined and implemented at relatively low cost, and supervision is easy to maintain, although it must be combined with internal mobility and flexibility. *Quasi-market relationships* will develop within the organization, with relatively weak hierarchy. Indeed, the recurrent possibility of trade-off between organizing activities internally or providing them through outsourcing limits the role of the discretionary power of hierarchy.[19]

b. When specificity of assets remains relatively low, but their arrangement involves an increasing number of identical internal transactions (see II), *observability* is simplified further since routinization can be developed. Therefore, contracts distinctive of 'primitive teams' are easy to write and to implement, so that the hierarchical structure can be expected to be decentralized and reduced to a few levels, while the number of members under its control can be expanded. This is typically a situation in which a network of well-coordinated *autonomous groups* prevails, with routines at the core of most decisions, and with self-monitoring and mutual controls as efficient modes of checking opportunistic behaviours. Allam (1995) analysed such an arrangement at a major car manufacturer, where plants have been restructured along 'Elementary Units of Work', with groups of twelve to twenty members, with hierarchical levels reduced to four.

c. The situation is quite different when assets become more specific and frequency of transactions is low (see III). *Observability of performance* comes to the forefront of the hierarchical structure, with contracts that are complex and largely open-ended, because they are relatively unadapted to transactions that are difficult to predict. Opportunism tends to develop, and monitoring by specialized agents must be implemented. Superiors must be close to subordinates and have similar competencies; but at the same time, they have to continuously exercise discretionary power in order to manage unpredictable and/or complex transactions. *Simple (or 'direct') hierarchy* should develop, where supervisors can easily be identified and where compliance depends on competence of orders. Firms oriented towards the development of highly nonstandardized technologies or towards the supply of very specific services provide illustrations.

d. With highly specialized assets combined with high frequency of internal transactions (see IV), problems of observability and of bilateral dependency are mitigated relative to the previous situation. Indeed, repetition of transactions allows some effective monitoring.

Supervision by specialized agents is possible, and relatively complex contracts can be implemented. This is the world of *complex hierarchies*, with multiple-layer structure, mixing decentralization of operational decisions with centralization of strategic ones, so that 'relational contracts' are preferred. Divisionalization is obviously a case in point.

This description does not pretend to provide a general typology of organizations. As indicated at the beginning of the subsection, it rather intends to identify specific modalities of the hierarchical relationship at work *within* formal organizations. The underlying premise is that the analysis according to transaction cost principle helps to account for differences among these modalities.

The analysis above also strongly suggests that contractual characteristics of labour relations are logically related to the typology of hierarchical relationships. Indeed, they are based on related criteria with asset specificity and problems of observability (influenced by the frequency of transactions) at the core. In other words, both the hierarchical relationship internal to the organization and the accompanying contractual arrangements depend on the attributes of transactions. I propose the following formalization of this link:

(P2)   Contractual labour arrangements typical of internal spot markets characterize *quasimarkets*; those typical of primitive teams characterize *autonomous groups*; labour contracts adapted to obligational markets meet the requirements of *complex hierarchies*; while contracts adapted to relational teams will largely prevail in *direct hierarchies*. This proposition obviously needs to be examined in relation to empirical studies. Ongoing research should help to develop preliminary tests.[20]

The role of unions   The suggested relationship between modalities of hierarchy and characteristics of labour contracts introduces a complementary question, that of the role of 'organized labour'. Indeed, hierarchies can only maintain the advantages of 'making' rather than 'buying' by combining incentives to cooperate with the use of 'fiat'.[21] Organizations confronted with specific human assets, nonobservabilities, and/or nonseparability of tasks will have to deal with *coalitions*,[22] such as labour unions or similar arrangements. There has been very little work done on this aspect from a transaction cost perspective. What follow are only rough indications for further research. I do not consider arguments about the existence or nature of unions; emphasis is rather on some of their roles when transaction costs are taken into consideration.

First, it is likely that unions or similar arrangements will develop within formal organizations along three basic patterns, moulded by characteristics of human assets. (i) When these assets are weakly specific, that is, easy to redeploy at low cost on labour markets, coalitions should form primarily about the conditions of this redeployability, particularly wages and monetary compensation. This is to say that under these circumstances the employment relationship tends to be ruled by *exit* (Hirschman, 1970). Therefore, we can expect the usual mode of unionization among employees, in which unions fight to obtain and maintain guaranteed wages and to implement a protective shield against uncertainties related to redeployability. (ii) Conversely, with highly specific assets that are nonseparable (or very weakly so), adjustments through labour markets involve considerable transaction costs. Bilateral dependency between employer and employees will be a powerful incentive to develop coalitions allowing *voice* to predominate over *exit*: negotiations on conditions in which these assets will be mobilized should prevail over market regulation. One can expect 'professional organizations' to emerge, with a strong emphasis on bargaining focused on arrangement of tasks and on the internal structure of hierarchy. (iii) Finally, in intermediate situations where human assets involved in a determined set of transactions are specific but redeployable at reasonable costs, we can predict a very active labour market, with a weak propensity to unionize and, when labour associations exist, with a strong propensity for multiple associations in competition with each other. It should be so because human specificity makes such a labour force valuable, while redeployability favours strong competition.

Second, some normative consequences can be predicted as well. High specificity and nonseparability of human assets engender situations of 'lock-in' among members, with more possibilities for opportunistic behaviour. In order to reduce this, it is likely to be advantageous for an organization operating under these conditions to contract with employees *collectively*, by negotiating with unions or similar arrangements (Klein et al., 1978; Williamson, 1985, Chapter 2; Muramatsu, 1984). Three factors motivate this strategy. (i) A union's reputation for reliability in contract observance will act to reduce implementation costs by procedures of self-control. (ii) The active contribution of unions in filling in blanks of contracts that are necessarily incomplete because of the specificity involved will significantly reduce costs of arbitration: internal negotiation will prevail over costly appeal to external parties (for example, courts). (iii) With highly specific assets, bargaining is likely to be the most cost-saving procedure for pairing hierarchical coordination with cooperation on the floor.

Both dimensions, positive and normative, demonstrate the role of unions in making *voice* prevail in the employment relationship, a role of particular importance for resolving conflicts in organizations with highly specific assets.[23] This analysis can also rebut a critique from Dow (1987), who accused Williamson of biased views on the role of discretionary power within organizations.[24] According to Dow, transaction cost economics would uniformly emphasize the role of hierarchy as an efficient instrument for allocating human assets and for fighting against employees' opportunism, while it would totally neglect the role of command as a powerful tool for opportunistic managers and employers to absorb the organizational rent. This critique is significantly mitigated if one recognizes the complementary role of unions in exerting institutional control over management abuses, thus reinforcing the comparative advantage of these organizations. In reducing downward opportunism of managers over employees, unions or similar arrangements could well reduce the costs of managing internal transactions, particularly when high uncertainty and/or high human specificity is involved. By providing a rationale for some monitoring of superiors by subordinates, transaction cost economics may explain why unions or similar institutional forms can minimize conflicts and reduce costs, thus contributing to the continuity and efficiency of the organization of work when transaction-specific skills are involved. Similar views could be extended to the role of *organizational culture*.[25]

To summarize, in this section I have suggested that attributes of transactions processed within formal organizations can help to explain some fundamental characteristics of *how human assets are organized within hierarchical relationships*, defining this governance structure that we label 'an organization'. There has so far been little work in this direction in transaction cost economics, and I am aware that the previous propositions and suggestions are hypothetical and controversial. But I have expressed all of them in order to facilitate investigations, tests and refutation.

3   Governing an organization

The modalities by which human assets are structured within formal organizations, in relation to their degree of specificity, will be embedded in the 'government' of the organization, and will define its *configuration*. Other factors will certainly be involved, such as technologies, dimensions of assets not examined above (site specificity, physical specificity, and so on), the nature of products or services to be provided, intensity of competitive pressures, and regulation.

But I want to emphasize here that transaction cost analysis can also shed light on how the government of organizations will be arranged. The guiding principle, again, is that of *the search for an internal governance that is appropriate for transactions at stake*, that is, what Williamson (1993) identified as 'the first-order economizing problem'. This economizing strategy does not mean that an organization works towards a well-defined end. But it indicates that attributes of transactions strongly contribute to the modelling of the internal government of organizations.

I will substantiate these ideas in two ways. The first subsection suggests a more explicit transaction cost interpretation of the structural forms of organizations identified by several authors (Chandler, 1962; Williamson, 1975; Armour and Teece, 1978; Aoki, 1988). The second subsection deals with a more complex and controversial issue, that of the specific composition of the governing *board* of an organization. 'What is' and 'what ought to be' are closely interconnected when it comes to these problems. I will stick to the former as much as possible.

Selecting a 'configuration'
As developed by Williamson (1975, Chapter 8), and tested by Armour and Teece (1978), Cable (1983, 1985) the Chandlerian distinction between U-forms and M-forms in modern corporations seems purely descriptive. No explicit reference is made to transaction costs in order to provide an explanation for this diversity of arrangements or for the trade-off between these forms. More recently, Aoki (1988, Chapter 2; 1990) developed a very stimulating analysis of a would-be new form, the J-form, which he explicitly positioned as complementary to the distinction between U-form and M-form. He then proceeded comparatively, examining respective capacities of these structures to adjust to uncertainty, to produce and process information, and so forth. These are familiar headlines in transaction cost economics, and their consequences deserve to be explored further.

A rationale for the differences in design   In his well-known analysis, Williamson (1975, Chapter 8) emphasized three factors that would explain the superiority of a multidivisionalized organization (M-form) over a functionalized one (U-form) for a firm involved in a strategy of diversification: (i) divisionalization, since this aligns the structure of the firm on its main lines of activities; (ii) the separation between strategic and operational decisions, since this improves decision-making; (iii) a higher degree of decentralization, since this extends possibilities of control. The underlying argument concerns relative efficiency: when a firm expands and diversifies, the increasing complexity of transactions it has to deal with makes it more and more difficult to allocate internal resources rationally and to keep control over members under the centralized U-form. Under these circumstances, the M-form would *comparatively* perform better. The reference test for that hypothesis was developed by Armour and Teece (1978), followed by several studies.[26] Their estimation, based on 28 firms in the oil industry during the period 1955–73, was designed to measure the respective performance of distinct organizational forms, approximated by an evaluation of their relative profitability.[27] The results provided strong statistical support to the hypothesis that organizational structure is an important factor in the observed variations in profitability: shifts from U-form to M-form induced a positive variation of about 2 per cent during the transition period, that is, before most firms adjusted to the more profitable form.

These results, comparing the relative efficiency of different organizational structures, are clearly in the spirit of transaction cost economics. But the connection remains loose, and Dugger (1983) justifiably argued that, if the explanation is not pushed further, it looks very much like an *ex post* justification for the development of modern corporations. I submit that much more can be said about this trade-off among structures by using recent research in the field.

First, we have learned through numerous empirical studies over the last ten years how crucial the concept of specific asset is. This concept should be applied to explain differences in organizational design. As they expand and diversify, organizations contend with increasingly complex internal transactions. This is the logical consequence of the advantages of the division of labour that organizations internalize (Demsetz, 1988). As a result, lock-in develops among members, with loss of control and opportunistic behaviour increasingly at risk. Multidivisionalization can be understood as a solution to the problem of retaining the advantages of discrete adjustments over strategic decisions while delegating to 'local' levels the management of routinized transactions, that is, those with less uncertainty, higher frequency, and less specificity. The development of the J-form can be seen as a refinement of the divisionalized firm when the latter is confronted by even more complex transactions because of the diversification of the products to be delivered and/or because of increased uncertainty. Indeed, it pairs strong hierarchical coordination with even more decentralized operational decisions in order to restore a continuous flow of information among human assets requiring more flexibility. Diffusion of accumulated know-how can reduce the incentive to behave opportunistically, which generates comparative advantages for the J-form under these circumstances. This analysis also implies that shifting from one form to another *is not irreversible*: new technologies, new products and new competitors may change the characteristics of transactions, for example, decrease the required specificity of assets, and initiate a shift back to a previous organizational design.[28]

Second, large organizations can develop by taking advantage of fiat when rapid adjustments are required (see the subsection on 'organizations as hierarchies' in Section 2, above). Managerial discretion has been a major topic in organization theory since Berle and Means (1932),[29] with notable contributions by Cyert and March (1963), Williamson (1964), Jensen and Meckling (1976). Notwithstanding their differences, these approaches address the same problem: if managerial discretion generates gains (otherwise large organizations would collapse), what is their limit to control efficiently (otherwise there would be one single 'big' firm – see Coase, 1937)? Possibilities of managerial abuse, towards employees as well as towards stockholders, are usually referred to in order to explain loss of efficiency. Such 'biases' can be explained by the fundamental behavioural assumptions of transaction cost economics: bounded rationality restricts the capacity to detect opportunistic choices made possible by the discretionary power delivered to managers holding specific assets. Again, U-forms, M-forms or J-forms must be compared in terms of their capacity to reduce these risks. Typically, multidivisionalization improves intrahierarchical controls over a U-form, by facilitating comparisons among divisions and by creating competition among heads of divisions. The J-form goes even further in this direction, since it combines hierarchical control of a multilayer structure with self-control implemented through the organization of work and the horizontal mobility of managers (Aoki, 1990; Coriat, 1991). Dissociation of strategic decisions from operational ones, in the M-form as well as in the J-form, delivers a supplementary advantage by economizing on the limited capacities of the Centre to solve problems, while making it easier for stockholders to focus on the control over major choices and their implementation.

Third, incentive problems operate in the same direction. Increasing specificity of human assets and related unobservabilities in organizations dealing with complex internal transactions raise the problem of how to induce members to cooperate, since monetary incentives are weakened (Williamson, 1991). Without getting into the complexity of incentives, I want to emphasize that, from a transaction cost point of view, organizations cannot prevail over markets or hybrid forms without complementing discretionary power with cooperative behaviour. The problem is that organizations develop because of the advantages of combining highly specific assets: but this specificity also increases the possibility of opportunism without the safeguard of high-powered incentives that are typical of markets. The larger an organization, the more likely that the M-form will prevail over the U-form, since it creates competition among divisions and among heads of divisions, thus improving incentives that are specific to a multilevel hierarchy (for example, promotion, status and power). These 'organizational incentives' are even more important in a J-form because of the priority given to a strategy of growth, which maintains the dynamics of the hierarchy by using mobility as a powerful stimulus (Aoki (ed.), 1984, Chapters 2 and 3; Aoki, 1988, Chapter 3; Aoki, 1990). Last, development of a 'mini financial market' within large organizations may operate as an incentive to reduce managerial opportunism: allocation of scarce funds among separate lines of business can be contingent on the access to information.[30]

To summarize, alternative configurations of internal governance structures can be viewed as different answers to problems raised by the specificity of (mainly human) assets involved, by the managerial discretion associated with large organizations, and by the resulting incentives to behave opportunistically. We can encapsulate these properties in the following propositions:

(P3)   The more diversified the organization is, the more specific managerial assets are and the more pressures there will be to shift from a U-form to an M-form.
(P3′)   The more endogenous uncertainty is added to the previous characteristics, the more pressures there will be to shift to a J-form.

Changing forms   I suggest relating this proposition to the representation developed by Williamson (1991), where M is for markets, H is for hybrids (more on this below), O is for formal organizations, and k is for the human assets, with human assets highly redeployable next to $k = 0$, and very specific when k is large (see Figure 2.2). Close to k_0, the U-form will predominate as an organizational structure. With more specific assets, organizations would shift successively to an M-form (k_1) and then to a J-form (k_2). In other terms, *incentives for shifting from one configuration to another* would be rooted in the logic of asset specificity described in the previous paragraphs, with *maladaptation* as the moving force.

However, a change in structures is extremely costly. Status and functions of human assets must be adapted, physical and financial assets must be redistributed, flows of information and communication must

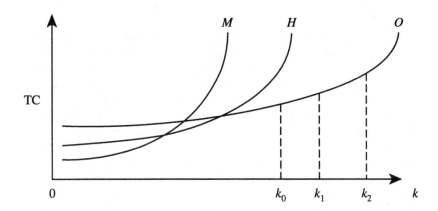

Figure 2.2 Organizational forms in relation to asset specificity

be rechannelled, and so forth. This is why organizations are highly conservative when it comes to their 'configuration'. Changes in structures will occur only when serious challenges develop, and *after* production costs *stricto sensu* have been seriously reduced. Three factors of structural change, related to maladaptation, need to be emphasized from a transactional point of view. (i) Pressures can come from the specific set of transactions in which a firm is involved. Development of new products related to its existing activities may oblige it *to diversify*: from a Chandler–Williamson perspective, this will almost always induce changes in organizational structure. (ii) Vertical integration is also a powerful incentive to change forms. Transaction cost economics strongly suggests that *integration* occurs because of development in asset specificity. Resulting problems of coordination explain the accompanying changes in internal structures.[31] (iii) Substantial changes in the institutional *environment*, for example, tax policy or regulations, can also push a firm to shift from one structure to another. Aoki (1990) thus insisted on the differential in adaptability among J-form, U-form or M-form, according to the degree of uncertainty of the environment. But we know very little about these interactions between institutional environment and internal structures (Williamson, 1993; Menard, 1995a).

A major qualification must be introduced here. Changing organizational structures to maintain advantages of 'making' over 'buying' does not necessarily involve shifting from one pure form to another. In transition periods, firms will often adopt 'intermediate' or 'degenerated' forms (Armour and Teece, 1978) such as holdings or conglomerates. Moreover, organizations confronted with radical incentives to change may search first for forms of coordination that mix the advantages of hierarchies' strong coordination with markets' powerful incentives. This is the domain of *hybrid forms*, a new and exciting field of research in transaction cost economics (Williamson, 1991, 1993; Menard, 1995a, 1996; Masten, 1996; Schanze, 1991). Examples are: networks of firms (Thorelli, 1986; Menard, 1996); franchising,[32] and agreements between service organizations and their customers when highly unobservable services are involved (Bowen and Jones, 1986; Jones, 1987).

Two fundamental questions raised by the existence of hybrid forms as well as by the coexistence of different organizational structures concern the *stability* of these forms and the *factors that could explain their coexistence*. These are questions still to be explored, by both theoretical and empirical studies.

Who is the pilot?

'Configurations' of organizations analysed in the previous subsection refer to structures through which transactions are monitored. But structures do not explain the mechanisms involved in making choices. This is typically an area where transaction cost economics has a great deal to learn from organization theory. Little has been done in the field so far. I will briefly develop two propositions here, one about the composition of external financial resources, and the other about the composition of the 'government' of a large organization.

Finance and the control of organizations[33]   Large organizations periodically need external financial resources. In the Modigliani–Miller approach, the source of these funds is irrelevant. If financial markets are competitive and therefore relatively efficient, the composition of capital has no substantial impact on the internal governance of an organization: whatever the source of the resources is, it maintains competitive pressures for managers to make efficient use of these resources.

In a pathbreaking paper, Williamson (1988) suggested a very different view, that can be completed by Aoki's analysis of the financial characteristics of Japanese firms (Aoki (ed.), 1984, Chapters 1 and 6; Aoki, 1988,

Chapter 4). Using transaction cost economics, Williamson interpreted the choice to finance new investments by debt, equity or other forms as having a significant impact on the internal governance of the firm. External funds will be invested in more or less specific assets: as such, they are not only financial instruments, they also directly influence the government of an organization. To illustrate, let us assume two relatively 'pure' forms of financial resources, debt and equity. Choice between the two can be related to that between 'to make' or 'to buy'; redeployability and, therefore, the possibility of opportunism should be taken into consideration.[34]

Debt is typically an outside procurement in the market mode. It is therefore preferred wherever the assets it finances are highly redeployable. With debt, indeed, transaction costs depend on contractualizable safeguards offered to debt-holders: fixed interest payments to be made at regular intervals; consecutive liquidity tests that the business must meet; principal to be repaid at the expiration of the term of the debt; and, moreover, the possibility for debt-holders in case of default to exercise preemptive claims against redeployable assets. When these guarantees become too costly because the funds are needed for acquisition of highly specific assets that either cannot be redeployed or are redeployable only at high costs, organizations have to turn to other financial resources, such as equity. Equity is a much more intrusive mode of financing than debt. In exchange for taking risks, suppliers of financial resources are awarded forms of control over the government of the organization: they can claim residual rights to the firm; they can and usually do have representatives on the Board of Directors; they share some of the discretionary power in the hierarchy; they vote, can replace managers and contribute to decisions on management compensation; they can authorize audits; they are involved in decisions about important investments as well as about some operational choices. Therefore, equity is rather in the hierarchy mode with similarities to integration because it brings equity-holders into the internal government of the firm. Thus, equity would be preferred when the need for new financial resources is associated with investments with highly specialized features, nonredeployable or very weakly so.

This analysis can be encapsulated in the following proposition:

(P4)   The trade-off between debt and equity or other forms of financial resources depends on the nature of the assets to be financed, and on the related transaction costs.

Debt would predominate for financing less-specific assets; equity would prevail with highly nonredeployable assets; and with intermediate degrees of specificity, we should expect 'hybrid forms' of financing, for example, convertible bonds, or shares without voting rights.

There are two major consequences of this analysis: (a) the origin of financial resources impinges on the government of an organization; and (b) the decision to finance through debt, equity or mixed forms depends on the managers' strategy regarding the extent to which they want to preserve their discretionary power from intruders.

Composition of the Board[35]   Similarly, the composition of the internal 'government' of an organization, for example, the composition of the Board in a corporation, is not neutral. If 'direction' is at the core of formal organizations, then 'judgement rules' play a major role. These rules are implemented and monitored by managers, which explains the traditional attention to the problem of managerial discretion. But this problem is of a much more general nature: in an arrangement where property rights are spread over different categories of holders, the relationship between corporate Board, which is an essential part of the internal governance structure, and constituents of the corporation, becomes a major issue.[36]

Transaction cost economics suggests an interpretation consistent with our analysis and significantly different from the agency theory. When transactions are plagued with high uncertainty, contracts among constituents are necessarily incomplete.[37] Constituents (for example, stockholders, managers, employees) being assets of the firm, the central difficulty of internal governance is related to the degree of specificity of these assets and to the type of guarantee constituents can get or want to get. These criteria may help to determine *ex ante* reasons that could explain why some groups will tend to be part of strategic decision-making, while others would rather be coordinated through contracts. We can expect that:

(P5)   Only those constituents holding highly specific assets *and* not in a position to obtain *ex ante* guarantees that could protect them against opportunism will systematically seek significant power in the government of formal organizations. To illustrate, let me consider some constituents.[38]

Most analyses of participation in the government of an organization (for example, the Board) are normative: they indicate what this government ought to be in relation to an 'ideal type' where market efficiency would determine the standards. A transaction cost approach rather suggests *what can be expected*: the Board is effective in so far as it meets the requirement of a hierarchical governance which is to improve, compared with other possible governance structures, the coordination of highly specific assets by protecting them against opportunism, while economizing on transaction costs. The crucial question then becomes: what conditions must a Board fulfil to reduce the possibilities of opportunistic behaviour? Agency theory looks for an answer in an *ex ante* set of contracts with adequate incentives. Transaction cost economics suggests that the number of constituents involved and the extent of unobservabilities inherent in the specificity of assets would make such a contractual system far too costly,[39] if it were possible at all. It is precisely to economize on such costs that hierarchical structures exist. In a corporation, which is such a structure, the Board is the *ultimate* court of appeal:[40] it is therefore predictable that constituents with highly specific and poorly protectable assets would be the most concerned about the government of the organization. Equity-holders will tend to be well represented, since they have few safeguards against expropriation related to mismanagement; in contrast, it can be expected that debt-holders would have a rather marginal place. Following the same logic, high-level managers, being a very specific asset, should be expected to press for representation on the Board, while the more redeployable intermediate and low-level managers would be less concerned. Last, and much more controversial, what about employees' representation on the Board? Expressed in transaction cost terms, this question becomes: could this kind of participation protect employees from the opportunistic behaviour of shareholders and managers? And could it reduce employees' incentives to behave opportunistically?[41] At this abstract level, transaction cost economics strongly suggests that *participation can reduce opportunism **if** opportunism is generated by the specificity of the assets involved and/or if exchange of credible information is crucial to reduce transaction costs within the organization.* Otherwise, contracts should prevail. As a consequence, one would expect unions or similar representation to be on the Board when they represent highly specific assets, but to prefer negotiations and contracts otherwise.

But transaction cost economics also emphasizes costs related to the participation of constituents. These costs delineate limits beyond which formal organizations lose their comparative advantages. First, there are 'informational costs'. One can expect them to be particularly high for those constituents peripheral to the decision-making process, as with generic suppliers or customers: other solutions will then be preferred (for example, networks of suppliers, specially crafted protection for consumers).[42] Second, there are costs related to the dilution of discretionary power. Formal organizations exist because the adaptive capacities of direction may be paralysed by the involvement of too many constituents. Williamson (1985, Chapter 12) gives the example of operational decision-makers in a multidivisional corporation: their participation on the Board can deflect strategic decision-makers from the main strength of the M-form, which is the separation of operational and strategic decisions. Third, extensive participation of many constituents provides incentives for opportunistic behaviour: for example, by facilitating logrolling and by suggesting the possibility of extracting additional concessions through bilateral bargaining. Firms then resemble the political coalition described by March (1988), losing their relative advantage over market governance even if transactions have attributes that would otherwise give a premium to formal organizations.[43]

To summarize, I have mainly *suggested* in this section *how* transaction cost economics provides useful concepts for investigating characteristics of *the structure of power within organizations*, a problem long neglected or regarded with scepticism by most economists. I have emphasized the consistency of the explanation, as applied to different problems, and I have tried to express these ideas in *refutable propositions*, that is, propositions that can be empirically explored.

4   Conclusion

In this chapter I challenge the view expressed by Alchian and Woodward (1988) that transaction cost economics has little relevance to the analysis of the internal structure of organizations. On the contrary, I argue that using this set of concepts provides a powerful tool for exploring some of the most fundamental characteristics of formal organizations.

In order to make my point, I have focused my analysis on a very restricted number of contributions, thus neglecting an impressive set of recent papers that develop specific arguments or propose empirical tests. As I indicated at the beginning, I also deliberately set aside some fundamental questions, such as the nature of vertical integration or the dynamic of organizational innovation. Last but not least, I emphasized what I consider an essential breakthrough of transaction cost economics, without paying attention to weaknesses and limitations, such as the difficulties we have considering chains of transactions or delineating transaction costs and production costs. Similarly, I barely mentioned problems of technological changes and their organizational requirements. I have also put aside the complex problems of interaction among firms, and between firms and other governance structures.[44]

These lacunae can partially be justified by my methodological choice, which was to explore specific contributions and propositions showing how transaction cost economics can help to explain the actual functioning of *specific governance structures*, namely, in this chapter, formal organizations. Moreover, and this is a major underlying guideline to this chapter, this approach shows that particularly significant progress could be achieved by bridging the gap between transaction cost economics and organization theory.

Notes

* A preliminary draft of this chapter benefited from extensive discussions with Marina Bianchi, Bart Nooteboom, Oliver E. Williamson, members from ATOM, and participants to conferences held at the Sorbonne (Paris) and at Erasmus Universiteit (Rotterdam). I alone remain responsible for all insufficiencies and errors.

1. For a detailed survey, see Klein and Shelanski (1995).
2. This also means that transaction costs are not solely the costs of using the price mechanisms; they are the differentiated costs of operating transactions through different governance structures.
3. I prefer the expression 'formal organizations' to that of 'hierarchy'. The latter, popularized by Williamson in *Markets and Hierarchies* (1975) tends to confuse a specific institutional arrangement and the relationship characterizing this arrangement. I will hereafter identify the arrangement as an *organization*, and I will refer to *hierarchy* as the key concept for understanding the nature of such an arrangement.
4. Paradoxically Coase backed up on this idea, which is at the core of his 1937 paper, in the same book where Masten substantiated the specificity of this relationship. See Coase (1988, Chapter 5) and Masten (1988).
5. Simon (1991) rightly emphasized that strict respect of contractual clauses by employees usually reveals discontent and introduces 'chaos' in the organization.
6. This section was written simultaneously to, and in total ignorance of, Bouttes and Hamamdjian (this book, Chapter 3): we first met at the conference, where our papers were discussed. It makes the convergence of our views particularly striking, and even more so by taking into account that their analysis is closely related to their experience as high-rank managers of a major corporation.
7. 'Engineering technologies', one of four classes of technologies used by Perrow (1967, 1986) to classify organizations, would also fit well here.
8. Williamson (1985, Chapter 10, p. 247) mentions the 'clan' form of organization described by Ouchi (1980).
9. This subsection draws on Menard (1994, 1995b) but with substantial changes.
10. This argument is shared by many authors working within different paradigms. See, among others, Alchian (1984); Grossman and Hart (1986); Tirole (1986); Demsetz (1988); Winter (1988).
11. A view also shared by many noninstitutional economists, for example, Holmstrom and Tirole (1989).
12. Usually reinforced by the implementation of incentives *to obey*: the theory of incentives focuses on some fundamental aspects of this problem.
13. Note that this may be combined with high decentralization of operational decisions, that is, the implementation of strategic decisions is left to those in charge of specific transactions.
14. Williamson (1985, Chapter 4, Section 3) initially identified four sources of specificity: site (related to geographical factors); physical (related to the characteristics of inputs

in use); dedicated (related to choice of investment a firm makes in relation to others' needs), and human. More recently (Williamson, 1993), he added brand-name specificity (the reputation factor) and temporal specificity (intertemporally dependent transactions).

15. As such, specific human assets are different from *skills* that can be measured through observable and redeployable qualifications.

16. This will be so for both strategic and operational decisions.

17. The fundamental rationale being that more frequent transactions tend to reduce problems of observability, and, therefore, of endogenous uncertainty, while higher specificity of human assets has the opposite effect.

18. Remember that we are within a formal organization: a minimum level of frequency as well as of specificity is necessarily involved. In his analysis of labour organization, Williamson (1985, Chapter 10; see my first subsection, above) assumed transactions as recurring and, therefore, frequency as given.

19. I suggest that a moving team, analysed by Alchian and Demsetz (1972), is more of this type than a 'primitive team' (as argued by Williamson). Indeed, in a moving team, the set of actions is relatively well known to the movers, which makes it easy to identify one who does not provide the expected efforts. Typically, moving teams are either weakly integrated or organized through market contracts.

20. In Chapter 3 (this volume), Bouttes and Hamamdjian have provided empirical indicators in this direction. See also Allam (1995). More investigations are required, though.

21. Organizations in which 'internal spot markets' can be implemented could be a possible exception. Such situations should be relatively limited though: according to transaction cost economics, organizations exist primarily because of the necessity of combining specific assets, which means that the value of k is most of the time *significantly* different from zero.

22. Tirole (1986) suggested an analysis of coalitions from a principal–agent perspective.

23. This may help to explain the role of unions in the J-firm (Aoki (ed.), 1984, Part One; Aoki, 1990; Coriat, 1991), as well as their positive contribution to structural adjustments in the co-management system implemented in Germany after World War II.

24. See also Dugger (1983).

25. Helpful studies in this direction are those by Jones (1983), Schein (1985), Cremer (1993), Hofstede et al. (1990), and Kreps (1991).

26. For a survey, see Klein and Shelanski (1995).

27. Defined as the ratio of their profit (after taxes) over stockholders' equities.

28. This may be what happened in the personal computer industry over the last decade. For an empirical study supporting this view, see Anderson (1988).

29. The problem has already been discussed by Smith (1776, Book IV) and Marshall (1920, Book IV, Chapter 12) among others.

30. This is the foundation of the model by Groves and Loeb (1979) on incentives into multidivisionalized firms.

31. For a very stimulating study of the difficulties of coordination in the M-form, see Eccles and White (1988). Analysing the formation of prices in thirteen multidivisional firms of the manufacturing sector, they showed how prices of internal transactions are 'socially constructed' through negotiations among managers.

32. See the excellent issue from the *Journal of Corporate Finance* on franchising (Vol. 2, No. 1/2), 1995.

33. This paragraph draws on Williamson (1988), with some differences in the interpretation.

34. Alchian and Woodward (1988) similarly emphasized that: 'It is not the riskiness, but the plasticity of the firm's asset that drives the cost of debt financing'. Surprisingly, they see this as a disagreement with Williamson.

35. This section greatly benefited from very helpful comments by Bart Nooteboom.

36. This is the core of agency theory, in which harmonization among constituents is

viewed as the search for an optimal contract that would allow the principal's interests to predominate over those of agents (managers), who are themselves in charge of implementing the appropriate decisions with employees through a chain of contracts and subcontracts. See Tirole (1986) and, for specific illustrations, Charreaux and Pitol-Belin (1985).

37. The behavioural theory of the firm (Cyert and March, 1963; Williamson, 1964) has already noted how incomplete contracts, complemented by discretionary power of managers, leads to choices nonreducible to profit maximization, except if one assumes perfect capital markets *and* perfect internal and external labour markets, assumptions that are often made in agency models. Firms rather operate as coalitions of interests.

38. What follows is partially based on Williamson (1985, Chapter 12), with significant differences in interpretation.

39. Rocketing costs of lawyers' services in American corporations may be an indicator of such inefficiencies. For a converging view, see Aoki (1988, Chapter 4; and 1990).

40. This does not fully apply to the contractual part, where courts play that role. But courts consistently refuse to consider cases involving conflicts between branches of formal organizations (except if personal rights are challenged).

41. Similar questions are raised from very different perspectives by Dow (1987) and by Alchian and Woodward (1988).

42. For a stimulating empirical study, see Jones (1987).

43. A similar analysis can be extended to the role of other constituents such as local or regional authorities.

44. Bianchi (1995) develops stimulating critiques in relation to these problems.

References

Alchian, Armen (1984), 'Specificity, Specialization, and Coalitions', *Journal of Institutional and Theoretical Economics*, **140** (March), 34–49.

Alchian, Armen and Harold Demsetz (1972), 'Production, Information Costs, and Economic Organization', *American Economic Review*, **62** (5), 777–95.

Alchian, Armen and Susan Woodward (1988), 'The Firm is Dead. Long Live the Firm', *Journal of Economic Literature*, **26** (1), 65–79.

Allam, Delila (1995), 'L'incomplétude des contrats', Ph. D. Université de Paris I, Panthéon-Sorbonne, unpublished.

Anderson, Erin (1988), 'Transaction Costs as Determinants of Opportunism in Integrated and Independent Sales Forces', *Journal of Economic Behavior and Organization*, **9** (2), 247–70.

Aoki, Masahiko (ed.) (1984), *The Economic Analysis of the Japanese Firm*, Amsterdam: North-Holland.

Aoki, Masahiko (1988), *Information, Incentives and Bargaining in the Japanese Economy*, Cambridge, UK: Cambridge University Press.

Aoki, Masahiko (1990), 'Toward an Economic Model of the Japanese Firm', *Journal of Economic Literature*, **28** (1), 1–27.

Armour, Henry O. and David J. Teece (1978), 'Organizational Structure and Economic Performance: A Test of the Multidivisional Hypothesis', *Bell Journal of Economics*, **9**, 106–22.

Barnard, Chester I. (1938), *The Functions of the Executive*, Cambridge, MA: Harvard University Press (2nd edn, 1962).

Berle, Adolf E. and Gardiner C. Means (1932), *The Modern Corporation and Private Property*, New York: Commerce Clearing House Inc.

Bianchi, Marina (1995), 'Markets and Firms: Transaction Costs versus Strategic Innovation', *Journal of Economic Behavior and Organization*, **28** (3), 183–202.

Bowen, David E. and Gareth E. Jones (1986), 'Transaction Cost Analysis of Service Organization–Customer Exchange', *Academy of Management Review*, **11** (2), 428–41.

Cable, John (1983), 'Hierarchies and Markets: An Empirical Test of the Multidivisional Hypothesis in West Germany', *International Journal of Industrial Organization*, **1** (1).

Cable, John (1985). 'Internal Organization, Business Groups, and Corporate Performance: An Empirical Test of the Multidivisional Hypothesis in Japan', *International Journal of Industrial Organization*, **3** (4).

Chandler, Alfred D. Jr (1962), *Strategy and Structure*, New York: Doubleday & Co.

Charreaux, Gérard and Jean Paul Pitol-Belin (1985), 'La Théorie contractuelle des organisations: une application au conseil d'administration', *Economies et Sociétés* (série Sciences de Gestion), **19** (6), 149–81.

Cheung, Steven (1983), 'The Contractual Nature of the Firm', *Journal of Law and Economics*, **26** (1), 1–22.

Coase, Ronald (1937), 'The Nature of the Firm', *Economica*, **2** (1), 386–405. Reprinted in Williamson and Winter (eds) (1991).

Coase, Ronald (1988), 'The Nature of the Firm: Origin, Meaning, and Influence', *Journal of Law, Economics and Organization*. Reprinted in Williamson and Winter (eds) (1991).

Coase, Roland (1992), 'The Institutional Structure of Production', *American Economic Review*, **82** (4), 713–19.

Coriat, Benjamin (1991), *Penser à l'envers*, Paris: Christian Bourgois.

Cremer, Jacques (1993), 'Corporate Culture and Shared Knowledge', *Industrial and Corporate Change*, **2** (3), 351–86.

Cyert, Richard M. and James G. March (1963), *A Behavioral Theory of the Firm*, Englewood Cliffs, NJ: Prentice-Hall Inc.

Davis, Lance E. and Douglass C. North (1971), *Institutional Change and American Economic Growth*, Cambridge, UK: Cambridge University Press.

Demsetz, Harold (1988), 'The Theory of the Firm Revisited', *Journal of Law, Economics and Organization*. Reprinted in Williamson and Winter (eds) (1991), pp. 159–78.

Dow, Gregory (1987), 'The Function of Authority in Transaction Costs Economics', *Journal of Economic Behavior and Organization*, **8** (1), 13–38.

Dugger, William (1983), 'The Transaction Costs Analysis of Oliver E. Williamson', *Journal of Economic Issues*, **17** (1), 95–114.

Eccles, Robert G. and Harrison C. White (1988). 'Price and Authority in Inter-Profit Center Transactions', *American Journal of Sociology*, **94** (supplement), S17–S51.

Fama, Eugene and Michael C, Jensen (1983), 'Agency Problems and Residual Claims', *Journal of Law and Economics*, **26** (2), 327–49.

Grossman, Stanford and Oliver D. Hart (1986), 'The Costs and Benefits of Ownership: A Theory of Vertical and Lateral Integration', *Journal of Political Economy*, **94** (4), 691–719.

Groves, Theodore and Michael Loeb (1979), 'Incentives in a Divisionalized Firm', *Management Science*, **25** (3), 221–30.

Hirschman, Alfred O. (1970), *Exit, Voice, and Loyalty*, Cambridge, MA: Harvard University Press.

Hofstede, Geert, Bram Neuijen, Denise Doval-Ohayv and Geert Sanders (1990), 'Measuring Organizational Cultures: A Qualitative and Quantitative Study Across Twenty Cases', *Administrative Science Quarterly*, **35** (2), 286–316.

Holmstrom, Bengt and Jean Tirole (1989), 'The Theory of the Firm', in R.D. Schmalensee and R.D. Willig, *Handbook of Industrial Organization*, Amsterdam: Elsevier, vol. 1, pp. 63–133.

Jensen, Michael and William H. Meckling (1976), 'Theory of the Firm: Managerial Behavior, Agency Costs, and Ownership Structure', *Journal of Financial Economics*, **3** (October), 304–60.

Jones, Gareth R. (1983), 'Transaction Costs, Property Rights, and Organizational Culture: an Exchange Perspective', *Administrative Science Quarterly*, **28** (3), 454–67.

Jones, Gareth R. (1987), 'Organization–Client Transactions and Organizational Governance Structure', *Academy of Management Journal*, **30** (2), 197–218.

Joskow, Paul L. (1988), 'Asset Specificity and the Structure of Vertical Relationships',

Journal of Law, Economics and Organization, Reprinted in Williamson and Winter (eds). (1991), pp. 117–37.

Klein, Benjamin, Armen Alchian and Robert G. Crawford (1978), 'Vertical Integration, Appropriable Rents, and the Competitive Contracting Process', *Journal of Law and Economics*, **21** (2), 297–326.

Klein, Peter and Howard Shelanski (1995), 'Empirical Research in Transaction Cost Economics: A Survey and Assessment', *Journal of Law, Economics and Organization*, **11** (2), 335–61.

Kreps, David (1991), 'Corporate Culture and Economic Theory' in James Alt and Kenneth Shapsle (eds), *Perspectives on Positive Political Economy*, New York: Cambridge University Press.

March, James (1962) 'The Business Firm as a Political Coalition', *Journal of Politics*, **24**, 662–78.

March, James G. (1988), *Decisions and Organizations*, Oxford: Basic Blackwell.

Marshall, Alfred (1920), *Principles of Economics*, 8th edn, London: Macmillan. Reprint 1969.

Masten, Scott E. (1988), 'A Legal Basis for the Firm', *Journal of Law, Economics and Organization*. Reprinted in Williamson and Winter (eds) (1991), pp. 196–212.

Masten, Scott E. (1996), *Case Studies in Contracting and Organization*, Oxford: Oxford University Press.

McManus, John C. (1975), 'The Cost of Alternative Economic Organizations', *Canadian Journal of Economics*, **8** (3), 334–50.

Menard, Claude (1994), 'Organizations as Coordinating Devices', *Metroeconomica*, **45** (3), 224–47.

Menard, Claude (1995a), 'Markets as Institutions Versus Organizations as Markets? Disentangling Some Fundamental Concepts', *Journal of Economic Behavior and Organization*, **28** (3), 161–82.

Menard, Claude (1995b), 'Inside the Black Box: The Variety of Hierarchical Forms', in John Groenewegen (ed.), *Transaction Costs Economics and Beyond*, Amsterdam: Kluwer Academic Press, pp. 149–70.

Menard, Claude (1996), 'On Clusters, Hybrids, and Other Strange Forms', *Journal of Institutional and Theoretical Economics*, **152** (March), 154–183.

Mintzberg, Henry (1983), *Structure in Fives. Designing Efficient Organizations*, Englewood Cliffs, NJ: Prentice-Hall.

Muramatsu, Kuramitsu (1984), 'The Effect of Trade-unions on Productivity in Japanese Manufacturing Industry', in Aoki (ed.) (1984), pp. 103–24.

Ouchi, William G. (1980), 'Markets, Bureaucracies, and Clans', *Administrative Science Quarterly*, **25** (March), 120–42.

Perrow, Charles (1967), 'A Framework for the Comparative Analysis of Organizations', *American Sociological Review*, **32** (2), 194–208.

Perrow, Charles (1986), *Complex Organizations*, New York: Random House.

Schanze, Erich (1991), 'Symbiotic Contracts: Exploring Long-Term Agency Structures Between Contract and Corporation', in Christian Joerges (ed.), *Das Recht des Franchising*, Baden-Baden: Nomos Verlagsgesellschaft, pp. 68–103.

Schein, Edgar H. (1985), *Organizational Culture and Leadership*, San Francisco: Jossey Bass.

Simon, Herbert (1945), *Administrative Behavior*, New York: Free Press.

Simon, Herbert A. (1951), 'A Formal Theory of the Employment Relationship', *Econometrica*, **19** (3), 293–305.

Simon, Herbert A. (1991), 'Organizations and Markets', *Journal of Economic Perspectives*, **5** (2), 25–44.

Smith, Adam (1776), *An Inquiry into the Nature and Causes of the Wealth of Nations*, Reed E. Cannan, Chicago: University of Chicago Press, 1976.

Thorelli, Hans B. (1986), 'Networks: Between Markets and Hierarchies', *Strategic Management Journal*, **7** (1), 37–51.

Tirole, Jean (1986), 'Hierarchies and Bureaucracies: On the Role of Collusion in Organizations', *Journal of Law, Economics and Organization*, **2** (2), 181–214.

Williamson, Oliver E. (1964), *The Economics of Discretionary Behavior*, Englewood Cliffs, NJ: Prentice-Hall.

Williamson, Oliver E. (1975), *Markets and Hierarchies*, New York: Free Press.

Williamson, Oliver E. (1985), *The Economic Institutions of Capitalism*, New York: Free Press/Macmillan.

Williamson, Oliver E. (1986), *Economic Organization*, New York: New York University Press.

Williamson, Oliver E. (1988), 'Corporate Finance and Corporate Governance', *Journal of Finance*, **43** (3), 567–91.

Williamson, Oliver E. (1991), 'Comparative Economic Organization: The Analysis of Discrete Structural Analysis', *Administrative Science Quarterly*, **36** (2), 269–96.

Williamson, Oliver E. (1993), 'The Economic Analysis of Institutions and Organizations. In General and with Respect to Country Studies', Working Paper No. 133, Paris: OECD.

Williamson, Oliver E. (1996), *The Mechanisms of Governance*, Oxford: Oxford University Press.

Williamson, Oliver E. and Sydney Winter (eds) (1991), *The Nature of the Firm*, Oxford: Oxford University Press. Reprint of a Special Issue of *Journal of Law, Economics and Organization*, 1988.

Winter, Sidney (1988), 'On Coase, Competence, and the Corporation', *Journal of Law, Economics and Organization*. Reprinted in Williamson and Winter (eds) (1991), pp. 179–95.

D23 D21 L14

3   Contractual relationships within the firm*

Jean-Paul Bouttes and Pascal Hamamdjian

1   Introduction

Although coordinating economic activities within firms is very common, it remains a mystery from a theoretical point of view.

Economics essentially considers that internal organization problems can be solved *ex ante*, either by setting incentive schemes that try to imitate market discipline within firms, or by allocating residual rights of control in advance. In both cases, the way of thinking is the same: economists try to approach an ideal world, that is, a world where people are, and know that they are, residual claimants of the consequences of their own actions on the global corporate performances.

Conversely, some branches of management theory, coming from the necessity of making people (organization members) coexist in a cooperative way, try to base this cooperation on the participation of all concerned in the different levels of the decision process: strategy, control and operation.

Economics and management theory may lead to a binary typology of organizational forms with, on the one hand, the Taylorian enterprise, working on the basis of routines and, on the other hand, the 'network firm'.

The objective of this chapter is to go beyond this typology, and it is based on the fundamental concepts of transaction cost economics. Starting from a reading of contract theory, we will try to define three elementary contractual modes: complete contract, residual rights allocation and project contract. We will then go on to study the way these contractual modes are put together within the firm through a double process of differentiation and integration.[1]

Our objective is to describe the mechanisms by which operators and activities are coordinated within large corporations. By a large corporation, we mean an organization in which no-one can be made residual claimant of the company's financial results. In that perspective, we tried to understand how coordination works and how it enables a collective body to pursue identified objectives.

Of course, we do not underestimate the difficulties of collective action and we know that speaking of the 'objectives of the firm' is a conceptual short cut behind which a great number of difficulties are hidden. We all know that collective objectives emerge only with difficulty, that it is difficult to distinguish the organizational objectives from those of a coalition of actors within the organization. At the limit, the collective body does not exist in so far as its own existence is being threatened by permanent infighting. When we think about it, there are few reasons why a corporation should succeed in elaborating credible and relevant objectives in line with those of its stakeholders: shareholders, regulators, and so on.

It turns out that at least some corporations succeed. The reasons for this success are twofold: first of all, objectives, in the case of commercial organizations, are embodied in physical assets, professional knowledge, and so on. This is why firms are generally better and more effectively organized than political parties. This is also why opportunism is much stronger at the top of a large corporation than at the bottom, where physical assets and professional skills are more salient. The second element of success is the setup within the firm of a special contractual arrangement that we call the project contract and whose function is, *inter alia*, to make collective objectives emerge.

Transaction cost economics has a deep influence on our way of thinking. The frame within which we studied coordination mechanisms, once we admit that collective bodies are able to set up pertinent objectives for themselves, is a Williamsonian one. Williamson called it the 'Fundamental Transformation' (1985, Chapter 10). But although an important part of the literature gives a central role to opportunism, the bounded rationality hypothesis is generally focused on the non-verifiability of actions and the difficulties of writing enforceable contracts. Beyond this important issue, we believe that the central problem is the difficulty actors have to define what they should do when they face a particular problem. Within firms, agents have to innovate collectively. In our opinion, this fundamental problem supersedes opportunism as far as coordination is concerned.

Economics considers internal organization as follows: opportunist agents are locked in a bilateral monopoly situation and they cannot write enforceable contracts. No third party able to help to implement a mutually advantageous solution exists. In our opinion, the story is different: locked-in agents have to solve problems collectively and they have to communicate on the solutions they have in mind. Collective innovation is the main coordination problem. Opportunism remains but as a second-tier element.

In the literature, the standard triad is something like:

asset specificity $<=$ opportunism $=>$ bounded rationality (non-verifiability).

Our triad gives to bounded rationality, interpreted as a necessity to innovate, a central role:

asset specificity $<=$ need for innovation $=>$ opportunism.

What we are interested in is the set of rules, procedures, institutions – specific knowledge that allows actors to innovate and act collectively.

In a world where bounded rationality means need for innovation, incentive schemes alone cannot create the conditions for an effective coordination of actors and activities. To a certain extent, incentive and coordination should be considered separately: the definition of objectives and learning mechanisms on the one hand, the mechanisms of reward and sanction on the other.

In Section 2, we try to show why incentive mechanisms and coordination mechanisms should not be linked too tightly, through a review of the formal literature on contract theory. We show in particular that the formal literature does not catch up with the Williamsonian conception of firms, as idealized in the Fundamental Transformation, where asset specificity and non-technological separability are mixed.

In Section 3, we try to describe the coordination mechanisms that work within firms: definition of roles, responsibilities, objectives and actions, and assessment of these roles, responsibilities, objectives and actions.

We describe these mechanisms using the word 'contract', in reference to the theoretical developments of Section 2. We distinguish three basic contracts: complete contract, allocation of residual rights and project contract. We show that management science specialists and social science specialists have developed categories close to ours.

2 A reading of contract theory

The aim of this section is not to give an exhaustive view of the literature. We will rather try to answer the following question: how does this literature allow us to understand the specificity of organizations, that is, major firms, as a coordination process of economic activities?

In Chapter 10 of *The Economic Institutions of Capitalism*, Williamson built a remarkable typology of industrial relations. We present here a summarized version of that typology which will help us to analyse the contribution of economic literature.

Industrial relations: a taxonomy

In his typology, Williamson crosses two criteria: the degree of asset specificity and the degree of technological non-separability.

Asset specificity makes long-term relationships between the firm and its employees necessary. Moreover, uncertainty makes these relationships difficult to manage, since unforeseen events may occur and make renegotiation imperative.

Technological non-separability creates measurement problems. When there is technological non-separability in an activity, the measurement of the global performance cannot be broken down to assess the individual contribution of the organization's members.

Williamson calls k_0 a low degree of asset specificity, k_1 a high degree of asset specificity, S_0 a high degree of technological separability, S_1 a low degree of technological separability. He then considers four cases:

1. k_0, S_0 *internal spot market*. Workers can join and quit the firm without bearing any particular cost and individual performances can be measured easily. High-powered incentive schemes can be set up and the firm can simulate the market. Actually, the organization is a subset of the marketplace.
2. k_0, S_1 *primitive team*. Human capital is not specific, but individual performances are difficult to assess. Monitoring mechanisms must be set up. However, long-term relationships are not required.
3. k_1, S_0 *obligational market*. Investments in human capital are specific to the firm, but there is no measurement problem. The firm should commit itself to a long-term relationship with its workers and can use simple and efficient incentive schemes.
4. k_1, S_1 *relational team*. This time we find the two difficulties together. One should enter into long-term relationships and give workers incentives to invest in specific assets. Moreover, assessing individual performance is a serious matter. The firm cannot imitate the market any more, using simple incentive schemes.

We will use this typology to reinterpret the economic formalized literature. We selected three basic settings. The first one, 'implementation theory', is the most general expression of the so-called complete contract approach; the second one, by Laffont and Tirole (1986), belongs to the complete contract world, too, but goes one step beyond by providing very intuitive results; the third one, Grossman and Hart's incomplete contract model, is in the formal literature the setting closest to Williamson's conceptions.

Implementation theory

To begin with, we will recall the general statement of the typical problem in implementation theory. We will then analyse the different 'fundamental' hypotheses, implicit or explicit, concerning four points: specificity of investments, links between individual and global performances, the stability of technology and the existence of a market for intermediary products.

General formulation of implementation problems A typical problem in implementation theory is the following: two agents should cooperate to maximize a social choice function. The timing of the cooperation is as follows: at date 0, agents sign a contract that defines mission and compensation rules. At date 1, agents make investments e_1 and e_2. To be more concrete, we may say that 1 is responsible for the technical side of the product and 2 is responsible for the marketing side. These investments give, as a result, two intermediate products θ_1 and θ_2 on a random basis. We assume that there is no market for θ_1 and θ_2. θ_i is known only by agent i. Let V_1 and V_2 be the intrinsic utility function of unit 1 and unit 2. Here V_1 and V_2 may be viewed as operational margins (before taking into account the investment costs). Let $x^*(\theta_1, \theta_2)$ be the functional maximizing

$$V = \sum_i V_i(x(\theta_1, \theta_2), \theta_i)$$

for a type profile (θ_1, θ_2). $x()$ can be seen as a set of characteristics of the final product chosen within a domain assumed to be known *ex ante*. At date 2, after 1 and 2 announced $\hat{\theta}_1$ and $\hat{\theta}_2$, action $x^*(\hat{\theta}_1, \hat{\theta}_2)$ is taken. At date 3, the final product is sold and V_1 and V_2 are realized. $V = V_1 + V_2$ is the global corporate performance, investment cost not included.

The basic problem is, on the one hand, to give agents incentive to choose the right levels of investments e_1^* and e_2^* and, on the other hand, to make them reveal their private information about parameters θ_1 and θ_2.

Fundamental hypotheses: a discussion We can reinterpret the model in the following way:

A. Specificity of investments and absence of market for intermediate goods. e_1 and e_2 are specific investments that allow the production of intermediate goods for which no market exists. Once the contract is signed, agents are locked in a bilateral monopoly situation and there is no longer any room for competition: no bid can be organized on θ_1 and θ_2. Furthermore, in this situation, people have private information and they can use it in an opportunistic way.

B.   Technological stability, links between individual and global performances. The functionals $x(.)$, $V_1(.)$ and $V_2(.)$ are known *ex ante*. So we can define *ex ante* the best action relative to θ_1 and θ_2 profiles, and the impact of that action on the utility levels $V_1(.)$ and $V_2(.)$ can be assessed precisely. Of course, technological separability is not total: on the one hand, $x(.)$ depends on θ_1 and θ_2; on the other, the choice of $x(.)$ has an impact on both $V_1(.)$ and $V_2(.)$. However, using monetary transfers, one can put individual performances and global performance on line by choosing appropriate transfers t_1 and t_2 such that 1 and 2 while seeking to maximize $V_1 + t_1$ and $V_2 + t_2$ would in fact maximize $V_1 + V_2$. It is therefore possible to give to 1 and 2 credible objectives and effective incentive schemes based on the global performance V.

One can summarize the characteristics of the model as follows:

- specific investments are needed to produce intermediate goods for which no market exists: we are in the frame of Williamson's Fundamental Transformation;
- one can define the characteristics of the final product *ex ante* since $x(.)$, $V_1(.)$ and $V_2(.)$ are known;
- credible objectives can be defined for each agent *ex ante* or *interim* starting from the global performance $V_1 + V_2$;
- effective incentive schemes can be set up based on these objectives.[2]

At this stage, we can define the firm as an institution which allows specific investments to be made, reliable information for activities' coordination to be gathered, and technical interdependence and utility function antagonism to be managed. Regarding Williamson's typology, we are in case number 3: k_1, S_0, obligational market.

Incentive theory
We will proceed here as for the implementation theory by recalling the general statement of the problem. Since the conceptual framework is about the same as the one of implementation theory, we will discuss fundamental and technical hypotheses more briefly and we will spend more time examining in detail the original results obtained by Jean-Jacques Laffont and Jean Tirole.

General formulation Jean-Jacques Laffont and Jean Tirole developed a set of models in 1985–90 that have been gathered in *A Theory of Incentives in Procurement and Regulation* (1993). In the basic version, the model has one period and two agents whose utility functions are antagonistic.

Laffont and Tirole's model is one of adverse selection (β) in which one introduces an action variable (an effort e) so that *ex post* observation of the agent's performances (a unit cost $c = \beta - e$ and the quantity produced q) does not allow a trivial resolution of the problem to be made.

In the one-period version, the model shows the existence of a trade-off between extracting informational rent and inducing effort. The optimal incentive scheme is implemented through a menu of linear contracts in which the compensation of the agent is a function of the announced performance P_a and the realized performance P: $W = A(P_a) + B(P_a)[P - P_a]$, with $A(.)$ and $B(.)$ increasing relative to P_a.

Discussion of the underlying hypotheses Regarding the fundamental hypotheses, incentive theory is close to implementation theory: the (implicit) presence of specific investments and the absence of a market for intermediate goods (the parameter β) create a situation of bilateral monopoly. In the same way, the stability of the functionals allows one to put the agent's and principal's objectives on line in return for the payment of a rent: one can describe the cost function for every state of the world (every β) and one can induce the agent towards the maximization of public welfare through a transfer payment.

Regarding the technical hypotheses, the sequence moral hazard–adverse selection is reversed: the agent knows his/her type before signing the contract and he/she chooses his/her effort after the contract is signed. Having only one agent (the principal has no productive function) makes things easier and allows interesting formal results to be obtained; the agent's risk neutrality and the nature of the individual rationality constraint (*ex post* for each β) explain the nature of the results obtained. Here and unlike in d'Aspremont–Gérard-Varet's construction, only a second best optimum is reached.

Intuitive results The model is a nice illustration of important – but intuitive – phenomena:

- Evolutionary incentive schemes exist within firms: operational units are committed to objectives they partially define. They are given incentives in order to be ambitious and to stick to their objectives.

- The ratchet effect: in a dynamic setting, it is very difficult to write contracts using the revelation principle. When there is more than one period, agents are less inclined to reveal their information since they fear a detrimental (strategic) use of that information in the following periods.
- Multidimensional adverse selection parameter: when the adverse selection parameter has several dimensions, incentive contracts become very tricky. Those contracts should therefore be reserved for specific activities, that is, activities where the expected performance is essentially monodimensional.
- Multi-agent model: when there are several agents, collusive behaviour may occur; agents may collude and lie in a concerted way to the principal, the latter having no means of discovering the truth.

All these phenomena are actually observed in firms and the merit of the model is to provide a formal treatment. Finally, the idea of evolving complete contracts is an important one for the internal organization of firms. On the other hand, hypotheses like specific investments and uncertainty, which explain and justify long-term relationships between a small number of agents, are not treated *per se*: the problem of resetting objectives to be reached and the institutions needed to improve the renegotiation outcome are not developed.

The main teachings of the model can be summarized as follows, as far as management issues are concerned:

- when expected performances can easily be assessed, it becomes possible to write contracts that look like Laffont and Tirole's contract model;
- these contracts are complete and evolutionary;
- when expected performances are complex, when there are several actions or dynamic problems, writing complete contracts becomes far more hazardous;
- similar problems arise when we assume risk aversion;
- managers need to be hyperrational to be able to write and implement such contracts.

Incomplete contracts: allocation of residual rights

We will examine here the concept of allocation of residual rights such as it has been formalized in the literature since the seminal paper by

Grossman and Hart (1986). After presenting the model and discussing the main hypotheses, we will assess its contribution to internal organization analysis.

General setting Two agents must cooperate for the production of a particular type of goods. The cooperation consists of two stages: stage 1 is the investment stage (we will call i and j the investment decisions of agent 1 and agent 2), stage 2 is the operating stage during which agents 1 and 2 take decision q_1 and q_2. *Ex post*, before transfer, the return is B_1 (i, j, q_1, q_2) for agent 1 and B_2 (i, j, q_1, q_2) for agent 2.

In an ideal world, we should be able to write a contract specifying that 1 must realize $[i^{OPT}, q_1^{OPT}]$ and 2 must realize $[j^{OPT}, q_2^{OPT}]$ to maximize B_1 $(i, j, q_1, q_2) + B_2$ (i, j, q_1, q_2). Grossman and Hart assume that such a contract cannot be written and make the following assumptions:

- one cannot contract at date 1 either over i and j or over q_1, q_2, B_1, B_2;[3]
- at date 2, q_1 and q_2 become contractible.

The model studies the impact of the choice of q_1 and q_2 at date 2 on the choice of investment variables. Grossman and Hart show how allocating residual rights of control *ex ante* on q_1 and q_2 between the two agents influences investment decisions at date 1.

The hypotheses of the model Basically, this model fits case number 4 of Williamson's typology (the *relational team*). However, an important difference from Williamson's setting exists: in Grossman and Hart's setting, there is no problem of coordination *ex post*, while this problem is essential for Williamson. Here, the renegotiation process allows one to reach the optimum *ex post*, given i and j. Apart from this, one is clearly within the frame of the Fundamental Transformation: the agents realize specific investments and there is no market for the intermediate goods q_1 and q_2 *ex post*. The stability of the technology is not guaranteed and the links between individual and global performances are not clear *ex ante* for the third party. This is how to interpret the non-verifiability of q_1 and q_2 and the non-contractability of B_1 and B_2. The firm is not able to describe *ex ante* what the operating conditions will be, cannot break up the global performance into clearly defined objectives for each agent, and cannot write enforceable contracts.

On the technical side, the hypotheses of the model are peculiar: there is no verifiable variable *ex ante* and there is no asymmetry of information. However, this does not affect the core of the model, and we will analyse the main results next.

The main results   The main contribution of the model is to formalize the concept of residual rights. Whereas Williamson allocates residual rights directly to investment decisions, Grossman and Hart allocate residual rights of control to operating variables.

To a certain extent, one may regret that the model does not go a little bit further. In the Grossman and Hart setting, the construction of the hierarchical structure and the control for the use of residual rights rest on a proxy that is impossible to implement in the real world: to allocate residual rights of control, Grossman and Hart pick the agent that would have spontaneously taken operating decisions close to the optimal ones. In a certain manner of speaking, the model falls into its own trap. Although it is the difficulty in linking global performance and individual performances that creates, in combination with uncertainty, the necessity of allocating residual rights of control, Grossman and Hart try to solve the problem by giving the control to the agent which embodies the firm in the least unsatisfactory way. The investment process is then influenced by the reinforcement of the bargaining position of the controlling party.

In the real world, this kind of proxy is often difficult to implement, because of the difficulty of linking residual rights and the associated income stream. Once residual rights of control have been granted, the firm will have to monitor the way the controlling party uses its discretionary power. For the same reason, we will have to imagine adapted schemes to make people achieve specific investments that are of the utmost importance to the firm.

Within firms, the link between individual and global performances is very difficult to assess because of the large number of agents involved in the production process and the spread of outcomes over time. The scope of complete contracts is therefore bounded: complete contracts only cover specific tasks during specific periods and they need to be renegotiated periodically. Other contractual forms must be designed to deal with uncertainty and the need for coordination and innovation it requires. Allocation of residual rights of control and project contracts are these contractual forms.

Conclusion of Section 2
The major contribution of the formal literature on contracts is to provide a rigorous treatment of a range of important issues, in particular informational asymmetry (between two agents, between agents on the

one hand, and third parties like the courts on the other) and its strategic use in a bilateral monopoly situation. Institutions like piece-rate salary, hierarchy and their limits are better understood than they have ever been. It also provides a precise vocabulary to describe internal organizational problems. This will help to reduce transaction costs in the research area.

The second contribution of the formal literature is to provide a framework to describe and differentiate two different kinds of contract: complete contract on the one hand, and allocation of residual rights on the other.

The limits of this literature, when applied to management issues, are twofold: first, it does not really succeed in formalizing case number 4 of Williamson's typology, which crosses asset specificity and technological non-separability. Consequently, it does not take into account the notion of governance structure. Williamson's insight that firms need to design low-powered incentive schemes and governance structures regulating the people who have been granted residual rights of control, remains without formal echo. Second, the formal literature underestimates the importance of cognitive issues.

3 Contractual arrangements within the firm

This section starts with case number 4 of Williamson's typology but modifies the relative importance of the elements of the triad 'asset specificity–limited rationality–opportunism'. We wish to interpret the concept of bounded rationality less in the sense of the non-verifiability of actions than in the sense of the need to innovate. When the emphasis is put on the non-verifiability interpretation of bounded rationality, everything rests on the opportunism hypothesis. Non-verifiability limits the intervention of third parties like judges and reinforces the bilateral monopoly situation. Opportunism therefore produces its maximum adverse effects. In our approach, opportunism remains a problem but the main difficulty is that people within the firm have to work together without always knowing exactly how to deal with and solve the problems they have to face. The need to innovate requires the establishment of dialogue between people. People need to communicate because they have to solve problems together. This is the main coordination issue. The three contractual arrangements we will discuss next are institutions created for making people communicate and think together. Of course, as we still consider opportunism to be an important question, we have to consider control issues as well.

The specificity of the integrated enterprise
Before examining the contractual arrangements themselves, we should explain our project more explicitly. For this purpose, we propose to go back to the elements that determine the specificity of the integrated company.

Hatchuel (1993) found two important elements for the understanding of what characterizes the modern firm. Recalling Weber's argument according to which a strong relationship exists between the nature of collective organizations and the rationality of these organizations, he sets the following propositions for firms:

- we should be aware of the existence of different forms of collective organization and of their permanent reconstruction over time since the beginning of the nineteenth century;
- these reconstructions are stimulated by permanently renewed rationalization schemes, the nature of which is to be explored;
- each of these schemes stimulates new learning processes embodied in the formulation of new rules and new actions.

Hatchuel defines rationalization as a fundamental driver for organizational changes and emphasizes the interconnection between organization and learning.

The propositions we would like to develop are close to those developed by Hatchuel, although using different words, that is, those of contract theory. At this stage, we need to emphasize the fact that the meaning of certain words in this chapter is somewhat different from the standard meaning they have. We enjoyed the lexical richness of contract theory but we felt free to broaden the definition of certain concepts.

From innovation to 'routinization'   Innovation characterizes the newly established firm. The entrepreneur is fundamentally an innovator. He/she is also the one that creates the conditions of his/her own success. For that purpose, he/she has to conceive tasks, rules and incentive schemes: in a word, he/she has to 'routinize' his/her own innovations.

Creating routines means breaking down complexity into tasks that become more and more common over time. This transformation requires specific contractual arrangements since they mean employing specific assets in an opportunistic world. Asset specificity and opportunism cannot by themselves justify the existence of the integrated enterprise. They explain rather earlier contractual arrangements like putting-out or inside contracting: a set of independent workshops or factories rather than an integrated firm since 'routinization' allows the writing of complete contracts.

The path innovation–routinization cannot explain the survival of integrated firms in the long run even if it explains the creation, at a given moment, of a firm.

The durability of the integrated company The very nature of modern economies breaks the path of innovation–routinization by introducing positive uncertainty such as technical progress, the evolution of consumer needs and the evolution of competition.

The domain of the integrated firm appears as soon as there are uncertainties that threaten the firm, but at the same time give it new opportunities, and as soon as it is worth trying to innovate by using an existing structure.

The integrated company is then driven by a double logic:

- simplify the complexity which is a necessary condition in order to make innovations profitable – this is the domain of complete contracts;
- innovate and prepare itself to innovate in the future by regularly modifying the organization of knowledge and the coordination process within the firm – these are the domains of what we will call project contract and residual rights allocation.

To do so, the integrated company should bring its members to make further specific investments in order for them to acquire a real capacity to change. It must put in place contractual arrangements to manage these somewhat contradictory logic systems. The firm should see itself in perpetual evolution in an uncertain world which requires it to adapt to every opportunity. The firm has to reconcile contradictory logic systems and it does so by putting into a hierarchy contractual arrangements that are by nature different.

Contractual arrangements in the integrated firm

Preliminary remarks The description of the contractual arrangements of the integrated firm will be made as follows.

First, we will try to differentiate three elementary contracts: the complete contract, the allocation of residual rights and the project contract. We will use for that purpose the following criteria: the nature of specific investments and the role of the contract in the coordination process; the relative role of quantified indicators and of dialogue for

Table 3.1   Main features of three elementary contracts

Criteria	Complete Contract	Residual Rights Allocation	Project Contract
Nature of Specific Investments*	Qualification, professional experience	Experience of different functions within the firm	Knowledge of the firm and its environment
Role in the Coordination Process	Weak	Very important	Important
Role of Quantified Indicators	Essential	Instrumental	Instrumental
Role of the Management Dialogue	Allows the evolution of the contract terms	Very important, *ex ante, interim* and *ex post* to appreciate performances	Important for the cohesion of the project team
Discretionary Power	Weak	Important	Very important
Veto Right	No	No, in general	Essential

Note: * Specific investments are the set of knowledge, procedures, institutions that make contracts change over time and adapt to new contingencies.

the performance assessment; the size of discretionary power and the existence of a veto right for general-purpose decisions.

Next, we will study each type of contract in detail. We will then analyse the way these contracts are put together within the firm.

General characteristics of contracts   Because the integrated firm must reconcile contradictory logic systems, there must be different contractual arrangements. We choose to distinguish three elementary contracts.[4] Table 3.1 summarizes the main features of each contract.[5]

Complete contracts

Complete contracts are the most familiar contractual arrangements. There is substantial literature on complete contracts in economics and in management science. After presenting certain characteristics of complete contracts, we will study their implementation within firms and the different existing forms. We should stress again that the expression 'complete contract' is taken in a sense that differs somewhat from the meaning it has in the literature.

General features   Complete contracts are those for which the effort of quantification is the most important, either for setting objectives or for assessing performances.

The operator who is required to make specific investments (training, team socialization, understanding of certain components of the information and management system) is expected to reach objectives defined over time with a given periodicity.

Facing these objectives, the agent has little leeway: simple decisions, choice of effort level. This, however, does not rule out technical skills.

Finally, the role of the operator in terms of coordination is at the same time informal and simple: informal because what is required of the agent is to match people within a small group where personal relations are essential (people know each other), simple since coordination is made easier by the existence of quantified objectives.

The implementation of complete contracts   The implementation of complete contracts is performed in two stages. First, the firm must be able to stabilize the environment of the agents it is signing contracts with. It must then make contracts evolve over time.

A. Stabilizing the environment. On this point, economic theory and management science share common views. The stabilization of the environment corresponds to the upstream part of the contract. From the economist's point of view, the principal who has been granted residual rights of control must define the tasks of his/her subordinates and the intermediate goods they have to supply. Using the formalism of Grossman and Hart (1986), the controlling party defines q_1 and q_2, i and j: he/she defines specific investment and performances to be reached.

In the same manner, when Mintzberg (1982) built his typology of coordination processes in five points, three referred directly to the concept of complete contract and more exactly to the effort made by the firm to stabilize the environment of some of its workers. Hatchuel (1993) clearly shows that Mintzberg's five coordination processes are of a different nature:

Mintzberg, in his attempt to synthesize organizational types . . . distinguished five coordination processes: direct supervision, methods standardization, output control, standardization through qualifications, mutual adjustment. . . . One can easily notice that some of these types are defined by reference to a relational model, the others through the acknowledgement of a certain distribution of knowledge between agents. Thus, direct supervision and mutual adjustment are respectively a hierarchical relationship and a bilateral agreement. On the other hand, the three other processes are based on a particular distribution of information and knowledge.

Hatchuel thus accepts the existence of contracts of a different nature. There is a close relationship between direct supervision and residual rights on the one hand, mutual adjustment and project contract on the other. We will go back to this relationship later on.

As far as complete contracts are concerned, we will bear in mind that the stabilization of the agents' environment can be obtained through different channels: through method standardization, through qualification standardization or through output control.

Method standardization consists in specifying how tasks should be performed. Output control consists in setting in advance product attributes or performances to be reached. Qualification standardization consists in specifying the training of the operators.

Standardization stabilizes the operator's environment and allows a description of the expected performance through a small number of dimensions to be made.

B.   Contract evolution.   The operator's environment cannot be stabilized once and for all. The firm therefore needs to make the stabilization process itself change over time. The essential question is thus the following: what is the role of the operator in the evolution of the contractual terms if we assume that this is one of the responsibilities of the controlling party? There are two possible solutions: one in which the operator does not play any role in the evolution of the routines or of the objectives to which he/she is held, another in which the operator plays a crucial role in defining the routines he/she will have to adopt and the objectives he/she will have to reach. The type of random shocks that affect the firm may help to discriminate between these two solutions since there is clearly no absolute answer.

Different forms of complete contracts   The ways in which the manager defines the room for manoeuvre of his subordinates vary a lot. First, they depend on the type of standardization selected. They also depend on the nature of the objectives assigned. One can list three kinds of objectives: routines respect, physical objectives assignment (quantity, quality, turnover) and monetary objectives assignment (constitution of cost centres, profit centres, and so on).

Let us summarize the difference between these three kinds of objectives in the following way:

A. Definition of routines. The manager should be able to give the operators precise instructions for every conceivable contingency. Conversely, he/she does not have to define quantified objectives, either physical or monetary. If local random events are not important, this system will work quite well. In particular, the upward level will be able to coordinate operators located upstream and downstream in industries where the quality of intermediate products cannot be easily controlled, either because of its complexity or because of the frequency of transactions. Of course, the occurrence of local random shocks may considerably disturb the coordination process.

B. Multidimensional physical objectives. The manager does not have to price the different elements of the expected performances. Of course, the objectives assigned to the different operators should be consistent with each other even if control processes exist (buffer inventories, and so on). This system is particularly well adapted when there is a high degree of technical interdependency between operators for the production of intermediate products and when quality is essential. We find here the arguments developed by Weitzman (1974) concerning the relative merits of objectives expressed in price terms and objectives expressed in quantity terms.

C. Monetary objectives. This is the system that leaves operators the largest leeway. Operators can perform trade-offs using the price system, should this price system be granted by the market or by the operator hierarchy. To make this system work, there should be little interdependence between operators. Clearly, we find this system in units that work close to the market (trading unit, for instance). Such a system is well adapted when units are in a better position than the centre to appreciate price evolutions in the marketplace and make the right trade-offs. Incentive schemes *à la* Laffont and Tirole stem from that system and so does the piece-rate wage.

Allocation of residual rights

We will proceed here as for complete contracts. After presenting some general features, we will go further into the way those residual rights of control are exercised and how the dialogue takes place between managers and the chief executive officer of the firm. Afterwards we will explain the central role played by managers of operational units in the coordination process.

Some general features Agents who are granted residual rights are generally executives with management or other responsibilities requiring special expertise. To carry out their missions correctly, these agents need to acquire a certain amount of specific knowledge.

Except for technical knowledge that we suppose is already acquired, these specific skills are the experience of different functions in the company, the knowledge of the information system and of the decision process, the ability to communicate, and so on.

The agent to whom residual rights are allocated has some discretionary power. This is justified by the fact that the hierarchy is not able to define precisely and *ex ante* what he/she is expected to do. The agent may therefore innovate, at least locally.

The agent may be an expert or a manager. In the latter case, he/she manages groups of operators with whom he/she signs complete contracts. It is up to him/her to stabilize the environment of the workers he/she is responsible for, and to make these contracts change over time as required by changes in the environment. Workers may be involved in the revision process through an information feedback system.

Residual rights should also be distinguished according to the freedom left to the manager. One can have three typical situations:

- residual rights involving the manager's adaptation to local shocks. One example could be a foreman who modifies the organization of his team to improve its productivity;
- residual rights consisting in introducing more durable changes in order to adapt to any modification of the local environment. To make these changes, executives should be able to interpret the global strategy of the firm and to adapt it to the local circumstances;
- residual rights over the definition of general policies. The object here is to create new intervention fields. Here we enter the domain of project contracts.

Residual rights: implementation and control   We will consider here the way residual rights are implemented and the way one can monitor those who receive residual rights. Having discretionary powers does not mean that executives act without any control. Firms oblige managers to work under tied controls and to meet objectives. The difference with complete contracts lies in the relative role of quantified indicators in the dialogue between executives and their hierarchy. Here, the assessment of the manager's actions is made by the firm's Chief Executive Officer (CEO). The CEO has to motivate his appraisal and executives should be able to justify their own decisions. However, arbitrary judgements can never be ruled out. That is why one should try to reduce the opportunism of both parties and generate a form of congruence of interest between executives and the general management of the firm.

The relationship between the manager and his hierarchy depends to a large extent on the type of residual rights allocated. We will distinguish residual rights for adaptation to local shocks from residual rights for adaptation to more structural changes.

A. Adaptation to local shocks. The executive takes part in the definition of quantified objectives with his/her hierarchy. However, each party knows that these objectives cannot summarize in a satisfactory way the expected performance. The quantified objectives serve another goal: to structure the dialogue *ex ante* and make the agent understand what he/she is expected to do, to structure the dialogue *ex post* for performance assessment.

   Even more important, executives should be able to explain to their hierarchy why they took such or such a decision. In particular, they should be able to describe the random shocks that occurred. We are therefore close to the world of complete contracts: the hierarchy and the executive define quantified objectives. However, residual rights allocations are not complete contracts: here, quantified indicators are essentially devoted to structuring the management dialogue. Only in a second stage and also indirectly, do they serve as an incentive device.

B. Adaptation to more structural changes. Here, the manager receives the power to allocate residual rights and to monitor the way these rights are exercised. Since the manager's room for manoeuvre is more important in that case, the dialogue *ex ante* is more important: projects are submitted to the hierarchy in a more formal way, and the manager can be helped by experts for whom he/she is not directly responsible during the preparation. The project is analysed from different points of view: financial, technical, social, and so on.

   The term of the mandate for high-level executives is generally long (several years). The manager's position is never clear: he/she must have a certain independence, but is subjected to periodic control. In the real world, it is relatively frequent to see executives, even at a high level, subjected to very tight control from the CEO. This shows how residual rights allocation is a difficult task.

The coordination of activities at the unit level Operational unit managers play an important role in coordinating activities. Product quality,

Table 3.2   Examples of coordination failures

Coordination Failures	Origins	Possible Remedy
Intermediate product or service not, or poorly, supplied	Antagonistic interests	Modification of complete contracts
Poor understanding of what the other does or requires	Absence of shared vision, absence of common logic	Implementation of a small project contract under the principal's control
Domination of one team	Attempt of one group to increase its influence over the other	Redefinition of the residual rights of each team, help in the exercise of residual rights

cost reduction and compliance with strict deadlines depend on the quality of coordination within units. We can analyse the problem as follows.

Let P be the manager of a unit composed of two teams, A1 and A2. A1 and A2 have to work with each other frequently, which raises coordination issues. One can distinguish two polar cases: in one case, interactions between A1 and A2 are stable. It is then possible to give A1 and A2 formal incentive to cooperate by properly using complete contracts. Typically, client–supplier relationships are of this type. The settlement of this kind of relationship can take on different forms: internal transfer prices can be freely negotiated between A1 and A2 or be imposed by P. Again, P may allow A1 or A2 to buy goods or services outside the firm, introducing second-source competition.

In the second case, interactions between A1 and A2 change in nature over a period of time. P should therefore make the cooperation process evolve over time too. If nothing is done, coordination failures may appear. We give some examples of coordination failures in Table 3.2.

Project contract

The identification of the project contract as one of the fundamental contractual arrangements within industrial corporations is motivated by our conception of bounded rationality. In the standard incomplete contract paradigm, the main effect of bounded rationality is in practice to make actions non-verifiable. People know what they have to do but they cannot sign enforceable contracts. Opportunism then produces maximal adverse effects. Here, bounded rationality means bounded knowledge. People do not know how to do their job, at least partially, and they are condemned to innovate collectively. This requires the setting of a common project, based on a common vision of the underlying difficulties.

Residual rights allocation and project contracts   There is a basic difference between residual rights allocation and project contracts. Those who have been granted residual rights receive authority by delegation of their hierarchy. They are then 'free' to do whatever they want. Conversely, the members of a project contract, like executive directors in a company, work in a different way. Even though they are technically specialized (there are financial directors, marketing directors, and so on), their first characteristic is to belong to a collective body.

The members of a project contract have a kind of veto right for any decisions, even those in which they are not directly involved. This process of collective decision is the real difference between allocation of residual rights and project contracts.

An example of project contract: the executive committee   The executive committee has essentially one mission: to define the company's strategic main lines. To do so, it begins by defining a strategic core: definition of the markets, of the commercial and financial targets, of the products, and so on. The strategic core is fed by the experts who work for the executive committee. Of course, each expert team has its own mental models or cognitive maps (technical, financial, marketing, and so on) and directors have to find compromises and focal points despite the heterogeneity of the points of view.

The strategic core is then translated into facts through decisions: appointment of senior managers, implementation of procedures for launching new policies. The coordination role of executive directors is to give impetus and define residual rights, then to allocate them.

Members of the executive committee should be residual claimants for their decisions. However, it often takes a long time for policies already engaged to produce tangible effects and this makes this kind of regulation sometimes ineffective. The control of the ruling team should be performed differently. In practice, one would check the following points:

- avoid letting the executive committee be in charge of too many things;

- limit the size of the committee – members of the committee should know each other;
- see to the quality of the information that the committee members receive;
- have a truly collective decision process;
- have a certain stability in the composition of the committee (as a commitment device).

Executive directors are granted substantial power and one might fear that they would misuse their power. This is a big problem since executive directors may appoint and dismiss whoever they want. However, to a great extent, executive directors work and make decisions under a veil of ignorance and this considerably limits their discretionary power: asymmetry of information acts as a sort of protection against an opportunistic use of power by executive officers.

Hierarchical organization of contracts

The integrated firm is an organization in which we find put together in the right way the three contractual arrangements we were talking about: complete contracts, allocations of residual rights and project contracts. This organization requires that the three forms be put together by a double move of differentiation and integration. Differentiation means preserving the nature of each contract. Each contract should be associated with certain types of responsibilities and with a certain language. Integration means putting together the three kinds of contract in order to facilitate the coordination of the innovation process and the adaptation of the firm to its environment. It requires information systems and incentive schemes.

The differentiation of contracts   Differentiating contracts helps to preserve the nature of contractual arrangements. One differentiates contracts by identifying them with logical levels, with temporal horizons and with languages of different kinds. We associate strategy, the long term and economic language with the project contract. We associate control, the medium term and techno-economic language with residual rights of control. We associate operation, the short term and technical language with the complete contract.

These links are not sufficient. The differentiation of contractual arrangements is effective only when the nature of contracts is preserved. We noticed that if the differences in the nature of the three elementary contracts are real, they are subtle. This is thus a source of ambiguity. Let us take some examples: collective decision process is a central characteristic of the project contract. But the general manager may gather all the power into his/her hands and transform the other members of the executive committee into simple executives with residual rights of control over their departments. In the same manner, at the operational unit level, an excessive use of quantified indicators may transform residual rights allocation into complete contracts.

This general motion is likely to occur when specific investments by the organization members are insufficient. This kind of organizational entropy can be stopped only if the executive committee takes considerable care and keeps under control the way people within the firm acquire specific knowledge.

Integration of contractual forms   The objective of integration is to coordinate the innovation process and the firm's adaptation. Integration requires the implementation of information systems and incentive schemes.

A.   Information systems.   Information systems allow the production of relevant information at a reasonable cost. It should also sort out information and dispatch it to the right places, that is, the places where it will be used in a profitable way.

Of course, information is generally not produced at the place it is going to be used. That is why organizing information flows upwards and downwards is very important: upwards, it allows the executive committee to take pertinent decisions, downwards it allows operational units to understand the corporate strategy.

Information systems have another role: they allow contracts to evolve: objectives, domains of action, coordination processes, strategic main lines, and so on. Their architecture is closely related to the technical characteristics of the industry. Sometimes the construction of information feedback that allows workers to take an active role in updating contracts is useless: updating contracts can be made in a centralized way. Sometimes, the operators' participation is imperative.

B.   Incentive schemes.   We have said little about incentive schemes up to now. If incentive schemes, that is, rewards and sanctions, are an important part of the contractual arrangements, they cannot by themselves guarantee the coordination of activities. Coordination and incentives are needed, but one cannot replace the other. How to design an incentive scheme in a world of bounded rationality is at the top of the agenda today. We believe that in large corporations, career concerns play an important role, even more important than extra money or a bonus as an incentive device. At least, what we should study is a certain number of incentive schemes that take into account problems like equity, collusion, allocation of resources within the firm, and so on. There may be particular links between certain incentive schemes and certain contracts: monetary rewards and complete contracts, carrier concern and residual rights, judgement by peers and project contracts. However, these links should not be considered as systematic.

One important function for incentive schemes is to create some form of congruence of interest between the members of the organization and the organization itself. Congruence of interest does not mean that the firm changes the 'utility function' of its employees. It simply means that the firm tries to conceive of situations in which the different parties have a common interest in participating. Thus, when an employee has made specific investments and proves that he/she has certain qualities, the firm should be able to offer him/her a job which is good for the firm and interesting for him/her.

Last but not least, the boundaries of firms are changing, as far as social relations are concerned. Earlier forms of organization are coming back, like putting-out or insider contracting. Some people work for corporations without being employed by them, at least not in the usual sense. At the same time, a new form of cooperation appears between corporations, such as joint venture, consortium. Things that used to happen within firms are happening in the marketplace and vice versa. To a certain extent, these changes confirm the existence of different contractual arrangements and the fact that incentives and coordination are two different problems that should be dealt with separately.

4   Conclusion

Trying to innovate using an existing structure and making the structure itself evolve are the main challenges for corporations today.

We really believe that big corporations can perform reasonably in a global economy in which uncertainty and rapid structural changes are an integral part. In that sense, the 'small is beautiful' device and the complete contract vision underlying it is only a part of the truth.

Transaction cost theory has been the cornerstone of our research. It has helped us to usefully interpret contract theory and to go beyond the world of complete contracts *stricto sensu* (to a certain extent, Grossman and Hart's residual rights allocation still belongs to that world).

Our conviction is that collective organizations do rest on a collection of contractual forms that need to be recognized *per se* and preserved. There is essentially no equilibrium in that 'game' because all contractual forms have a natural tendency to degenerate into the most stable one: the complete contract.

We hope concrete studies will help to support and clarify our vision of big industrial firms.

Notes

* This chapter is the first part of a paper written in May 1994. The original paper described and analysed in a second part the significant changes introduced in the management process at Electricité de France during the last years. This chapter is part of an applied research programme on management carried out in the corporate planning and strategy division of Electricité de France under the responsibility of the authors.

1. The way we tried to conceptualize internal organization problems reflects our professional experience as managers in a large industrial corporation with more than 120,000 employees. We would have written very different things had we worked in a law firm or a medium-sized industrial enterprise.

2. We need further hypotheses to characterize the incentive schemes set up. We generally assume that agents are risk neutral and that one can sign contracts *ex ante*, that is, before agents learn their types (θ_1 and θ_2). Inasmuch as we only impose individual rationality constraints *ex ante*, that is, on average over the types, one can find mechanisms that push people to internalize the global performance $V_1 + V_2$. Then the question of budget balance arises: the sum of the transfers should be equal to 0, whatever the values of θ_1 and θ_2. D'Aspremont and Gérard-Varet (1979) showed that in a model without investment where agents learn only their types, one can obtain the first best and satisfy the budget balance condition at the same time, even off the equilibrium path. The budget balance condition is important since only when it is fulfilled is the credibility of threats guaranteed. When the budget is not balanced, one needs a third party to act as a counterpart and clear the mechanism. If that third party is missing, the mechanism will not work as well. In a model with moral hazard, one could show that the budget is not balanced off the equilibrium path. See Holmström (1982) for further development.

3. There may be two reasons why those variables are not contractible at date 1: either the parties cannot describe *ex ante* the outcome of investment and operation decisions, or they can describe such outcomes but not in a way formal enough to be verifiable by a court. In both cases, they cannot write enforceable contracts.

4. These three elementary contracts correspond to three fundamental tasks within the firm: innovate, coordinate, realize.

5. A contract is signed between two persons located at two different levels in a hierarchy: level n and level $n+1$. Except when specified, we consider things from the point of view of level n.

References

Aghion, P. and P. Bolton (1989), 'The Financial Structure of the Firm and the Problem of Control', *European Economic Review*, **33**, 286–93.

Aghion, P., M. Dewatripont and P. Rey (1989), 'Renegotiation Design under Symmetric Information', mimeo, MIT.

Alchian, A. and H. Demsetz (1972), 'Production, Information Costs, and Economic Organization', *American Economic Review*, **62**, 777–95.

Aoki, M. (1986), 'Horizontal *vs.* Vertical Information Structure of the Firm', *American Economic Review*, **76**, 971–83.

Aoki, M. (1990), 'Toward an Economic Model of the Japanese Firm', *Journal of Economic Literature*, **28**, 1–27.

Baron, D. and R. Myerson (1982), 'Regulating a Monopoly with Unknown Costs', *Econometrica*, **50**, 911–30.

Bouttes, J.P., P. Lederer and J.M. Trochet (1990), 'Incentive Regulation of EDF', miméo EDF.

Brousseau, E. (1993), *L'économie des contrats, technologies de l'information et coordination interentreprises*, Paris: Presses Universitaires de France.

Butera, F. (1991), *La métamorphose de l'organisation*, Paris: Les éditions d'organisation.

Chandler, A. (1977), *The Visible Hand*, Cambridge, MA: Harvard University Press.

Chung, T. (1991), 'Incomplete Contracts, Specific Investments, and Risk Sharing', *Review of Economic Studies*, **58**, 1031–42.

Coase, R. (1988), *The Firm, the Market and the Law*, Chicago: University of Chicago Press.

d'Aspremont, C. and L.A. Gérard-Varet (1979), 'Incentives and Incomplete Information', *Journal of Public Economics*, **11**, 55–66.

Dewatripont, M. and J. Tirole (1992), 'A Theory of Debt and Equity: Diversity of Securities and Manager–Shareholder Congruence', *European Research Conferences*.

Farrell J. (1987), 'Information and the Coase Theorem', *Journal of Economic Perspectives*, **1**, 113–29.

Fudenberg, D., B. Holmström and P. Milgrom, (1990) 'Short-Term Contracts and Long-Term Agency Relationships', *Journal of Economic Theory*, **51**, 1–31.

Fudenberg, D. and J. Tirole (1991), *Game Theory*, Cambridge, MA: MIT Press.

Grossman, S. and O. Hart (1986), 'The Costs and Benefits of Ownership: A Theory of Lateral and Vertical Integration', *Journal of Political Economy*, **94**, 691–719.

Hart, O. and J. Moore (1988), 'Incomplete Contracts and Renegotiation', *Econometrica*, **56**, 755–85.

Hatchuel, A. (1992), 'Frédéric Taylor: une lecture épistémologique', *Communication aux journées Histoire et Epistémologie des Sciences de gestion*.

Hatchuel, A. (1993), 'Fondements des savoirs et légitimité des règles', *Communication au colloque de Cerizy*, 'Rationalité limitée et constitution du collectif'.

Holmström, B. (1979), 'Moral Hazard and Observability', *Bell Journal of Economics*, **10**, 74–91.

Holmström, B. (1982), 'Moral Hazard in Teams', *Bell Journal of Economics*, **13**, 324–40.

Holmström, B. and P. Milgrom (1991), 'Multitask Principal–Agent Analyses: Incentive Contracts, Asset Ownership, and Job Design', *The Journal of Law, Economics and Organization*, **7**, 24–52

Holmström, B. and J. Tirole (1987), 'The Theory of the Firm', in R. Schmalensee and R. Willig (eds), *Handbook of Industrial Organization*, Amsterdam: Elsevier, pp. 63–133.

Holmström, B. and J. Tirole (1991), 'Transfer Pricing and Organizational Form', *Journal of Law, Economics and Organization*, **7**, 201–28.

Joskow, P. (1991), 'The Role of Transaction Cost Economics in Antitrust and Public Utility Regulatory Policies', *Journal of Law, Economics and Organization*, **7**, 53–83.

Joskow, P. and R. Schmalensee (1986), 'Incentive Regulation for Electric Utilities', *Yale Journal on Regulation*, **4**, 1–49.

Kaplan, R. (ed.) (1990), *Measures for Manufacturing Excellence*, Cambridge, MA: Harvard Business School Press.

Kaplan, R. and H. Johnson (1987), *The Rise and Fall of Management Accounting*, Cambridge, MA: Harvard Business School Press.

Laffont, J.-J. and J. Tirole (1993), *A Theory of Incentives in Procurement and Regulation*, Cambridge, MA: MIT Press.

Leban, R. (1993), 'L'élaboration de la régulation des services publics en France: le cas de l'électricité', miméo CNAM, Paris.

Marschak, J. and R. Radner (1972), *The Economic Theory of Team*, New Haven: Yale University Press.

Midler, C. (1991), *Evolution des règles de gestion et processus d'apprentissage*, Paris: Cahiers du Centre de Recherche en Gestion, Ecole Polytechnique.

Mintzberg, H. (1982), *Structure et dynamique des organisations*, Paris: Les éditions d'organisation.

Montmillon, M. and O. Pastré (eds) (1984), *Le taylorisme*, Paris: Editions La Découverte.

North, D. (1981), *Structure and Change in Economic History*, New York: Norton.

North, D. (1990), *Institutions, Institutional Change and Economic Performance*, Cambridge: Cambridge University Press.

Ponssard, J.-P. (1992), 'Formalisation des connaissances, apprentissage organisationnel et rationalité interactive', Miméo Laboratoire d'Econométrie de l'Ecole Polytechnique.

Revue Economique (1989), 'Numéro spécial sur l'Economie des Conventions', Presses de la Fondation Nationale des Sciences Politiques.

Reynaud, J.-D. (1993), *Les règles du jeu: l'action collective et la régulation sociale*, Paris: Armand Colin.

Riordan, M. (1990), 'What is Vertical Integration?' in Aoki, Gustafsson and Williamson (eds), *The Firm as a Nexus of Treaties*, London: Sage.

Shapiro, C. and J. Stiglitz (1984), 'Equilibrium Unemployment as a Worker Discipline Device', *American Economic Review*, **74**, 433–44.

Shavell, S. (1979), 'Risk Sharing and Incentives in the Principal and Agent Relationship', *Bell Journal of Economics*, **10**, 55–73.

Tanguy, H. (1989), 'La réhabilitation des modèles et des plans dans l'entreprise: le cas d'une grande maison de champagne', *Cahiers d'économie et de sociologie rurales*, **10**, 26–64.

Tirole, J. (1986), 'Procurement and Renegotiation', *Journal of Political Economy*, **94**, 235–59.

Tirole, J. (1988), *The Theory of Industrial Organization*, Cambridge, MA: MIT Press.

Weitzman, M. (1974), 'Prices *vs* Quantities', *Review of Economic Studies*, **44**, 477–91.

Williamson, O. (1975), *Markets and Hierarchies*, New York: Free Press/Macmillan.

Williamson, O. (1985), *The Economic Institutions of Capitalism*, New York: Free Press/Macmillan.

4   Privatization in Russia: what should be a firm?*

Paul L. Joskow and Richard Schmalensee

1   Introduction

The effort to create a market economy in Russia and the other states that made up the former Soviet Union (FSU) is an enormous political and intellectual challenge. The design and implementation of a programme to transform a large centrally planned economy into a well-functioning market economy supported by a democratic political system test the theoretical, empirical and policy design skills of social scientists in a large number of disciplines. For students of organizations, especially those interested in the boundaries between firms and markets, the opportunity to apply what we have learned in the past 10–15 years is particularly challenging. These challenges are especially great in Russia, as a consequence of its large size, the industrial legacy of Soviet central planning, the primitive and fluid state of many fundamental institutions of capitalism (such as property rights, contract law, bankruptcy laws and the banking system), and Russia's limited historical experience with markets. These challenges are magnified by a turbulent political environment characterized by profound disputes about the appropriate means and ends of economic reform.

The transformation of state-owned enterprises into private firms subject to market discipline and shareholder control is generally viewed as being critical to the creation of democratic market economies with desirable efficiency properties out of centrally planned economies. The ongoing privatization initiative that began in Russia during 1992 was conceived as part of a wider programme to create an efficient market economy – though most of the other elements of that programme are proceeding slowly, at best. The Russian privatization programme has also been structured as a political instrument. Privatization's most influential proponents have viewed it as being critical to creating an effective constituency that supports the continued movement towards a democratic market economy, with the institutions required to support it, in the face of active opposition by powerful incumbent interest groups in the bureaucracy and among the managers of large state enterprises and industrial associations (Boycko et al., 1993). As a consequence, the privatization programme that began in 1992 has been heavily influenced by the view that speed – getting state-owned enterprises into private hands quickly before reactionary elements can stop reform – is of the essence.

Theoretical discussions of privatization of state-owned enterprises in Eastern Europe and the FSU often argue that institutional restructuring should precede privatization (see, for example, Tirole, 1991). From this perspective, restructuring is required both to create private firms with reasonably efficient organizational, managerial and governance structures, as well as to create market structures that will support reasonably competitive markets. The recommendation to 'restructure first' is generally based on the sensible observation that it is likely to be easier to shuffle assets around and to accommodate the associated wealth transfers before rather than after clear ownership rights are established. Some have argued that it is particularly important to restructure first to promote competition in Russia, because many products were produced by only one or two production entities under central planning and imports are unlikely to be a significant competitive constraint for many products. However, privatizing these entities without first restructuring would create a market economy dominated by monopolies. (JST argue, however, that the monopoly problem is considerably more complicated than a glance at Soviet statistics typically suggests.) In contrast, restructuring to promote competition could inhibit the creation of efficient organizational structures.

The 'new learning' of transaction cost economics (see, for example, Williamson, 1991, 1993) should, in principle, provide us with useful insights into how industrial restructuring should occur. After all, an important goal of research in transaction cost economics is to develop a framework for understanding the organization of firms, the boundaries between firms and markets, and the nature of relationships between firms, all from a comparative institutional choice perspective. The purpose of this chapter is to examine from a transaction cost perspective a variety of issues associated with the restructuring of Russian industry prior to privatization. This perspective is useful for understanding both the structures of Soviet industrial hierarchies and the implications of this legacy for post-Soviet restructuring.

We will argue that it has been very difficult in practice to effect a finely tuned administrative restructuring of Russian state-owned enterprises prior to privatization. The perceived need for speed has been a significant barrier to developing any explicit, comprehensive industrial restructuring policy. Other significant barriers include the de facto control rights held by incumbent workers and managers; the uncertain state of the future institutional environment in which firms will operate; the lack of information available to the privatization authorities about prevailing organizational and buyer–seller arrangements; the difficulty of predicting how the industrial structure will respond to dramatic changes in the structure of demand, subsidies, price controls, import and export opportunities; and potential conflicts between competition policy goals and organizational efficiency goals. Nevertheless, the privatization authorities have made a number of decisions regarding the initial structure of privatized firms that, we argue, have, partly by accident and partly by design, often represented the best that could be done, given the multiple objectives and constraints that these authorities faced.

In what follows, we examine the initial structuring of organizations for privatization, taking into account the prevailing uncertainties about the future institutional environment and industrial structure, as well as the informational and political constraints under which the privatization authorities have operated. Because of these uncertainties, the ability of the initial privatized firms to adapt and evolve in response to the inevitable (if uncertain) changes that they will face is especially important. Finally, we also consider potential tensions between the goals of restructuring firms for efficiency and restructuring markets for competition.

We do not try to articulate a complete normative framework for designing the ideal institutional environment and private organizational arrangements for the Russian economy. It should be obvious that a centrally planned economy such as that of Russia lacked most of the basic legal institutions of capitalism (including private property rights, contract laws, bankruptcy laws and securities laws),[1] as well as compatible industrial, financial, distribution and other service sectors ultimately necessary for a market economy to thrive. It would be convenient if all these institutions and organizations could be created instantly or in a carefully orchestrated sequence. However, for both practical and political reasons, the changes necessary to support a well-functioning market cannot be made all at once, or even in a fully predetermined order.[2]

Russia is proceeding with privatization before many of these institutional and organizational structures are mature and, in some cases, while they are very primitive. For a variety of reasons, privatization is the primary component of the 1992 reform programme that continues to be supported by those in power in Russia. Therefore, much of the rest of the development of the Russian institutional environment and organizational structures will have to be pulled along by the needs of the firms that are being created by privatization. Indeed, the ultimate success of the privatization programme will turn on whether or not it can 'pull' the creation of other necessary institutions along with it, despite a resistant bureaucracy and a sceptical public. Therefore, while we accept the distinction of Davis and North (1971) between the 'institutional environment' and a set of 'institutional arrangements', and the symbiotic relationship between them (Williamson, 1993, pp. 110–116), the privatization programme in Russia has not been able to wait for a stable institutional environment to be created. These two aspects of economic institutions will have to evolve together over time.

The next section provides a brief discussion of the structure of Russian industry that has been inherited from the Soviet central planning system. We then examine a variety of issues that the privatization authorities have had to confront and that are associated with the organization of firms prior to privatization. These include the carving of Soviet industrial hierarchies into firms for privatization, the treatment of voluntary spin-offs of fragments of incumbent industrial enterprises, and the treatment of proposals for aggregations of enterprises into holding companies and financial industrial groups.

2 The organization of industry in the command economy of the FSU[3]

Many discussions of the privatization and restructuring of Russian industry speak loosely about the transition from central planning to the market as if the institutions that characterized central planning were irrelevant for the transformation process and as if the institutional characteristics of a 'market economy' were simple to identify and very similar from one country to another. None of these assumptions is valid (Milgrom and Roberts, 1992, Chapter 16; Williamson, 1993). At least in Russia, the institutional legacy – especially the Soviet industrial hierarchies – imposes important constraints on the privatization and restructuring process. Furthermore, because there are wide variations in the detailed institutional environments and industrial structures that characterize developed economies' markets (Williamson, 1991, pp. 286–94; Milgrom and Roberts, 1992, Chapter 16), there are likely to be different views about the most desirable institutional environment and associated industrial structures for Russia to emulate.

It is important, therefore, to understand the characteristics of the industrial system that Russia has inherited from the FSU. Moreover, this understanding must go beyond the elementary textbook description of the central planning agency (Gosplan) establishing a plan and then trying hard, often without great success, to have that plan implemented.

The FSU had a complex industrial structure that was the primary institutional framework through which information passed from factories to
the centre, and through which plans and orders from the centre were
implemented. Gosplan is gone but much of the rest of Soviet industrial
structure, including portions of the government bureaucracy responsible
for various industries, exists in some form and generally seeks to restore
its previous authority. Unfortunately, our knowledge about the structure
and behavioural relationships that characterized these industrial hierarchies is relatively limited. This reflects, in part, the fact that many
Western economists interested in centrally planned economies focused
on normative models of planning and largely ignored issues of bureaucracy, organizational structure, information channels and the
development of informal institutions both to complement and bypass
the formal planning process (Williamson, 1993, p. 123).

Hierarchical structure of Soviet industry[4]
At the top of economy of the FSU were the primary state-pricing and
-planning entities responsible for developing each five-year plan,
developing targets for individual industrial sectors and enterprises,
arranging for materials and supplies to be available so that individual
enterprises were able to meet their planning targets, establishing prices,
allocating capital and providing for the clearance of debts between
enterprises. The most important of these central-planning entities were
the State Planning Committee (Gosplan), the State Committee on
Prices (Goskomtsen), the Ministry for the Distribution of Material
Production (Gosnab) and the State Bank (Gosbank). Beneath these
institutions, the entities of the Soviet economy that produced goods and
services were organized into industrial sectors, each producing related
products. Each sector was organized according to a fairly rigid hierarchical structure. A simple schematic diagram of these industrial
hierarchies is depicted in Figure 4.1. Our discussion will focus on the
attributes of these industrial hierarchies rather than on the highest-level
central-planning entities.

Industrial or branch ministries   Each industrial sector was headed by
a Union or Union-Republic branch ministry with primary responsibility
for that sector and for dealing with the higher-level organs of state
planning. The structures of these hierarchies follow a surprisingly similar
pattern from one industrial branch to another. Producing entities under
the control of All-Union ministries were run directly from Moscow.
Union-Republic ministries, however, had offices both in Moscow and
in the republic involved, and orders could come from either office. In

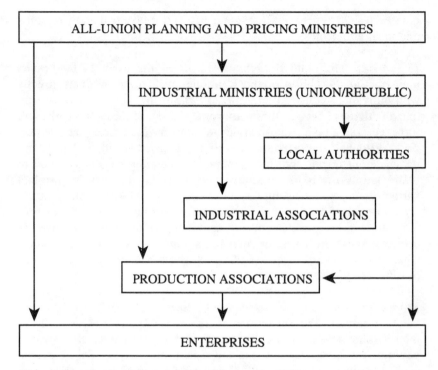

Figure 4.1   Soviet industrial hierarchy, early 1980s

the early 1980s, there were roughly 50 branch ministries responsible for manufacturing, energy, communications and transportation sectors at the Union and Union-Republic levels, nine of which were in the military-industrial complex (MIC).

Beneath the Union or Union-Republic ministries were often symmetrical ministries in each republic that were responsible primarily for strictly local enterprises, and further disaggregation to agencies at the regional level also occurred for some goods and services. Each branch ministry was responsible for negotiating the planning targets for its industry, obtaining the material and financial resources required to fulfil these targets, and inducing the enterprises within its hierarchy to meet these targets. In the mid-1980s, the Union and Union-Republic ministries controlled roughly 80 per cent of the 46,000 industrial enterprises located throughout the FSU, of which about 25,000 were located in Russia (World Bank, 1992, p. 83; IMF, 1991, p. 287). The smaller local enterprises (20 per cent of total enterprises) were controlled by regional and local authorities.

Enterprises   Until the Brezhnev reforms of the early 1970s, branch ministries at the Union or the Republic level primarily dealt directly with individual industrial 'enterprises' within their branch and coordinated activities between these enterprises. Each of these enterprises, in turn, received a plan from the relevant ministry (some very large enterprises also had direct contacts with Gosplan), had an 'independent' management responsible for meeting the planning targets assigned to it and had its own books of financial accounts. Each enterprise also had various financial responsibilities for the payments of wages and bonuses, reinvestment of profits, and payments for various social services provided to workers (such as housing, canteens, health clinics and day-care centres). What the Russians refer to as 'enterprises' were the smallest legal economic entities in the FSU; all assets had to be on the books of some enterprise.[5]

Production and industrial associations   In the early 1970s, the government promoted the development of two types of association at intermediate levels of the command and control hierarchy, located between the ministries and the individual enterprises.[6] The first type was a 'production association'. These were intended to integrate their associated enterprises to realize economies of scale and specialization, to improve the coordination of the enterprises and reduce information and transaction costs, and to encourage R&D and its application. In some cases, these production associations merged into single enterprises but, in many cases, they did not, and the association was much looser (Freris, 1984, pp. 4–10; Hewett, 1988, p. 248, Spulber, 1991, pp. 175–6). By 1980, when a new set of reforms stopped the pressures for further consolidation, production associations accounted for about half of industrial production in the FSU.

Production associations generally reduced the independence of the associated legal entities called enterprises. Indeed, the term 'enterprise' came to be used loosely to refer to entities that were legally enterprises, to production associations made up of several such entities and even to larger administrative aggregations of enterprises formed by individual branch ministries. Moreover, these different notions of what constituted an enterprise in the FSU encompassed organizational structures with wide variations in actual managerial independence from other enterprises within their respective ministries (Hewett, 1988, p. 251, n. 50).

The other type of association created in the early 1970s was the 'industrial association', which consisted of a much larger number of individual enterprises and production associations. The industrial associations were designed to replace departments within branch ministries, which had responsibilities for sets of closely related enterprises and production associations, and to rationalize overlapping responsibilities between departments within each industrial ministry. The associations were intended to lead to improved industrial performance, by moving those responsible for planning and coordination closer to the enterprises and further from the branch ministries. However, many observers argue that the industrial associations never achieved any significant independence from their ministries and did not achieve the expected efficiencies (see, for example, Kroll, 1991, p. 148; Spulber, 1991, p. 165).

Thus, as the Gorbachev reforms began in 1985, many of the managerial functions normally found within firms in market economies were not located in the enterprises – or even in associations – but, instead, they were performed in one or more departments of the branch ministries. These branch ministries selected enterprise managers and controlled planning targets, resource availability, flows of capital, R&D, product introductions and the distribution of output by the production associations and enterprises. They also coordinated vertical and horizontal relationships between associations and enterprises within their direct control and under the control of other ministries.

Industrial organization at the enterprise and production association levels

In the Soviet era, the relevant ministries aggressively pursued the concentration of production of particular products in a relatively small number of individual enterprises and production associations. They also pursued a high degree of product specialization within enterprises. In other words, rather than producing a wide range of related products, each enterprise produced a very narrow range of products. Both goals reflected mainly a belief that all industrial production processes were characterized by important economies of scale at all relevant output levels. In addition, a relatively small number of highly specialized production enterprises simplified the tasks of the central planning, pricing, and supply and distribution ministries. These policies are generally viewed as having created an industrial structure in which the production of individual products was dominated by national or regional monopolies, and the associated enterprises were unusually large when compared with Western firms that produced similar products.

As JST and Brown et al. (1993) pointed out,[7] the medium-term monopoly problem has probably been significantly overstated by a focus on very narrow product market definitions and a corresponding neglect of enterprises' opportunities for diversification into related products. Nevertheless, monopoly and oligopoly problems are of significant potential concern in the short run, and any privatization and industrial restructuring programme must be concerned with them.

It is clearer that the widely held view that Russian enterprises are 'gigantic' firms by Western standards is largely a myth.[8] If we view what the Russians call 'enterprises' (strictly defined) as being equivalent to what we call 'firms' in developed market economies, then the largest Russian enterprises are not unusually large by Western standards. The top ten civilian Russian industrial enterprises, by employment, had 50,000–125,000 workers in 1991. The top ten US industrial firms had 128,000–750,000 workers in 1992. The fiftieth largest Russian civilian industrial enterprise had about 17,000 workers in 1991, while the fiftieth largest US industrial enterprise had 52,000 workers in 1992.[9]

What is striking about the size distribution of Russian enterprises is not so much the presence of unusually large enterprises but, instead, the absence of a large number of small manufacturing enterprises. In the US, more than 300,000 companies are engaged in manufacturing. In Russia, there were roughly 25,000 enterprises in the industrial sector (which excludes retail shops, small service enterprises and agriculture-related enterprises). Perhaps more importantly, large Russian enterprises are structured quite differently from large US firms, which generally have multiple establishments and facilities at many different locations around the country and often abroad. Russian enterprises tend to have their facilities located in or near a single city, and are often built around large integrated production complexes. Therefore, large Russian enterprises tend to look like Henry Ford's River Rouge plant. Branch ministries and industrial associations historically performed the sort of coordination functions for enterprises producing similar products that are performed within large national multi-establishment firms in the US. This functional structure suggests that it may be more appropriate to treat Russian enterprises as if they were what are called 'establishments' or plants in the US: producing facilities located on a single production site. JST pointed out that, if we view what the Russians call 'enterprises' as being similar to what are called 'establishments' (plants) in the US, then Russian enterprises are (on average) unusually large plants by US standards.

This structure creates some potentially difficult problems for implementing a demonopolization strategy based on the dissolution of existing enterprises and associations. Breaking up these enterprises into multiple viable competing firms may be very difficult, both because of the way that they are structured physically and organizationally, and because much of the information necessary to effect workable separations is possessed by people in the branch ministries and the enterprises who are unlikely to want to reveal it to those who might want to break them up.

Vertical integration Because of infirmities of Soviet planning, which made it difficult for enterprises controlled by different ministries to rely on each other for supplies, the branch ministries pursued policies of material input self-sufficiency (autarky) that largely ignored scale economies.[10] This resulted in a high degree of vertical integration (IMF, 1991, p. 293). Many branch ministries established enterprises that built machinery and equipment required by other producing enterprises for which they were responsible rather than purchasing from enterprises under machinery or equipment branch ministries. They created their own construction enterprises, repair enterprises, food distribution facilities and even farms. Enterprises, production associations and ministries often produced their own raw materials, such as cement and timber, and even consumer products, such as washing machines and refrigerators, for their workers. Finally, enterprises often provided their workers' housing, food supplies, canteens, day-care centres, health-care facilities and other social services.

The MIC Enterprises located within the branch ministry hierarchies that constituted the MIC also produced significant quantities of civilian products (see Cooper, 1986, 1991). While information on these enterprises is sparse, it is quite clear that they have produced a wide range of civilian products, both for use by the military and government agencies (and their workers), and for distribution to civilian enterprises and the public. Furthermore, enterprises in the MIC produce many military products using facilities that could, in principle, be readily converted to civilian production of goods such as trucks, engines, ovens and machine tools.

Distribution of inputs to enterprises, wholesale and retail trade In developed market economies, manufacturers often compete directly for the patronage of wholesale and retail distributors, and sometimes integrate forwards into the wholesale and retail service functions. Unfortunately, Russia inherited a distribution system quite ill suited to a modern market economy.[11] Manufacturing entities in the FSU generally did not compete for the patronage of wholesale and retail distributors; did not develop special relationships with specific retailers; and did not vertically integrate downstream into wholesale or retail trade. Instead, the distribution of raw materials and producer goods was accomplished through a complex set of planning arrangements that involved administrative agencies at every level of government.

Russia had a very undeveloped retail sector, partly as a direct consequence of the Marxist view that the services ordinarily associated with the marketing and distribution of products to consumers are an unproductive activity.[12] There were far fewer retail sales and service outlets per capita (in aggregate and by sector) than in Western countries or even compared with Eastern Europe. Retail margins were consciously kept low. Advertising, brand names, franchising and other familiar aspects of modern retail sectors were, with a few exceptions, non-existent.[13]

Breakdown of central control

The highly centralized governance structure described above persisted until about 1987. The first two years of the Gorbachev reforms (1985–86) were devoted mainly to efforts to streamline, strengthen and further consolidate the central planning process.[14] A set of 'superministries' was created to oversee related groups of previously independent industrial branch ministries, and industrial concentration was encouraged through mergers and the expansion of closely-knit production associations. Industrial associations were phased out to strengthen direct ties between the branch ministries and the enterprises and production associations, but they were often simply replaced by industrial departments in the branch ministries.

The Gorbachev government appears to have changed course after 1986 and embarked on a programme designed to decentralize decision-making authority.[15] The independence of production associations and enterprises from both the central planning authorities and their respective branch ministries was increased considerably by 1990, despite ongoing efforts by the central bureaucracies to retain control or at least a major role. Legislation passed in 1990 accelerated this trend and, during the last two years of the Gorbachev government, both the de facto power of enterprise managers and the control rights of local and regional governments were substantially increased (see, for example, World Bank, 1992, p. 84).

By 1991 these changes also stimulated an accelerating process of so-called 'spontaneous privatization' or '*nomenklatura* privatization',[16] which represented local assertions of control rights in response to the centre's withdrawal of control. Initially, workers or managers simply diverted profits to their own use. This led to the transfer of assets to new private ventures at very low prices and the creation of de facto independent ventures within existing enterprises. The other main process was worker-management buy-outs of assets at their book values – because of the rapid inflation that began in the late 1980s, these book prices were much lower than market values. It appears that a large number of enterprises, especially smaller enterprises in light industry and services, gained a sort of de facto private status by 1992 (see JST, pp. 327–30).

These developments, along with the collapse of the Soviet Union in late 1991, sharply diminished the authority of the former branch ministries and forced state-owned enterprises increasingly to fend for themselves by creating business relationships to obtain inputs and sell outputs. As the branch ministry system began to collapse in 1990–91, the ministries became progressively less able to maintain links between enterprises and their suppliers and customers, or to serve as enforcers of supply obligations between enterprises. Although informal mechanisms had emerged under the old regime, to help enterprises to obtain the supplies that they were supposed to get according to the state plan (Greif and Kandel, 1993), after 1990, the creation and maintenance of supply relationships fell much more heavily on the enterprise and association managers than was the case under the old regime.

Trade associations   By 1992, there were almost no branch ministries left in Russia. However, the bureaucrats who ran them, and their functional roles, did not simply disappear. Usually, both were transferred during 1991 and 1992 into trade associations that grew out of the branch ministries during this period. The management of these associations was often the same as in the former branch ministries (World Bank, 1992, p. 84). Typically, though not universally, an association contained the enterprises that had been controlled by a branch ministry or one of its constituent departments. Collectively, the trade associations represented an attempt by the bureaucrats from the branch ministries to retain their positions of authority as well as a safety net for the workers and managers who had been cut loose fairly suddenly from central planning without a working system for arranging inputs and distributing outputs, and little knowledge or capability to fend for themselves in emerging markets.

Most of the associations were active in lobbying for subsidies and special preferences, and provided R&D support well into 1992. Furthermore, some of them successfully developed marketing and financial services. While the associations continued to be involved in coordinating input supply and distribution, their role here gradually became less important over time as control over resources became dispersed. However, the associations had valuable long-term relationships with key managers and state bureaucrats, and they were usually staffed with the best people from the corresponding branch ministries.

Conflicts between the regions and Moscow   Another source of disruption and breakdown of historical relationships has been the tension between the Russian Federation government in Moscow and the roughly 80 regional governments.[17] When we first began working in Russia in mid-1992, many regional authorities were laying claim to assets located on their territory, including pieces of the electric power, telephone, railroad and airline systems. They were also actively involved in protecting some products (especially food) produced in their regions from being 'siphoned off' by other regions. The actions of regional authorities and concerns in Moscow about the further dismemberment of the Russian economy and the undermining of Moscow's authority have had important effects on the structure of the privatization programme.

Contracts and prices

Contracts and their enforcement   Contracts, as we know them in market economies, and the associated laws that govern contractual enforcement, were not important features of the command economy of the FSU. In theory, all producing entities were supposed to produce according to planning targets specified by Gosplan and their respective branch ministries. Gosnab and the branch ministries were supposed to specify how the supplies produced by enterprises were to be allocated among enterprises and how finished goods were distributed to the wholesale and retail sectors. These planning targets were the basis for de facto contractual commitments between industrial enterprises. In practice, however, enterprises frequently did not meet their targets and other enterprises that relied on this production could not all be satisfied. Moreover, the quality of products produced by different enterprises varied widely. Therefore, disputes between enterprises about who would set what and when naturally arose (as discussed earlier, the vertical integration and 'autarky' policies were partially a response to these allocation problems, which were particularly difficult when more than one ministry was involved).

Disputes about the alleged failure of one enterprise to fulfil its commitments to another could, in principle, be resolved by the branch ministry, by Gosplan or by Gosnab. Enterprises could also bring their disputes to the State Arbitration Committee for resolution, although this mechanism was apparently not frequently used. Not surprisingly, enterprises evolved more informal arrangements to create and enforce credible supply arrangements, based on long-term relationships between enterprises and built on mutual dependence, exchanges of goods and services outside of normal planning channels, and sometimes violence (see Greif and Kandel, 1993). These relationships appear to have been especially close within production associations and enterprises under the same department of a branch ministry.

Therefore, as the central planning system collapsed, enterprises had to rely increasingly on bilateral arrangements negotiated with other enterprises. However, they had to do this in a country that effectively had no formal mechanisms to enforce contractual commitments. As a result, enterprises had to rely on private enforcement mechanisms of various kinds to support contractual commitments (Greif and Kandel, 1993). Historical relationships between enterprises were especially important at this time, and the skills of those managerial personnel who had been responsible for developing and maintaining those relationships were at a premium.

To deal with the absence of meaningful mechanisms to reform contracts, the Gaidar government established the Arbitration Court system to handle commercial disputes (including disputes that arose from enforcement of the antitrust laws; see JST). However, the arbitration courts enforce hasty revisions to the pre-existing Civil Code that are not well adapted to dealing with complex commercial disputes. Moreover, the arbitration court judges are not properly trained to deal with complex commercial disputes that arise in a market economy and have inadequate resources to deal with the volume of disputes that have been brought to them (JST; Greif and Kandel, 1993). As a result, enterprises have had to rely primarily on private enforcement mechanisms (Greif and Kandel, 1993, pp. 36–42). These private enforcement mechanisms are widely viewed as being inefficient (and, in some cases, incompatible with democracy), but these inefficiencies are almost certainly at least as much a consequence of an unstable economic situation, an unstable government and the breakdown of traditional relationships as of the absence of good contract laws and public enforcement arrangements. Nevertheless, the absence of effective formal contract enforcement mechanisms and the increasing reliance on peculiar organizational arrangements – particularly with thugs and associated threats to life and limb – to enforce contractual promises is widely and properly viewed as a very serious problem.

Prices Until 1992, all prices in Russia had to be approved by the State Committee on Prices (Goskomtsen). Prices played more of an accounting role than an allocational role in the central planning process, although prices did affect enterprises' bonuses and the availability of cash for some investment and social service activities.[18] Wholesale prices were set by applying a 'profit margin' to the sum of labour costs, materials costs and a depreciation allowance. Over time, the margins applied came to vary to reflect differences in capital intensity and political decisions regarding where production should be expanded or contracted. At the retail level, margins were applied to the wholesale prices of individual products (such as bread and milk).

In November 1991, the new Russian government announced its intention to decontrol prices early in 1992. In reaction to arguments that, without regulation, Russia's many monopolists would reduce output and create shortages,[19] the Federation and regional antimonopoly committees created earlier in 1991 were instructed to compile 'registers' of the 'monopolies' (using a 35 per cent market share standard) under their jurisdictions. Many prices were actually decontrolled in January and March of 1992, and there was a rapid run-up in prices.[20] Unfortunately, the inflation that had exploded in 1991 (142 per cent at the retail level) resumed after this initial price spike. Most outside observers blamed the continued rapid expansion of the money supply, undertaken both to finance huge government deficits (the Russian deficit was 31 per cent of the GDP at the end of 1991 (World Bank, 1992, p. 7)) in the absence of an effective tax system and to provide continued subsidies to favoured enterprises. Influential officials in the Russian government and parliament, however, pointed to the monopolies, and the shortages that they supposedly caused, as a major source of the inflation. They argued for the use of price regulation rather than tighter monetary policy to restrain inflation.

In August 1992, Prime Minister Yegor Gaidar authorized the Federation Price Committee and its local counterparts to regulate the prices of the firms on the 'monopoly registers'. These controls remained in effect until 1 January 1994.[21]

Other federal, regional and local authorities continued to regulate prices after the price liberalization in early 1992, and many still do so. The goods and services subject to price controls for reasons other than being on the monopoly register have been enumerated by JST. As a general matter, it seems that price controls have been applied primarily to energy, various 'public utility' services viewed as necessities and to basic food products (including vodka).

Thus, before 1992, Russian enterprise managers had no experience of setting prices to maximize profits in response to supply and demand conditions and marketing opportunities. Moreover, they lacked accounting systems that would have made it possible to monitor profitability, to estimate costs of different products or to provide useful information to shareowners. Finally, prices for many products continued to be regulated after general price liberalization, so that reliance on quasi-legal and illegal informal markets and barter arrangements also continued to be of considerable importance, at least through 1993.

3 What should be the boundaries of firms to be privatized?

As the previous discussion should make clear, the individual industrial sectors in the FSU were organized as complex hierarchies made up of interrelated 'enterprises', 'production associations', 'industrial associations' and 'branch ministries'. In general, the governance structure gave enormous power to the branch ministries at the top of each industrial sector. However, it is quite clear that the last 20 years of industrial reforms in the FSU reflected an effort to find 'the right mix' of centralized and decentralized authority within each branch. These hierarchies, their constituent entities and the relationships between all these structures were created by decree rather than by the evolutionary process of natural selection in a market. Because of ideology and the peculiarities of central planning, many of the managerial functions performed by firms in a market economy (including raising capital, selecting quantities and prices, developing product lines and brand names, advertising and distribution) were either performed within the ministry bureaucracies rather than in the enterprises, or were not performed at all in any recognizable form.

The activities of individual enterprises were often closely linked with other enterprises within the same production or industrial association, or were controlled by the same branch ministry. Therefore, an enterprise might depend heavily on other enterprises within or outside its ministry for services that a firm in a market economy would ordinarily provide for itself. However, as a consequence of historical 'autarky' imperatives, some enterprises produced goods and provided services that a firm in a market economy would ordinarily purchase from third parties.

How should the various pieces of these complex industrial hierarchies be aggregated for privatization to create both reasonably efficient private firms and reasonably competitive markets? The branch ministry hierarchies each had some attributes of a (very large) centrally managed firm and some attributes of a (very large) multidivisional firm. The complex relationships linking enterprises with production associations and both with their branch ministries were no doubt supported by meaningful physical and human investments in specific assets, to help to respond to the infirmities of the Soviet planning system. In thinking about how these hierarchies should be transformed into private firms, several factors must be considered.[22]

Efficient integration
It is quite clear that fragmenting the branch ministry industrial hier- archies would destroy important relationships between the enterprises and production associations, which had evolved over decades, and would require the privatized fragments to perform important managerial func- tions that had previously been performed higher up the hierarchies. The loss of these relationships could be very costly indeed, without a credible system for writing and enforcing contracts, without workable markets for raw materials or manufactured goods, without managers used to operating in a market economy, and with potential monopoly problems resulting both from opportunistic exploitation of relationship- specific capital and from the concentrated structure of many Russian industrial sectors.[23] Precisely how important these relationships would be for the efficient adaptation and evolution of privatized firms was and is highly uncertain, however. This uncertainty is magnified by the widely held view that many Russian enterprises – especially in heavy industry and the MIC – are very inefficient and produce products for which there is no longer much demand. Many of these enterprises will have to downsize or close when state subsidies are removed.

From this perspective, efficient restructuring prior to privatization might have involved formal horizontal and vertical integration between what were technically separate enterprises under the control of the same branch ministry or production association, to retain important vertical and horizontal relationships and to avoid hold-up problems after privatization. Indeed, many Russian industrialists (the so-called 'Red Barons') argued that aggregations of enterprises had to be created prior to privatization, to preserve important technical, organizational and managerial relationships. However, deciding how such multidivi- sional firms should be carved out of the branch ministry structures would have required a lot of information about how the various enter- prises worked together, what important managerial functions were being accomplished by the branch ministries and the trade associations created from them, and a lot of foresight regarding the economic forces that would face these entities in the future. Branch ministries hoarded information, however, and foresight is always scarce.

Efficient disintegration

There were also reasons in favour of breaking up the industrial hier-archies inherited from the FSU into small pieces for privatization. The huge Soviet industrial hierarchies contained the lumbering bureauc-racies that were at the heart of the failure of the central planning system. Managers and bureaucrats within these hierarchies were often chosen for attributes other than conventional managerial skill (although the early Gorbachev reforms apparently did lead to the replacement of many incompetent managers with more highly skilled and more honest individuals). Converting large portions of these hierarchies into large private firms would be unlikely to lead to the creation of firms that could adapt rapidly and efficiently to the many impending changes in their institutional and the economic environments. Moreover, the most likely future path for many of the large state enterprises is bankruptcy, reorganization and perhaps liquidation. The industrial bureaucracies are likely to fight rather than facilitate these adaptations and redeploy-ment of labour and physical assets.

On the political level, such large entities would probably be con-sidered to be 'too big to fail' and would probably become potent political forces, lobbying against pro-competitive reforms and for tar-geted protection and special subsidies. Therefore, rather than adapting to the changes in the institutional and economic environments, such large entities, employing tens of thousands of workers, would become a major obstacle to change.

Because Soviet enterprises tended to be highly specialized and mono-polies of narrowly defined products were correspondingly common, the primary hope for developing competitive markets in Russia in the medium term rests with promoting competition between enterprises that were within the same branch ministry hierarchies (JST develop this point at length). If these hierarchies are not fragmented, then that hope is lost. In addition, competition can be enhanced by making available on the open market input production that was previously dedicated to a particular enterprise or group of enterprises (or their workers) through some type of exclusive vertical relationship. Finally, the branch ministry structure had broken down by 1991 and had been replaced by trade associations and other less formal, more or less volun-tary coordination arrangements. These remaining structures had at least some claim to reflecting the most important relationships between enterprises, since the enterprises chose to rely upon them for assistance in coping with the turmoil that has characterized Russia's transition to a market economy.

Simple and complex strategies

These considerations suggest that neither pasting together large firms for privatization out of the existing branch ministry structure (most plausibly by focusing on industrial associations, trade associations and major trading partners) nor completely ignoring the existing industrial hierarchies and simply privatizing the smallest entities with books of accounts – the enterprises – was fully satisfactory. The first approach would retain important vertical and horizontal relationships during a period of transition when these relationships might be very important to maintaining output. However, the large entities implied by this approach had unattractive economic attributes: they would be unlikely to adapt efficiently to changing institutional and economic environments, and would probably possess substantial monopoly power. Indeed, on the competition front, several influential reformers argued that privatization should not go forward until the enterprises that were monopolies were also broken up.

These considerations also suggest that an appealing approach to privatization in Russia would have involved a 'fine-tuning' strategy to restructure both for organizational efficiency and for competition. This would have involved creating firms out of the existing branch ministry structure, with a view to retaining the most important horizontal and vertical relationships within a single firm when this did not lead to serious structural competition problems. It would also involve putting contractual arrangements in place to support relationship-specific capital when internal organization would have led to enterprises that were unreasonably large by Western standards or created serious competitive problems, and breaking up the very largest enterprises (horizontally and vertically) when they posed serious structural monopoly problems. Such a restructuring could have gone forward by relying on information about the key linkages between the components of the industrial hierarchies in Russia and, perhaps more importantly, by seeking to mimic the structures of firms that produced similar products in developed market economies.

With a lot of time and a lot of information about each industrial hierarchy and the nature of the relationships between its various pieces, armies of analysts could have had a great time structuring new entities for privatization out of these hierarchies and creating transitional contractual arrangements to govern relationships between entities at different levels of the vertical chain that were supported by relationship-specific human and physical capital. They could have balanced organizational and transactional efficiency considerations against competitive considerations (Joskow, 1991), and come up with a set of organizations and contractual arrangements that were better adapted to success in a market economy than were any of the individual pieces of the old industrial hierarchies.

In practice, such a comprehensive fine-tuning approach to restructuring was infeasible for both technical and political reasons. Even with the latest learning in organization and contract theory, and the best of intentions, it would have been impossible to determine with any precision what an 'efficient' firm should look like in most sectors, given the limited knowledge that we have about how to design such organizations from outside, and the likelihood that the structure of the Russian economy and the basic institutions that evolve to support it will change dramatically in the future. Any serious attempt to fine-tune the structure of thousands of privatized firms would have consumed huge quantities of economic and managerial expertise relative to the available supply. Moreover, the information required to perform such a restructuring exercise was largely concentrated with the enterprises, production associations and, most importantly, among the former authorities in the branch ministries, each of whom had incentives to hide vital facts about the nature of the relationships within and between the enterprises.

In addition, throughout the post-Soviet period, there has been an overriding political need to proceed quickly with privatization, so that the reactionary forces that exist throughout the Russian government and enterprise structure cannot re-exert control and stop reform entirely. The kind of fine-tuning programme outlined above would have taken many years to implement and would have been blocked at every turn by those who remained in powerful positions within the large state-owned enterprises, in various ministries (most importantly, the Defence Ministry, the Ministry of the Economy (formerly Gosplan) and the State Committee on Prices) and in the trade associations that replicated the branch ministries.

Finally, the pace of *nomenklatura* privatization was accelerating by late 1991, as were efforts to create holding companies and cross-ownership arrangements between enterprises that had been previously linked together in the branch ministry structure. Furthermore, efforts by regional and local governments to obtain control of assets that were located on their territories (including pieces of important network industries) were also accelerating as the authority of the central government began to collapse in 1991. Thus, the assets that made up the Russian economy were already in the process of being privatized in one way or another, through legal, quasi-legal and clearly illegal means. As a result, if the official (legal) privatization process did not move forward quickly, there might be little left to privatize.

4   Russian privatization programme in brief

The actual privatization programme that the Gaidar government
initiated in 1992 did not attempt to fine-tune the restructuring of Russian
industry.[24] Of particular relevance to the issues that are of interest to
us here was the decision to build the privatization programme around
the entities called enterprises, that is, the entities at the lowest level of
each industrial hierarchy. The privatization programme was based on
the propositions that enterprises would be privatized independently
and that certain implicit ownership rights of incumbent managers and
workers of these enterprises would be recognized. While the government would entertain proposals to privatize horizontal and vertical
aggregations of enterprises, as well as proposals to privatize pieces
(breakaways) of existing enterprises, such proposals required the mutual
agreement of the enterprises involved, and special approval from the
privatization authorities and, in the case of aggregations of enterprises,
from the antimonopoly authorities. Below, we discuss further how the
privatization authorities treated these alternatives.

The decision to build the privatization programme around the existing
enterprises at the lowest level of the industrial hierarchies did not result
from any detailed functional or structural analysis of the best way to
restructure the existing industrial hierarchies. It appears that privatization was built around the existing legal entities called enterprises
mainly for convenience and to move privatization along quickly.

This is not the place to discuss the details of precisely how these
enterprises were privatized (see Boycko et al., 1993). However, there
are some elements of the Russian privatization process that are worth
understanding. The privatization programme was, and is, administered
at the level of the Russian Federation by the Committee on the Management of State Property (GKI), and at local and regional levels by its
local and regional analogues. As a first approximation, the privatization
programme divided all Russian enterprises into three categories.

1. *Small-scale enterprises*   In the first category were small enterprises
    (200 or fewer employees) engaged in wholesale and retail trade,
    construction, agriculture, food and trucking. These were given to
    local governments to sell for cash.
2. *Special-interest industries*   In the second category were enterprises
    for which privatization posed special economic, political or security
    problems. These industries included natural gas, petroleum, coal,
    electric power, railroads, telecommunications, TV and radio,
    defence enterprises, medical facilities, all enterprises with more than
    10,000 workers (about 200 enterprises), enterprises that produced

certain foods (including vodka and wine), and various social, cultural and entertainment organizations. Enterprises in some sectors were excluded altogether from the 1992 programme; others were to be privatized only according to special decrees of the government (making privatization very difficult during 1992 and most of 1993); and privatization of still others required the approval of privatization proposals by GKI after consultation with the relevant branch ministries. Several of the industries in the special-interest category provide important 'infrastructure' services and several have subsectors with natural monopoly characteristics that may create a need for public regulation and/or a demand for continued public ownership.

3. *Medium- and large-scale industries* All the remaining (large and medium-sized) enterprises were placed in the third category; they were slated for mass privatization. These enterprises were also to be corporatized initially. After corporatization, workers and managers were to decide by vote between three options for the initial distribution of equity (Boycko et al., 1993, pp. 149–50). More than 80 per cent of the enterprises in this category have chosen an option in which workers and managers together get 51 per cent of common stock at a low price. Up to 5 per cent may be set aside for them to purchase after privatization. After approval of the privatization plan by GKI or its local analogue (and, in many cases, approval by the appropriate antimonopoly committee), most of the remaining shares were sold to the public, usually at auction for vouchers[25] which are freely tradable and were distributed to the entire Russian population between October 1992 and January 1993. Disposition of the remaining shares has varied but some shares are typically retained by the relevant state property committee. These shares may ultimately be sold for cash. When enterprises that fall into the special-interest category have been privatized (or have issued shares to the public, subject to continuing state control), similar distributions to workers and managers and voucher auctions for residual shares have generally been utilized.

The mass privatization programme ran from late 1992 until 1 July 1994. During this time period, roughly 14,000 industrial enterprises were privatized, including a significant number of enterprises that fall in the 'special-interest' category (especially those that were separated because of their large size). By July 1994, private firms employed about two-thirds of Russian industrial workers.[26] In addition, a large fraction of the businesses subject to small-scale privatization had been privatized by the end of 1993, but some regional and municipal governments have resisted implementing this programme.

Two important corporate governance consequences of this approach to distributing the ownership interests in the enterprises are worth noting. First, the generous benefits given to workers and managers to buy their support for the privatization programme have translated into strong insider control of most newly privatized firms (see Boycko et al., 1993, pp. 152–4).[27] Boycko et al. (1993) presented data from two surveys showing that, for at least two samples of privatized firms, post-auction acquisitions had raised insider ownership shares to 60–70 per cent on average.

Second, heavy reliance on voucher auctions has led to very dispersed share ownership, so that privatized Russian firms generally lack large outside shareholders who can effectively oversee the actions of managers and workers. Boycko et al. (1993) suggested that the emerging voucher funds (which issue their own shares for vouchers and invest the proceeds in voucher auctions) and individuals looking for opportunities profitably to change management control of enterprises that exhibit poor performance, will eventually help to exert effective control over these enterprises. A presidential decree issued in late October 1993, that strengthens the rights of outside shareholders, may facilitate this process.[28]

A significant fraction of Russian industry remains to be privatized. This includes enterprises that fell into the 'special-interest' category, as well as enterprises that, for one reason or another, were able to resist being sold off for vouchers as part of the mass privatization programme. Precisely how these remaining enterprises will be privatized is uncertain at present. However, it appears that this round of privatization is more likely to be combined with restructuring for many of these enterprises, and sales of assets for cash through tender offers are likely to play a much more important role in the future. Privatization approaches that lead to less-dispersed ownership and provide a more favourable climate for private investment are likely to be given much more favourable consideration in the post-1994 round of privatizations.

It is also important to recognize that, so far, the privatization programme has been concerned primarily with the reallocation of ownership rights. The programme did not raise significant amounts of cash, did not provide any investment capital for the privatized enterprises and did not lead to any fundamental restructuring at the enterprise level. As a result, these enterprises have had to rely on retained earnings (minimal), bank loans (mostly short-term), state subsidies and accounts payable to finance their activities. These are not satisfactory mechanisms for raising investment capital and newly privatized firms are going to need to find ways to obtain long-term financing for productive investments. This will not be easy until control rights are rationalized, bankruptcy laws are operating, securities laws are in place, and opportunities to purchase equity in these enterprises and to enter into joint ventures are made more attractive generally. Moreover, many inefficient enterprises will have to be restructured or closed. This process will not be easy and without a concerted effort to create a meaningful safety net for displaced workers, will carry a significant human cost.

5 Failure to restructure prior to privatization?
The Russian privatization programme is often criticized for not taking the time to restructure enterprises prior to privatization, to enhance organizational and transactional efficiency and to promote competition. At the same time, the programme has been criticized by many Russian industrialists and former officials of the branch ministries for creating too many private firms, for privatizing enterprises separately without taking into account vital horizontal and vertical linkages between enterprises that were previously part of the same industrial hierarchy, and for subsequently destroying critical organizational and managerial relationships that private firms need to adapt to a difficult and uncertain economic, political and legal environment. At the other end of the political spectrum, the programme has been criticized by some reformers for not going further and breaking up the enterprises at the lowest level of the industrial hierarchies into even smaller firms prior to privatization, to mitigate structural monopoly problems.

These diverse criticisms must be taken seriously. However, it is important to understand that the privatization programme did restructure the Russian industrial structure inherited from the Soviet regime. By focusing on the privatization of enterprises at the lowest level of the industrial hierarchy, the privatization programme supported the final destruction of the FSU's industrial hierarchies and the trade associations that grew out of the branch ministries in 1991 and 1992 (JST, pp. 327–30), and the horizontal and vertical relationships that characterized this structure. The contrasting view, that the privatization programme did not restructure Russian industry, rests on the invalid assumption that the enterprises inherited from the Soviet system had boundaries and internal organizational and management structures that made them correspond naturally to firms that have evolved in developed market economies.

As we shall see, while the privatization programme did not absolutely bar the aggregation of enterprises to recreate important pre-existing relationships, it made such aggregations difficult if they had anticompetitive implications and if their sponsors could not provide a compelling efficiency argument to support their creation. Moreover, since voluntary agreement of the enterprises as well as agreement by the government for pre-privatization aggregations of enterprises was required, the 'threat point' for such reorganizations was defined by the enterprise structure at the lowest level of the industrial hierarchies. Finally, the reservation of some equity for top management under the main privatization options provided a disincentive for joining enterprises together.

Thus, the privatization programme brought about the decentralization of Russian industry compared with its highly centralized hierarchical structure in the Soviet era. By focusing on the individual enterprises as the basis for privatization, the Russian programme effectively involved substantial deconcentration compared with programmes that might have been based on other aggregates within the existing industrial hierarchies and that could, arguably, have been viewed as more closely resembling firms in developed market economies. Moreover, the Russian privatization programme involved much more decentralization and deconcentration than did the leading alternative programmes[29] and, as we shall see presently, the Russian government generally resisted holding-company and financial-industrial group proposals that would have maintained or restored centralization and market concentration.

There are two aspects which should be addressed here.

1. *Breakaway divisions of enterprises*   A second way in which privatization deconcentrated Russian industry was through the privatization of subunits or 'breakaway divisions' of enterprises. The law and decrees governing privatization made it possible for the workers' collective of a subunit or division of an existing enterprise to propose that the subunit or division be privatized by itself, as an independent joint-stock company. Subunits with little capital did not require any approval on the part of the original enterprise to privatize independently. Otherwise, the approval of the original entity's workers' collective or a special decision of the relevant state property committee was required. GKI's approach to voluntary breakaway divisions of enterprises will be discussed further in the next section.

2. *Special-interest industries*   As noted above, a significant fraction of Russian industry, including all enterprises with more than 10,000 workers, was not subject to the provisions of the mass privatization programme. Special privatization packages had to be negotiated for these enterprises. Such a package could have involved a further

disaggregation to promote competition, although, aside from voluntary breakaways, we are not aware of any mandatory break-ups of Russian enterprises that have occurred to date. A special privatization package could also involve further aggregation of enterprises to promote organizational and transactional efficiency. For example, when the automobile and truck producer ZIL was privatized in 1993, with more than 100,000 workers, it sought to be effectively merged with various smaller enterprises with which it had been affiliated previously. GKI would not approve formal vertical integration but it did approve long-term contractual arrangements between ZIL and these enterprises. More fine-tuned restructuring prior to privatization is taking place in the oil industry (several vertically integrated enterprises are being created), in the electric power industry and in other industries.

All things considered, it is wrong to think of the Russian privatization programme as reflecting a decision not to restructure prior to privatization. Instead, it should be viewed as proceeding according to the following restructuring principles.

1. For enterprises subject to the mass privatization programme, effectively ignore the pre-existing industrial hierarchies. Begin with the presumption that individual enterprises are to become individual private firms.
2. For industries that fall into the special-interest category, try to fine-tune the restructuring to match the special conditions of these industries. Begin with the presumption that enterprises should not be aggregated unless a compelling efficiency argument is advanced to do so. Clearly, some aggregation of this sort is taking place, especially in the 'network industries' which are likely to have components that either remain in state hands or are subject to economic regulation (the rail, electric power and telecommunications systems, for instance, each consist of many enterprises).
3. Provide an opportunity for managers to seek voluntary agreement of all involved managers and workers for privatization of vertical and horizontal aggregations of enterprises. However, the burden of showing that the proposed aggregation should be approved prior to privatization is on those proposing it; they must show that it will promote efficiency and will not undermine competition goals.
4. Encourage voluntary spinoffs of subunits of enterprises. We turn next to this subject.

6   Voluntary separation of subunits of enterprises?

Although the Russian privatization programme was based on the privatization of the individual enterprises that comprised the lowest level of the FSU's industrial hierarchies, the privatization of subunits of enterprises could not be ruled out, for two primary reasons. First, many enterprises were thought to occupy monopoly or near-monopoly positions in the supply of individual products. Although JST show that there are relatively few industries with enterprises that account for more than 60 per cent of industry production when we aggregate production nationally at roughly the four-digit US SIC code level, there are many more enterprises with very high national market shares when we measure industry output at roughly the seven-digit level of aggregation. Taking into account the historic regional focus of much Soviet industry and the barriers to the creation of national markets posed by Russian transportation and distribution systems raises concerns about regional monopolies in a variety of sectors. In any case, monopoly problems were a significant concern of many influential groups in Russia, including some reformers, and a response to these concerns was clearly necessary.

However, as we noted above, any proposal for further deconcentration of the enterprises as the lowest level of the old industrial hierarchies had to confront the fact that many of these enterprises were effectively single plants or integrated production complexes. This meant that they were much harder to break up than multiplant firms. Not only would the privatization authorities have required a lot of information but their physical organization would have limited opportunities for efficient restructuring and would have raised opportunism problems caused by site specificity. While mandatory division of enterprises prior to privatization was problematical, at least some effort had to be made to accommodate 'voluntary' proposals for privatization of subunits of enterprises, since this would increase the number of competitors.

The second reason for considering privatization of subunits was that a large number of managers and workers in large enterprises desired to become independent from those enterprises. In part, this reflected a continuation of the *nomenklatura* privatization process discussed earlier. However, it was also a consequence of the incentives created by the distribution of ownership rights under the two most popular privatization options. The reservation of some equity for top management under these options provided an incentive for such secessions. At the same time, precisely this same factor provided an incentive for incumbent top management to oppose breakaways. Since its equity would be valuable only if the breakaway venture survived, there was no economic incentive to spin off non-viable operations. However, the managers of the original enterprise could always be expected to describe the dissolution as threatening the viability of what remained, and to point to real and imaginary monopoly and hold-up problems.

Clearly, one way to create more competitive market structures in the short run (that is, given existing assets), in a way that does not violate the constraints that militate against the widespread mandatory break-up of enterprises, is to encourage voluntary separations of subdivisions from existing enterprises. Such reorganizations can increase the number of horizontal competitors as well as improve market access to suppliers of inputs that new entrants will need to consume to operate efficiently. For economic, legal and perhaps political reasons, it is likely to be easier to effect deconcentration in this way during the privatization process rather than afterwards. Furthermore, such an approach could be designed to exploit better the information advantage that the enterprises and subunits of enterprises have about their interdependence, their independent viability and the need for supporting contractual arrangements to replace vertical or horizontal integration.

The voluntary separation of subdivisions of enterprises is unlikely to be objectionable if the primary effect is to reduce the concentration at one or more levels of the production chain. For example, a proposal to privatize separately a textile mill that is part of a multiplant textile enterprise is unlikely to lead to any competitive problems and may help to promote competition at one or more horizontal levels. As another example, a subdivision of a vertically integrated oil extraction and refining enterprise that consists of oil fields and some refining capacity (two horizontal layers) into two or more vertically integrated private firms is unlikely to be objectionable, since it will increase competition at both the oil extraction and refining levels of the product chain. Furthermore, this industrial structure is found in the oil sectors of many developed market economies. Therefore, a policy of establishing a rebuttable presumption that voluntary separations that are primarily horizontal will be approved appears to be sensible from a transaction cost perspective.

Similarly, there are enterprises in Russia that produce many different products that are neither in direct competition with one another (no horizontal integration) nor are part of the same production chain (no vertical relationship with other products produced by the enterprise). For example, enterprises in the MIC in Russia also produce many consumer products. Without compelling evidence of economies of scope, separation proposals for divisions that produce such products can also be routinely approved. Furthermore, since a voluntary separation is not likely to be forthcoming when there are significant economies of scope, the presumption should be that voluntary separations involving 'conglomerate' subdivisions will be approved. To rebut this presumption, the incumbent enterprise would have to demonstrate that the proposed separation would carry with it an important input also used in the production of other enterprise products and without which costs would increase significantly.

A situation in which voluntary separation of subdivisions may not be socially desirable is when it conflicts with longer-term restructuring goals for an industry. For instance, continuing with the oil industry example, one might argue that the creation of several oil enterprises that are vertically integrated between oil extraction and refining, while being better than a single vertically integrated firm, would be inferior to an industry structure with several independent oil producers and several independent refiners. The decision to approve or reject the proposed separation would then require a policy decision about whether or not the theoretically superior industry structure is technically and politically feasible.

Efficiency problems with voluntary separations are most likely to arise in situations which involve either a vertical separation or the separation of a piece of an integrated network. We deal with these in turn.

Let us consider the example of a manufacturing industry in which the market is national and where five vertically integrated enterprises currently produce output (downstream) and all of certain key inputs (upstream). None of the enterprises has more than a 35 per cent market share. The manufacture of cars and trucks in Russia has roughly these characteristics. One of the input-producing subdivisions of one of the enterprises proposes being privatized as a separate venture, and the managers and workers of the parent enterprise object. Since both levels are reasonably competitive, the only way that vertical separation could lead to efficiency losses is if there are relationship-specific assets that link the two levels of the enterprise and if economic circumstances give significant bargaining power to the separating division – a short-run monopoly or bilateral monopoly situation. Thus, the issues here would be whether or not there is significant transaction-specific capital at stake and whether or not contractual arrangements can mitigate opportunism problems in the absence of vertical integration. Information about the organization of similar industries in developed market economies could be very useful in gaining insights into the probable importance of asset specificity. There is, for instance, quite a lot of research on automobile manufacturing in other countries.[30]

Let us consider another hypothetical market in which, without any restructuring of enterprises, there will be very high levels of concentration upstream and downstream. Let us assume for simplicity that there will be only a single enterprise that controls all the production in the manufacturing sector (downstream) and in the raw materials sector (upstream). Without vertical integration, there would be market power upstream and downstream, and a potential double-marginalization problem. By solving this problem, vertical integration would lower downstream prices and increase welfare. In theory, the upstream and downstream subdivisions could both be made better off by staying together. However, information imperfections, bargaining costs and other considerations could lead the managers of the upstream subdivision, for example, to think that they would be better off by separating. The managers of the remaining divisions of the enterprise are likely to object. Should GKI reject the application to privatize a vertical segment of an enterprise? We think not, except in unusual circumstances.

While there may be static efficiency losses that result from double marginalization, the fact that both vertical levels are monopolies implies that a vertically integrated monopoly may be in a position to make entry more difficult into these markets. A merger of two monopolies at different levels of the production chain would almost never be approved in the US or the EU on the grounds that it would be anticompetitive. Thus, allowing vertical separation could help to facilitate entry at both levels and increase competition in the long run. Therefore, the expectation should be that vertical separations of enterprises where one or both levels of the vertical chain is highly concentrated should be approved.

The one clear exception to this rule is a situation in which the vertical segment that seeks to separate is a true natural monopoly in the long run. If the natural monopoly is thought to be limited to the vertical segment that seeks to separate, then it should be permitted only if the resulting firm is subjected to effective regulation of prices and required to deal with all demanders. This would then ensure access to the natural monopoly product and promote competition in the potentially competitive downstream market. The most likely candidates are transportation facilities characterized by high sunk costs and significant economies of scale. More generally, these situations are likely to involve services that are regulated or publicly owned in most OECD countries.

Approval also should not be automatic when the subunit that requests to be privatized as a separate firm is part of an integrated network, such as a long-distance telephone network, a railroad network or a pipeline network. There are significant complementarities between the pieces of the network but owners of some of the pieces may be able to gain a strategic advantage over the others by separating (one can think of this case as involving significant specific investments, since individual segments are of little value alone and, usually, the network has significant market power). Significant network economies may be lost by disintegration. The managers of other components of the network are likely to complain that the value of their assets will be reduced by the loss of coordination with, and strategic behaviour by, separate entities that are physically part of an integrated network. Therefore, it would be desirable to reject applications to privatize subdivisions of integrated networks in which complementarities and economies are significant.

Again, information about the organization of the relevant industry in other OECD countries and associated analyses of their performance can be useful to ensure that a 'network externalities' exception can be used only in cases where such problems are significant. Networks of this sort are almost always industries or segments that are subject to regulation or are owned by the government in OECD countries.

Precisely these kinds of consideration governed GKI's approach to voluntary separations.[31] GKI has been sympathetic to almost all voluntary separation proposals except those for which evidence from existing trading relationships or comparative data for other countries have suggested that such separations would sever important organizational, technical or economic linkages. Furthermore, GKI has attempted to get the parties to enter into contractual arrangements that would mitigate short-run disruptions in commercial relationships and opportunism problems.

Voluntary separations of subunits have often been opposed by the management of the enterprises from which these subunits have sought to secede. Disputes between would-be breakaway subunits and their parent enterprises became so common that, in November 1993, GKI and GKAP issued a joint regulation on the resolution of such disputes. Even though the antimonopoly committees were not initially sympathetic to separation proposals, the general tone of this regulation encouraged separations. Though most early discussions of the Russian privatization plan say little or nothing about the ability of subunits to secede from enterprises,[32] the secession provision has turned out to be of considerable importance. Of the 10,663 entities with privatization plans approved as of 1 July 1993, 1,237 (11.6 per cent) were formed from subdivisions of state enterprises (Boycko et al., 1993, p. 153).

7 Aggregations of enterprises into larger firms prior to privatization

At the same time that the privatization authorities were under pressure to be more aggressive towards breaking up enterprises at the lowest level of the traditional industrial hierarchies, they found themselves under even more pressure to approve the privatization of aggregations of enterprises. In some cases, this involved replicating portions of the old industrial hierarchies via holding companies. In other cases, the pressure was to create large conglomerates (so-called 'financial-industrial groups') to replicate real or imagined structural characteristics of the Japanese and Korean economies rather than a more decentralized 'Anglo-Saxon' structure for a market economy.

Holding-company proposals

In response to the corporatization and privatization requirements associated with the mass privatization programme announced in June 1992, most of the trade and industrial associations discussed above came to GKI with proposals for creating holding companies made up of their member enterprises. These proposals typically involved the creation of a holding company owned by the constituent enterprises. The holding company, in turn, would own a controlling interest in each of the enterprises. The holding-company management would be drawn from the trade associations, which had been created from the former branch ministries.

At first, these proposals seemed to be efforts by the former branch ministry officials to reassert control of their industries. However, by mid-1992, these officials were not in a position to impose their will on the enterprises and interviews with association officials confirmed that managers were actually the driving force behind these proposals.

Many managers were concerned that their enterprises would not survive the chaotic transition to a decentralized market economy. Some no doubt felt that the holding companies could recreate some of the familiar features of the old regime, while others saw these institutions as sources of expertise on functions that had been performed by branch ministries in the Soviet era. Furthermore, the holding companies, by eliminating outside shareholders, effectively gave managers much more control over their enterprises (at least collectively) than would have been the case if they had privatized separately and shareholding had become more widely dispersed.

While the desire to preserve historical commercial relationships and to retain the skills of senior officials previously located in the branch ministries and trade associations had a plausible efficiency basis, many of the holding-company proposals also had objectionable attributes.

Many of the proposals were blatantly anticompetitive. As JST discuss in detail, the primary way in which competition can emerge in the medium term in Russia is if the former members of individual branch ministry hierarchies compete with one another, diversify their product lines and, in many cases, expand their geographic coverage. This mechanism was blocked by holding-company proposals that typically linked together enterprises that were part of the same production association or branch ministry division, and that typically accounted for the vast bulk of the production at the four-digit level of aggregation.

A second objectionable attribute of the proposed holding companies was their size. They involved aggregations of enterprises with hundreds of thousands of workers. By the summer of 1992, one of the primary functions of the trade associations had become lobbying the government, the parliament and the central bank for protective legislation, for subsidies and for central bank credits. Because of their size, it appeared probable that the holding companies would be perceived as being 'too big to fail' and that they would become an impediment to weaning the enterprises from subsidies, imposing hard budget constraints, and moving towards macroeconomic stability.

A third objection to the proposed holding companies was that they were structured in a way that effectively removed them from public control by outside shareholders. In the most complex proposals, each holding company was majority-owned by its constituent enterprises, the holding company, in turn, had a controlling interest in each of the enterprises and each of the enterprises owned significant shares of the other enterprises in the group. This structure precluded any meaningful external control of either the holding company or the constituent enterprises immediately following privatization.[33]

Finally, many of the proposed holding-company structures were far more complicated than appeared to be necessary to create efficient multidivisional firms. Indeed, there is little (if any) evidence that these entities had made any significant efforts to develop an accounting framework or management system that would provide for the kind of balancing of centralized and decentralized management that characterizes large multidivisional firms in developed market economies. The entities seemed to be designed more to protect the positions of the incumbent managers than to preserve or create efficient organizational arrangements that would help the enterprises to adapt to the changing and uncertain economic conditions and the immature institutional environment.

Nevertheless, even in the light of the political, informational and competitive constraints that GKI operated under, it would not have been appropriate simply to ban all pre-privatization holding-company proposals or similar forms of aggregation. As we have noted, there could very well have been important efficiencies associated with retaining some of the interenterprise relationships within the existing industrial hierarchies and trade associations. What was needed was a 'screening' policy. Because the costs of denying applications for 'good' aggregations prior to privatization were mitigated by the opportunity to merge after privatization, subject to the antimonopoly law[34] and because of the serious anticompetitive potential of 'bad' aggregations, it made sense to design a policy to reject quickly what are apparently 'bad' proposals and to look more carefully only at proposals that posed minimal competitive risks.

In November 1992, GKI adopted a policy towards proposed holding companies, that embodied this screening concept and reflected the competition and corporate governance concerns identified above.[35] This policy involved an absolute ban on cross-ownership among subsidiaries in a holding company (or any other similar organizational structure). Subsidiaries, or 'daughters', of a holding company were not allowed to own shares in each other's company, or in the holding company itself. In the light of competitive concerns and opportunities for mergers after privatization, GKI decided to take a tough stand against holding companies that led to commonly owned enterprises whose aggregate market share exceeded a 'safe harbour' level. Proposals were approved only for holding companies which would not control more than 35 per cent of a relevant market, defined more broadly than was typical in the Russian government, and which could make a reasonable case that the proposed structures would bring about substantial efficiency gains.

This strict holding-company policy almost certainly deterred many anticompetitive proposals that would otherwise have been presented to GKI.[36] The GKI experts' commission set up to review holding-company proposals received only about 20 proposals between October 1992 and January 1993, and it approved several. In some cases, however, industries whose proposals were rejected were able to bypass GKI and obtain permission from the government for holding-company structures that GKI would have barred.

Financial-industrial groups

The 1992 holding-company proposals mainly involved agglomerations of enterprises in the same industry or those previously subject to control by the same branch ministry. In the summer of 1993, a new set of proposals for financial-industrial groups (FIGs) – encompassing enterprises in different industries – gained considerable support within the government and parliament.

The argument for FIGs usually begins with the observation that an economy with many thousands of one-plant, worker- or manager-controlled joint-stock companies and without a real banking system, uniform accounting standards or efficient securities markets is not likely to have either efficient private firms or an effective market for corporate control. Since most of the incumbent managers had inherited their positions from the previous system, there was no reason to believe that the correct hands were on the wheels or that the dispersed shareholding and worker-manager control would lead the market for corporate control to effect a smooth process of replacement of inefficient managers by efficient managers.

Moreover, workers and managers who control their firms will have a strong preference (at least, if they are even moderately myopic) to distribute profits to themselves in the form of wages and bonuses rather than to themselves and others in the form of dividends. Without efficient banks or workable financial markets, cash-poor firms may have great difficulty in financing even very attractive investments and the necessary restructuring process may operate very slowly.

FIG proponents argued that the only way to deal effectively with these problems was to force the creation of a number of large, geographically dispersed (for political reasons) conglomerate organizations, covering between a quarter and a half of Russian industry and modelled vaguely after the FIGs of Japan or Korea. The basic plan was to merge 'cash cows' with enterprises that have attractive investment projects, to operate an internal capital market within each FIG and to rely on talented top management to ensure that constituent enterprises are competently run. Mechanically corporatized enterprises slated for inclusion in an FIG would be held off the voucher auction market and a majority of their equity given to a holding company. A majority of the FIG holding company's shares would then be auctioned for vouchers. The rest would be held in trust for the FIG's top managers, to be given to them as a bonus if and only if they met legislatively fixed short-term performance targets, and to be auctioned otherwise.

There is nothing inherently uneconomic about allowing FIG-like structures to emerge over time in Russia as they have in other countries.[37] Such structures would probably then be generally consistent with the institutional environment that emerges in Russia. However, the fact that such groups have evolved over time in Japan and Korea does not mean that industrial groups with similar performance attributes can be recreated overnight by decree or random draws in Russia. There are several problems.

First, FIGs created in this way are likely to be inefficient. Multi-industry enterprises in market economies have worked well only when they have been built carefully over time (Milgrom and Roberts, 1992, pp. 542–3): the conglomerates patched together quickly in the US in the 1960s generally performed poorly.[38] The FIGs proposed in the summer of 1993 would be slapped together even more hastily than these unworkable aggregates, and they would be modelled after structures that evolved in economic and institutional environments very different from those in Russia today. Because these FIGs would be both inefficient and 'too big to fail', it is very likely that they would need and receive substantial state subsidies soon after their formation, making these inefficiencies enduring.

The formation of FIGs on a large scale would also necessarily slow privatization significantly. Unless enterprises are to be selected by drawing names from a hat, in which case the level of inefficiency would be staggering, individual FIGs would take months (at least) to construct. This means that many, if not most, corporatized enterprises would have to be held off the voucher auction market, in some sort of public–private limbo, until the process is concluded. This outcome would have been inconsistent with a programme designed to privatize reasonably quickly, for important political reasons.

Using these and other arguments, pro-reform forces in the government managed to prevent the adoption of the FIG proposals under discussion in the summer of 1993. Unfortunately, however, a compromise proposal was adopted by presidential decree in December 1993. This decree puts the Russian government on record as being clearly in favour of FIGs in general, calls for the near-term formation by the government of at least two FIGs composed of state enterprises, and provides for debt write-downs for enterprises included in privately formed FIGs. It should be noted that FIGs must be 'established in conformity with antimonopoly legislation of the Russian Federation', but it is unclear whether or not the antimonopoly committees have any general right of prior review.

Although this decree could lead to the creation of large, inefficient enterprises that further diminish competition, the privatization programme has not yet been seriously affected and the worst fears of the FIGs' opponents have not yet been realized. However, with the end of the mass privatization programme, there is still much to be privatized. There are also large numbers of trade associations, holding companies and bank-centred groups that appear to be in the process of formation (often without necessary approvals from the antimonopoly committees), and it is very possible that the next stage of privatization and industry restructuring will rely heavily on FIG-type organizations.

8   Concluding comments

Those responsible for identifying the boundaries of the firms that would be subject to privatization in Russia have had to confront many intellectual, economic and political challenges. Russian industry had been built on a set of large industrial hierarchies that relied extensively on formal and informal relationships between their constituent 'enterprises'. These enterprises, in turn, did not possess many of the managerial and organizational attributes of firms in developed market economies. On the one hand, preservation of at least some of the relationships within these industrial hierarchies may have been necessary to preserve important supply, financing, R&D and managerial relationships to create viable private firms with good adaptation properties. On the other hand, however, creating such firms out of these industrial hierarchies meant confronting serious information barriers, monopoly issues and political constraints. There was enormous uncertainty about the most efficient structures for firms that must operate in an economy that was expected to change radically and that still lacked many of the basic institutions of capitalism.

The ultimate decision by the Gaidar government to build the privatization programme around the enterprises at the lowest level of the industrial hierarchies, to treat industries with special characteristics and very large firms on a case-by-case basis, to evaluate applications for vertical and/or horizontal aggregations on a case-by-case basis, with a focus on market power issues, and to encourage voluntary separations, except where they would lead to significant efficiency losses, seems to have made eminently good sense. Whether or not the Russian privatization programme ultimately proves to be a success, however, must depend on its ability to pull along the many other institutional reforms – at both the microeconomic and macroeconomic levels – that are necessary to support a market economy with attractive efficiency attributes. The evolution of these institutions, along with the laws that govern competition policy and regulation of natural monopolies[39] will help to determine how the major post-privatization industrial restructuring that must now occur will proceed. Privatization is the beginning and not the end of industrial restructuring in Russia. Over the next few years, we are likely to see major industrial restructuring take place in Russia as privatized enterprises merge, diversify their product lines,

Privatization in Russia: what should be a firm?   123

spin off unrelated business activities, and are liquidated or restructured following bankruptcy.

Notes

* Much of the factual material contained in this chapter comes from Joskow, Schmalensee and Tsukanova (1994), which we will refer to as JST in what follows. JST, in turn, relies heavily on interviews conducted by the authors and their associates (especially Natalia Tsukanova) in Russia from mid-1992 to early 1994. The authors have advised the Russian Federation Committee for the Management of State Property (GKI) and the Russian Federation Antimonopoly Committee (GKAP) regarding some of the issues discussed in this chapter.
1. Perhaps surprisingly, Russia passed and antitrust law in March 1991, before the post-Gorbachev privatization programme began. As JST note, this reflected deep concerns about monopoly felt by a broad cross-section of the Russian bureaucracy and intellectual community.
2. Since these institutions took decades to evolve in developed market economies, it should not be terribly surprising that they cannot be created with the wave of a wand in Russia either. In both cases, history matters. As we discuss below, institutions inherited by Russia from the FSU already performed functions such as those observed in developed market economies, but did so in ways and in structures incompatible with such economies.
3. This section draws particularly heavily on JST.
4. Much of the discussion in this subsection is based on Freris (1984, pp. 1–48), Hewett (1988, pp. 94–250) and Spulber (1991, pp. 9–29).
5. For example, the Soviet Air Line Aeroflot's planes were on the books of individual airports in the FSU. When the Soviet Union collapsed, each airport (each one an 'enterprise') claimed the planes on its books.
6. See, generally, Freris (1984, pp. 5–11), Kroll (1991, p. 148) and Hewett (1988, pp. 245–50).
7. See also Kahn and Peck (1991, pp. 63–70) for an insightful early discussion.
8. See Brown et al. (1993) and JST for more detailed analyses of the size distribution of enterprises in Russia prior to privatization.
9. The US data come from *Fortune*, 19 April 1993, p. 222. The Russian data come from a database obtained from Goskomstat. The Russian data are consistent with the World Bank (1992, p. 83) report of 952 large Russian enterprises with average employment of 8,558 in 1987.
10. Hewett (1988, pp. 170–76) provides an extensive discussion with numerous examples.
11. See Spulber (1991, Chapter 11) and IMF (1991, Chapter V.2) for informative general discussions.
12. On the issues addressed in this paragraph, see IMF (1991, pp. 32–9), Spulber (1991, pp. 214–20) and BCG (1993).
13. Cigarettes, automobiles and a few food products (such as chocolates) developed some brand identity. However, the development of this brand identity was generally not accompanied by the kind of advertising and promotion activities that are common in the US. The brand identities seem to reflect instead customer perceptions about product quality for products that were in short supply.
14. See, generally, Hewett (1988, pp. 335–40) and Spulber (1991, pp. 268–9, 279).
15. See, generally, Hewett (1988, pp. 322–33) and IMF (1991, pp. 296–300).
16. For discussions, see World Bank (1992, p. 85) and Cooper (1991, pp. 53–9).
17. The breakup of the Soviet Union in 1991 was also a source of serious economic dislocation, since the planning system planned for the entire FSU and not for individual republics. The production of goods and raw materials was not evenly distributed across the FSU, and its breakup left net surpluses and shortages of goods and raw materials between the republics, that had to be handled through

international trading relationships. The rationale behind the Commonwealth of Independent States concept was partly a response to the desire to develop in an orderly way trading relationships to replace those that had operated under the central planning system.

18. Spulber (1991, pp. 44–8) provides an informative discussion.
19. Soviet academic economic thinking associated monopolies with shortages (see Tsapelik and Yasin, 1990).
20. World Bank (1992, Chapter 1) describes these changes and their aftermath.
21. Some local authorities may have continued to try to regulate the prices of goods produced by 'monopoly register', even after this date. As JST discuss, these controls appear to have been ineffective on most wholesale products, in any event.
22. Kahn and Peck (1991, pp. 71–3) discuss several of the factors considered here and make recommendations consistent, in practice, with the programme adopted by the Gaidar government.
23. An additional complication is posed by the 'social assets' owned by many larger enterprises. These assets include housing, commissaries, clinics and hospitals, and vacation facilities. In Russia, the corresponding services have traditionally been provided by large enterprises, particularly those located outside major urban areas, and have been intimately tied to employment. The Russian government has not yet constructed anything like the social safety nets that exist in OECD nations. Therefore, continued subsidies to large, unprofitable Russian state and private enterprises have been defended as being necessary to support the provision of essential social services to workers who would otherwise be unemployed and be cut off from those services. It is clear that the responsibility for providing essential social services must be shifted – to the workers themselves (such as by giving them ownership of their apartments), to the private sector, or to local, regional or national governments. The failure of the Russian reformers to deal effectively with social assets and the associated services has proved to be a significant impediment to gaining support for the reform programme from workers dependent on their enterprises for a wide array of basic services, and has greatly impeded the massive reallocation of labour necessary to produce a modern market economy in Russia.
24. On the issues discussed in this paragraph, see JST (especially pp. 332–5, 343–8).
25. As Boycko et al. (1993) discuss, bidders in each auction mainly just submit vouchers and set however many shares they buy at the equilibrium price, which is determined simply as the ratio of shares available to vouchers submitted.
26. Data obtained from Russia Privatization Centre, October 1994.
27. Workers also received substantial benefits, equal to 30 per cent of the sales price, when small-scale enterprises were sold by local governments (see Boycko et al., 1993, p. 154, n. 17).
28. See 'Further to Rise', *The Economist*, 13 November 1993, p. 90.
29. The leading alternatives proposed by the Gaidar government's opponents involved very slow privatization of state-owned enterprises and reliance on vague concepts of 'democratic socialism', under which the state would continue to own the bulk of industry for many years.
30. Another example of such a situation might be an electricity-generating plant built to supply the needs of an isolated aluminium plant that, in turn, supplies the entire Russian market for some product, such as widgets. The generating plant is of much less value without the aluminium plant as a customer, since it would have to build a transmission line to connect with other potential buyers. Similarly, the aluminium plant would need to incur the cost of a transmission line if it could not buy from the generating plant. Since the two parties depend on each other, integration is a natural outcome. Without integration, the generating plant and the aluminium plant will both seek the bulk of monopoly rents in the widget markets. The result of this struggle is likely to be elevated costs and prices. If the aluminium market is competitive, however, there are no monopoly rents for which to contend and failure to strike an efficient bargain would place both parties' survival at risk.

31. This may be more than a fortuitous coincidence, since the authors advised GKI on these issues in October 1992.
32. Compare World Bank (1992, Chapter 6) and Lainela and Sutela (1993).
33. In contrast, since the mass privatization programme effectively only distributed control rights and raised little (if any) capital for the enterprises, inside control would probably have had to diminish over time, when holding companies sought additional investment capital from banks, investment companies and the public.
34. JST discuss this law and its enforcement in detail.
35. This may not be a coincidence, since the authors helped GKI's expert team to develop a policy for responding to holding-company applications.
36. See JST (pp. 346–8) for further details.
37. There are, of course, ongoing debates about the costs and benefits of industrial economies built around bank-controlled industrial groups, as in Japan and Korea, and more decentralized economies, as in the US and the UK (see Grosfeld (1994) and the references cited therein).
38. See, generally, Ravenscraft and Scherer (1987).
39. In early July 1994, the cabinet of the Russian government adopted a new law on natural monopolies which the authors helped to write. A revised version of the law was passed by the Russian Parliament in 1995.

References
Boston Consulting Group (BCG) (1993), 'Food Distribution in Russia', Unpublished Report for GKI, BCG.
Boycko, Maxim, Andrei Shleifer and Robert W. Vishny (1993), 'Privatizing Russia', *Brookings Papers on Economic Activity*, 2, 139–92.
Brown, Annette N., Barty W. Ickes and Randi Ryterman (1993), 'The Myth of Monopoly: A New View of Industrial Structure in Russia', mimeo, Washington, DC: World Bank, 6 August.
Cooper, Julian (1986), 'The Civilian Production of the Soviet Defence Industry', in R. Amann and J.M. Cooper (eds), *Technical Progress and Soviet Economic Development*, Oxford: Basil Blackwell.
Cooper, Julian (1991), *The Soviet Defence Industry*, New York: Royal Institute of International Affairs.
Davis, Lance E. and Douglass C. North (1971), *Institutional Change and American Economic Growth*, Cambridge: Cambridge University Press.
Freris, Andrew (1984), *The Soviet Industrial Enterprise*, New York: St Martin's Press.
Greif, Avner and Eugene Kandel (1993), 'Contract Enforcement Institutions: Historical Perspective and Current Status in Russia', *John M. Olin Program in Law and Economics, Working Paper Series*, Stanford, CA: Stanford Law School.
Grosfeld, Irena (1994), 'Comparing Financial Systems: Problems of Information and Control in Economies in Transition', mimeo, May.
Hewett, A. (ed.) (1988), *Reforming the Soviet Economy*, Washington, DC: Brookings Institution.
International Monetary Fund (IMF) (1991), *A Study of the Soviet Economy*, Vol. 3, Washington, DC: International Monetary Fund.
Joskow, Paul L. (1988), 'Asset Specificity and the Structure of Vertical Relationships: Empirical Evidence', *Journal of Law, Economics, and Organization*, 4, 95–117. Reprinted in O.E. Williamson and S. Winter (eds), *The Nature of the Firm*, Oxford: Oxford University Press, 1991.
Joskow, Paul L. (1991), 'The Role of Transaction Cost Economics in Antitrust and Public Utility Regulation', *Journal of Law, Economics, and Organization*, 7, 53–83.
Joskow, Paul L., Richard Schmalensee and Natalia Tsukanova (JST) (1994), 'Competition Policy in Russia During and After Privatization', *Brookings Papers on Economic Activity: Microeconomics*, 301–81.
Kahn, Alfred E. and Merton J. Peck (1991), 'Price Deregulation, Corporatization, and

Competition', in M.J. Peck and T.J. Richardson (eds), *What Is To Be Done?*, New Haven, CT: Yale University Press, pp. 38–82.

Kroll, Heidi (1991), 'Monopoly and Transition to the Market', *Soviet Economy*, **7**, 143–74.

Lainela, Seija and Pekka Sutela (1993), 'Russian Privatization Policies', in Pekka Sutela (ed.), *The Russian Economy in Crisis and Transition*, Helsinki: Bank of Finland.

Milgrom, Paul and John Roberts (1992), *Economics, Organization, and Management*, Englewood Cliffs, NJ: Prentice-Hall.

Ravenscraft, D. and F.M. Scherer (1987), *Mergers, Selloffs, and Economic Efficiency*, Washington, DC: Brookings Institution.

Spulber, Nicolas (1991), *Restructuring the Soviet Economy*, Ann Arbor, MI: University of Michigan Press.

Tirole, Jean (1991), 'Privatization in Eastern Europe: Incentives and the Economics of Transition', in O. Blanchard and S. Fischer (eds), *The NBER Macroeconomics Annual 1991*, Cambridge, MA: MIT Press and National Bureau of Economic Research.

Tsapelik, Vladimir and Evgeny Yasin (1990), 'Puti Preodoleiya Monopolisma v Obshestvennom Proizvodstve', *Planovoye Khosiaistvo*, 35–41.

Williamson, Oliver E. (1991), 'Comparative Economic Organization: The Analysis of Discrete Structural Alternatives', *Administrative Science Quarterly*, **36**, 269–96.

Williamson, Oliver E. (1993), 'Transaction Cost Economics and Organization Theory', *Industrial and Corporate Change*, **2**, 107–56.

World Bank (1992), *Russian Economic Reform: Crossing the Threshold of Structural Change*, Washington, DC: World Bank, September.

5 Illegal markets and new institutional economics*

Margherita Turvani

1 Introduction

The illegal economy concerns a far from negligible part of overall economic activity[1] and includes various phenomena often interconnected with legal activities. Illegality is established at a social level, where the boundaries defining the set of exchanges, permitted in various possible circumstances, are drawn. When an economic agent is involved in an exchange (of a right or good) which is in conflict – either in its nature or its method of production – with the permitted transaction structure, then we speak of it as an illegal transaction, and the agent's behaviour is defined as deviant or criminal.

The economist may approach the subject by considering either the illegal behaviour, and proceed to study the economic rationality of individual choices, or the illegal transactions, their nature, the ways they take place, their structure and organization, that is, the development of organized crime and how the criminal markets function.

Becker (1968) and Stigler (1970) belong to the former. Developing some of the ideas already found in Beccaria (1764), they interpret turning to crime as an individual rational choice. The latter approach is due to Schelling (1967) and Buchanan (1980); market structure is determined by the interplay of two forces: addiction on the demand side and economies of scale on the supply side.

This chapter sets out to adopt a third approach, using the tools offered by new institutional economics. Such tools enable us to reinterpret the forms of economic behaviour of those operating in illegal markets (consumers and producers) and offer a clearer understanding of the special features of criminal organizations.[2]

Section 2 applies the conceptual tools of the new institutional economics to the analysis of behaviour in illegal markets; transactions are not cancelled by prohibition but they are embedded in another institutional environment, a different order with its rules, norms and enforcement institutions. As Schelling (1980) observes, illegal markets are the product of politics.[3] Thus they are the outcome of institutionally defined rules and the degree of their enforcement. The definition of these rules directly affects the transaction costs which the agents must bear to complete illegal transactions. The forms of relations between parties, that is, the organization forms, are modified as a consequence.

Section 3 discusses the two most widely recognized economic models of criminal behaviour – the rational criminal model, which asserts that illegal activity will be chosen when it offers the individual greater utility than legal activity, and the monopoly model, which describes organized crime as an organization driven by the goal of preventing or ending competition in illegal markets.

Section 4 presents the organization of the prohibited psychoactive substances market. The new institutional economics provides insights both to understand the prevailing flexible organizations of supply and to interpret consumers' behaviour in the drug market. Conclusions follow in Section 5.

2   New institutional economics and illegal markets

Why employ the new institutional economics?
Why does the new institutional economics offer an analytical framework useful for studying illegal markets? Its relevance is summarized in the following quote from Williamson (1993, p. 457):

> Institutional economics works at two levels of analysis. The macro variant, which is especially associated with the work of Douglass North, deals with the institutional environment. The micro variant deals with the institutions of governance. Lance Davis and North distinguish between these two as follows.
>
> > The institutional environment is the set of fundamental political, social and legal ground rules that establishes the basis for production, exchange and distribution. Rules governing elections, property rights, and right of contract are examples. . . . An institutional arrangement is an arrangement between economic units that governs the ways in which these units can cooperate and/or compete. It . . . [may] provide a structure within which its members can cooperate . . . or [it may] provide a mechanism that can effect a change in law or property rights.
>
> The way that I propose to join these two is to treat the institutional environment in which a transaction (or related set of transactions) is embedded as a set of shift parameters, changes in which elicit shifts in the comparative costs of governance.

The prohibition (in this case of the production, distribution and consumption of psychoactive substances) offers a paradigm of how an agreement reached in an institutional environment between members of a community leads to the definition of laws banning certain forms of behaviour. Prohibition classifies as illegal widespread forms of behaviour which may previously have been legitimate.[4]

In this case not only are forms of behaviour outlawed, but also consumer commodities. With the disappearance of the legal market, the black market opens up. Participating in transactions is illegal and it is in relation to such participation that the behaviour of agents and organization forms may be analysed using the model proposed by transaction cost economics.[5]

Transaction cost economics is based on two sets of assumptions. The first concerns the characteristics of economic agents: human beings have bounded rationality and are capable of opportunistic behaviour. The second refers to the nature of the transaction. Selected as the micro-analytical unit, a transaction differs in a number of attributes: uncertainty, frequency and asset specificity. Given the behavioural assumptions concerning agents, the combination of the critical attributes will give rise to transactions characterized by various levels of transaction costs. In order to keep such costs down, organizational forms able to complete transactions will be diversified. Organizational variety, therefore, is the outcome of human strategic capacity.

If prohibition does not actually prevent a set of transactions, but significantly changes the conditions in which the transactions can take place, then new institutional economics offers a valuable framework for understanding the organizational forms of the market and the ways in which transactions are redefined.

An institutional view on prohibitions and sanctions

Economists have embraced the well-known paradigm of human nature as consistently characterized by the pursuit of self-interest: given stable preferences, opportunities and constraints, economic action is the epitome of rational action, that is, the action which, through an optimizing calculus of advantages and disadvantages, is best able to satisfy the individual. Assuming there is an underlying utilitarian calculus to mental processes that result in action, we have a general principle for interpreting, assessing and guiding other people's actions.

This becomes important when authority is to be given a legitimate power: individuals, for example, can agree on the need to adopt an authority entrusted with the powers to govern conflicts and, by referring to the calculativeness of the human spirit, this authority will intervene in situations of conflict. The principle of individual utility defines the agent's areas of freedom and at the same time the limits to its applicability. These limits are defined by the interference with other agents and especially by the fact that such interference is harmful. The main tool used by the institution to maintain its own authority and guarantee stability is the sanction. In this way the individual is subject to an external power attenuating his or her self-interest.[6]

Prohibitions and sanctions may have the aim of identifying, that is, making visible, whoever violates the stability of the arranged order: some behaviours are thus stigmatized within a society and a kind of *moral suasion* will operate. But prohibitions and sanctions act primarily by modifying the set of conditions underlying the individual's decision-making procedures. Sanctions regulate behaviour, changing the constellation of advantages and disadvantages surrounding the individual. Systems of sanctions created by an agreement between agents to govern mutual interference sustain the institutions, which through the definition and enforcement of rules make such systems effective. These systems of sanctions must be characterized by certainty, suitable severity and timeliness: the strength of the utilitarian principle applied to the sanction lies in its capacity to place effective constraints on the agents' calculus.[7]

The utilitarian principle makes it possible to set limits to individual freedom, writing and enforcing rules supported by a system of sanctions. Sanctions are powerful and effective, precisely because they enter the agent's calculus of 'pain and pleasure'. The utilitarian principle, according to Beccaria (1764), opens up the possibility of stable institutional arrangements. Not only will rationality sustain such arrangements, which will be neither unfair nor arbitrary, but each individual will be defined as deviant (criminal) or rule-abiding with respect to the ongoing systems of rules.[8]

The multiplicity of institutional orders

> All prescriptions of behaviour for individuals require enforcement. Usually the obligation to behave in a prescribed way is entered into voluntarily by explicit or implicit contract. . . . When the prescribed behaviour is fixed unilaterally . . . we have the regulation or law. Departures of actual from prescribed behaviour are crimes or violations. (Stigler, 1970, p. 55)

According to economic theory, spot exchanges are able to ensure the smooth functioning of the market, that is, to ensure that desired transactions are completed in zero transaction cost conditions. The transaction can be so simple that no contract, either implicit or explicit, is required. The incentive to complete a transaction lies in the certain and immediate attainment of the object of self-interest; sanctions are provided by market competition. In this way we associate the idea of a perfect market with the notion of a self-regulating market and thus with the idea of order, albeit spontaneous order.

Contract involves a greater degree of complexity: in defining a contract we model a system of incentives and sanctions to ensure that the transactions will be completed. This is a way, to use Williamson's expression, of relying on private ordering, that is, the capacity of self-interest to create forms of collectively accepted orders and rules (by the parties, not necessarily only two, involved in the transaction).

Transactions between individuals do not always take place within a set of formal laws; more frequently they take place in the realm of some form of private ordering, supported by the proper authority and sanctions. Several private orders may coexist and interplay with the purpose of guaranteeing the completion of transactions. Rules need not be consistent with each other, or be based on the same principle, in so far as their purpose is to govern specific transactions. Each level of private ordering will be accompanied by a system of sanctions – they, too, are not necessarily consistent, as many inconsistent institutional arrangements may exist side by side.[9] Inconsistencies between institutional arrangements, with bounded rationality, challenge the cost–benefit calculus in the agent's mind, which now takes place across several levels of orders; human behaviour becomes much less predictable, the outcomes of transactions more uncertain, and opportunistic behaviour potentially more harmful.

For sure, private ordering promotes order in transactions and among agents; yet a set of laws or general rules is required. Both the functioning of a self-regulating market and of private orders require an external authority, that of the courts, when disputes occur. Using courts may be very expensive, yet the guarantee of contracts enforcement promotes the smooth functioning of markets and private orders.

Illicit exchanges: opportunism and violence

The first, obvious but essential, remark to be made about the working of an illegal market is that all the transactions that pertain to it are defined as illegal. Since transactions are illegal, the challenge posed by opportunistic behaviour is potentially more harmful. Should we expect that agents will behave more opportunistically? There is no easy answer to this question.

No recourse to the set of institutionalized laws and rules, guaranteeing the flow of transactions on the legal markets, is possible. The fact that a universally recognized public authority cannot be relied on for enforcement does not mean there are no underworld substitutes. As a matter of fact, private ordering prevails: transactions in the underworld take place within governance structures, within rules supported by sanctions, and private agreements are enforced. The illegal market is very powerfully governed from within, as is the individual behaviour. The power of such forms of private ordering may be so strong as to challenge the socially recognized order: through their own recourse to violence, the public, absolute, legitimate monopoly of the use of violence is denied.

Violence, as a form of sanction, is a widely used tool to govern disputes in illegal markets, but it is not the only means available for agents involved in illegal transactions. On the contrary, this tool is used sparingly, since it leads to conspicuous illegal behaviour and as such is more likely to elicit public enforcement.

In the underworld there exists a powerful form of internal control: complicity. The law of silence within the gang and between gangs is the rule, and it is enforced without exception. The harsh treatment meted out to defectors discourages short-term opportunistic behaviour. Becoming a repentant, and cooperating with the police, is seldom a paying strategy: complicity fundamentally transforms the structure of relations between the parties. Each party becomes hostage to the other.[10] Not only is everybody hostage to one another, but the exchange of hostages involves other individuals: they may be other members of the organization, or relatives. The obvious example is the feuds between criminal groups which extend the sanction – that is, violence – to individuals not involved in the transaction, for example, the family or other members of the gang.

Limiting vertical integration is the second tool at hand to control opportunism and eventually to limit its destructive potential for the criminal organization.

While conditions of bounded rationality and opportunism in legal markets are frequently controlled by means of impersonal forms of organization, such as firms, where human behaviour becomes more predictable, allowing substantial specific investments and extensive division of labour, in illegal exchanges agents must look for different solutions. Interdependency is controlled to reduce uncertainty: we expect agents to be more short-sighted and less specialized. Survival, with high level of risk due to both legal enforcement and violence, may push firms to look for niches and to break up the transaction chain: small firms and low level of vertical integration should be expected.

Small business firms serve the purpose of preserving flexibility in transactions. With face-to-face relations within each firm it is easier to enforce the law of silence: information is local and specific to each transaction and the overall span of control on the business organization is very limited.

Information and uncertainty play different roles in legal and illegal transactions. A well-functioning legal market produces information; organizational forms serve the purpose of making the market more transparent and reducing transaction costs. The opposite is true in the prohibited market: the tendency to obscure signals, making them indecipherable for agents outside the organization, continually encoding information in new ways, is the condition of survival for the business. Low vertical integration and continuous restructuring within the industry guarantees opacity and limits the amount of shared information.

Violence, the law of silence, reorganization of transaction, and monetary incentives all serve the purpose of mitigating the usual problems of incentives and information distortion generated by the principal–agent relationship in criminal organizations.[11]

3 Conventional wisdom about illegal markets

Choosing crime
Economists who follow the utilitarian approach to crime explain human behaviour solely in terms of self-interest: deviance, crime and law-breaking are all manifestations of self-interest. It is assumed that there is no such thing as the criminal personality, and that any individual, without any particular skills can become a criminal. Individuals become criminals when pursuit of their self-interest leads them not to respect the agreements sanctioned by orders.

The economics of crime (of deviance and law-breaking) elaborated from the work of Becker and Stigler, offers a rigorous reworking of this reasoning: the principle of individual utility makes it possible for institutions to govern individual action, changing the conditions in its calculus. Given that the effectiveness of sanctions depends on their certainty, severity and timeliness, these elements can be suitably scaled to attain the anti-crime objectives the community has set itself as a function of the resources it decides to dedicate to the purpose.[12]

We thus come to a key point in the argument: such a reductive vision of human behaviour implies that it is much easier to govern behaviour than might have been expected. Although not fully conscious of their own calculus, individuals will react in predictable ways to changed pleasure–pain conditions, and the authority's measures will attain the expected results, given the limits in terms of public resources to be dedicated to the purpose. Thus the prohibition of some types of behaviour will be respected if sufficient resources are spent on enforcement. Unfortunately, this line of reasoning fails to take into account strategic behaviour by agents and their ability to respond to regulations reorganizing transactions.

Organized crime

The theory which has long dominated the field (and is still unreservedly accepted in various spheres, especially by the enforcement agencies), describes illegal markets (and narcotics markets in particular) as monopoly markets. This theory, first developed in the United States by drug enforcement agencies and to varying degrees influenced by the experience of alcohol prohibition (or rather its myths), has also been accepted in some academic literature. The starting point is that, apart from a few exceptions, organized crime[13] always tends to operate under monopoly conditions: a non-monopolized market offers low profits and is left to common criminals. Thus, organized crime is the outcome of the creation of illegal or black markets which may be monopolized through the use of the tools specific to the criminal firm. The deservedly most famous writings on this subject (Schelling, 1967) begin with the observation that if many of the principles valid for the 'upperworld' are also valid for the underworld, the formation of the monopoly criminal firm – organized crime – arises from the opportunity that some illegal markets offer for exploitation of scale economies in the production, distribution and management of risk.

The core markets for forming and maintaining organized crime are the 'monopolizable' black markets. Not all 'black' markets (prohibited by law) are monopolizable: it depends – as it does for legal markets – on the characteristics of the demand and the organization of the supply. Both may by shaped by illegality, as in the case of illegal narcotics trading: firms face growing consumer demand and enjoy a special market power because of the consumer's addiction. By prohibiting this market, the law, or rather politics, creates organized crime.[14]

Why is an illegal market able to guarantee higher profits than legal markets? Resorting to their usual toolbox, economists analyse a prohibited market in exactly the same way as a legal market. Prohibition is considered simply to push up the supply curve: the cost of supplying the market with the same quantity of commodities is made higher. But in considering the new costs, the costs contributed by illegality, only production costs are reevaluated to take risk into account, while transaction costs are not considered.

The increased production costs elicit a selection process: the most skilful and unscrupulous firms (firms more likely to become the embodiment of organized crime) will be successful and may eventually become a monopoly by a process of concentration, reorganizing to reduce additional costs through corruption, violence and disguise. Unlike the legal competitive market, on the black market, in principle, there is no mechanism pushing prices down. Operators on the illegal market enjoy protection, rather along the same lines as a normal industry might be protected by tariffs. True competition – where there is complete freedom of entry – is impeded because potential competitors unwilling to embark on a criminal career are debarred from entering the market. Only criminal firms operate on the illegal market. There is a moral entry barrier.

Of illegal firms, organized crime is the most expert, unscrupulous and initially the most violent: once it has established a monopoly, organized crime cuts back on the use of violence. According to Schelling the industry has a collective interest in reducing violence so as to avoid trouble with the public and the police, but it cannot do so until it has achieved a monopoly.

This view is an elegant rationalization of the image of the black market monopolized by organized crime; it also suggests what should or should not be prohibited and how to improve enforcement strategies. The theory of criminal monopoly has justified the notion that organized crime is socially preferable to unorganized crime. If demand for the prohibited commodities responds to prices, then the amount of undesired commodities sold to consumers will fall as a function of increases in enforcement and strengthened market monopoly: this is the main advantage of criminal monopoly (Buchanan, 1980). Moreover, competition between criminal firms selects the most efficient, those able to impose a more 'disciplined' arrangement on the market.

4 The illegal drug market

The organization of narco-traffic
Results of field research have called into question the monopoly theory: rather it seems that the narcotics markets are the arena for 'disorganized' crime. Firms are small or even tiny and short-lived. Transactions and their organization are not standardized or standardizable: agents do not look for economies of scale but for secrecy and dissimulation.

As early as 1977, Moore[15] explored the impact of illegality on the behaviour of those involved in the black market, especially dealers and consumers, and on the structure binding them together. Moore focused on the effects of prohibition on the forms of market organization and on their distinguishing feature: the modes of retail distribution defining the consumer–dealer relationship. Moore concludes that illegality shapes the structure of the industry and the market through the concrete actions of the agencies entitled to enforce prohibition (that is, agents behave dynamically and continually react to regulation). Depending on their market position and the nature of enforcement, the conditions of illegality alter the agents' opportunities. 'In describing the calculus of heroin dealers, it is important to talk in terms of utility rather than simply money profit and to remember that utility will be affected not only by changes in money profits, but also by changes in levels of risk to the dealer' (Moore, 1977, p. 11).

When enforcement is increased, the traffic is reshaped to control for uncertainty. Therefore, higher risk in dealing does not lead to higher prices, but generally it leads to business reorganization. The purpose is to curb losses but above all to guarantee the smooth functioning of transactions. New strategies are introduced in order to conceal the connections between the individual and the industry, to avoid leaving traces, and to corrupt and manipulate enforcement agencies.[16] The industry is continuously reshaped, new transactions are created and new agents enter the business.

These processes work towards controlling the size and segmentation of the market. It means systematically reducing the information held by others, increasing individual incentives, redistributing exposure to risk, and rapidly establishing new forms of complicity. Cutting back the scale of operation ensures that connections are reduced in absolute terms (each agent is involved in a smaller number of transactions), and allows the supply to control its customers by combining both parties' interests in the market. Moreover, it entails face-to-face relations, facilitating direct disciplining behaviour (control of opportunism), while smaller scale ensures greater operational flexibility (control over uncertainty).

Empirical studies shed a new light on consumer behaviour. The illegal nature of transactions brings consumers into contact with the criminal world: they are vulnerable because of both the illegality of transaction and the poor quality of the products. Consumer access to the market is more difficult; and the conditions in which transactions take place are less transparent. Consumers react rationally to the new information constraint by creating and remaining loyal to small local markets; frequently consumers become dealers, a form of upstream integration, in the attempt to develop a better control of quality and regular supply.

Becoming dealers, they can go over to the other, better-informed, side of the market, reshaping the division of labour.

Summing up, all changes in the industry tend to create a very fluid situation, the only one that can guarantee products and information flows when enforcement continuously changes the rule of the game: a certain instability in roles in the division of labour follows, and consequently the transaction chain is continually redefined. Agents modify the way the business is organized to control uncertainty and to complete transactions: the new institutional economics paradigm suggests that restructuring organizational forms within the industry is the response to frequent, sudden and unforeseen changes in transaction costs. The story told so far applies not only to the United States. In other markets too – for example, the British market – the rise in drug consumption has not been accompanied by the formation of a monopoly, but by the expansion of disorganized crime.[17]

Organization and uncertainty

A detailed description of all the operations involved in the transaction chain – gathering and refining raw material, transportation to the area of consumption, distribution to consumers and redistribution of the earnings among the agents involved – shows clearly that some transactions entail greater transaction costs than others, both in terms of uncertainty and specific investments.

In the transaction chain (in which steps in the production and distribution of the illegal product can be logically separated), only a few links actually require physical contact with the goods. The illegal nature of the traffic and transactions involved is directly connected to the nature of the commodities handled. Within the production process a number of transactions require relations with the upperworld while others require some technical and financial sophistication.[18] They vary, therefore, as a function of the technological nature and degree of illegality; that is, some are blatantly illegal, while others, although part of the production process, are more difficult to prove to be illegal.

The continual reorganizations of the supply are revealed by the constant changes in the composition of the substances supplied in each outlet market and the corresponding continual turnover in routes (for example, the French connection, the Balkan, Indian or Nigerian routes). It must be remembered that a change in routes does not simply mean that the same organization changes the itinerary of the traffic, but involves changing organizations operating in new places.

Vertical integration seems very limited. Many operators deal only with a very well-defined set of transactions and are not involved in other criminal activities. Thus they may be considered as single-product firms.

From a conceptual point of view, illegal markets cannot be described simply by using the legal market transaction chain – from the gathering of raw material to the outlet markets – and modifying it to take into account the effects of differences in risk on costs. Unlike what happens on the legal market, to guarantee the completion of illegal transactions, strategies are often adopted that are intended to increase the degree of uncertainty. Those operating in the prohibited market develop their own organization and adopt technology designed to dissimulate, thus promoting a division of labour ensuring that no traces of the transactions remain.

While in the legal market the division of labour allows specialization, and specialization creates a firm's reputation, a firm's identity and differentiation among the many, in the prohibited market, the division of labour is instrumental to the necessity to conceal agents and to cut links between transactions. Thus the transaction circuit is systematically interrupted by *ad hoc* firms whose function is to produce dissimulation; they do not serve any 'productive' purpose, working as interfaces among transactions, re-encoding information, making it unintelligible to outsiders. The dimensions of such firms are small because the interfaces are unstable; the firms will be short-lived because stability conflicts with the need for dissimulation. Paradoxically, the prevailing, global condition of uncertainty in the prohibited market works as a safety net around each transaction, reducing local uncertainty.

In the legal market something similar exists and its name is flexible specialization. This phenomenon is a response to uncertainty which prevents the standardization of products and of procedures with a consequent continuous recombining and redefinition of the transactions needed to complete the final product. In the case of the illegal market, flexible specialization appears to be a response to the state of uncertainty affecting all transactions. It is usually assumed that specialization within a network makes the firm more stable, increasing its chances of survival. This does not hold for illegal markets, which are characterized by the greatest specialization and the greatest instability.[19] This suggests that the skills necessary for specialization are widespread, that is, easily reproduced (a case of low-asset specificity) and that the advantages due to specialization decrease over time.

Kopp (1992, pp. 524–5) also reaches a similar conclusion:

> The network ensures the functional relationship necessary to communication between markets placed at the interface of links along the chain. The deter-

minant feature is that the way the network works does not follow a unique vertical path such as when activities of firms are based on the arrangement of productive operations. On the contrary, many parts of the network progress up or down along that network, bypassing intermediaries and dealing directly with each other ... Agents transacting on the drug market operate in an environment characterized by a high uncertainty. They continuously experiment with new rules, changing the prior organization of markets and giving rise to new ones. (Translation)

As Schelling claimed (1980), there are parallels between the markets of the upperworld and underworld; however, differences are more meaningful. The transaction chain, *la filière*, from production to consumption, is not made up of the same links: the institutional definition of a prohibited commodity shapes and constrains the kinds of transactions needed for the survival of the business. As Schelling admits, the form of the market is created by politics: institutional economics goes further and suggests that the division of labour may be transformed by the definition of different sets of rules.

Consumers and prohibition

Utilitarianism strengthened the idea of the importance of the consumer in the economic system: the consumer is the king of the market. The idea of the sovereign consumer is important in economics and paradoxically is associated with the passivity of the consumer, characterized not only by unchanging tastes and desires, by a stable, ordered and consistent system of preferences, but above all fixed in his or her role as the final link in the transaction chain in the economy. What this model rules out is economic agents' ability to learn, that is, to elaborate their past experience and to orient the course of future actions through learning.[20] Agents combine goods and their labour services to reach their utility target in consumption; if they need a chair, for example, they can either buy it or make it, buying wood. Therefore consumers, combining in different proportion goods and labour to increase utility, may modify their own position within the transaction chain. As a result, consumers' actions affect the overall transaction organization.

If consumers are not automatons, but users of an illegal market, how will the regime of prohibition affect their behaviour? Is it conceivable that the market only reorganizes its supply side and not its demand side as well?

Prohibition modifies the institutional environment within which a given economic activity of production and consumption takes place: in this new institutional environment consumers play an active role. They choose a technology of consumption, shaping their role as final consumers and changing the original division of labour. Consumers' reactions to the new conditions, in term of prices and risks, may include active strategies to preserve consumption habits. Since now illegality affects the access to the market, consumers will eventually spend more time in search activity, gathering information about prices, quality, supply conditions, and so on. Their life organization may change substantially.[21]

In the prohibited market the consumer carries out various activities which interact with the division of labour; eventually, the ideal line dividing consumers from producers will fade out. A classic example is the dealer–consumer: dealing in psychoactive substances is not a generic delinquent activity, but it could be explained as a way consumers react to the external conditions governing the satisfaction of their needs.[22] If both consumption and dealing are liable to similar sanctions, there is a greater tendency to deal – not more punishable than consuming – because the individual enjoys a scope economy in terms of risk-taking, integrating the roles of dealer and consumer.

Consumers may attempt to reduce their transaction costs (which are increased by a lack of information) by going over to the other, better-informed side of the market, and becoming dealers. Integrating upstream in the prohibited industry, they will cover two distinct economic roles, changing the existing division of labour within the market and the organization of transactions.

In extreme cases, dealing may become a way of life; when more and more time is combined with goods (drugs) to attain consumption targets, consumers' lives may change dramatically. This is the view put forward by the sociologist, Ruggiero (1992, p. 102), who describes the life and the economy of the most marginalized consumers, in poor urban areas. It is an 'industrious bazaar' where agents, to preserve their consumption habits, not necessarily drug addiction, become addicted to a certain life style, where illegality is the distinctive feature:

> the lack of social status associated with a permanent job makes it much more difficult to come off drugs and leave the scenario in which heroin is exchanged and consumed. In short, for the unemployed, the addiction to drugs is combined with the addiction to a life style connected to the use of and dealing in drugs: and this life style becomes a job able to offer an albeit debased form of status.

The scenario consists of a set of activities carried out at the border between informal economy and an illegal economy:

> although having a previous criminal career more often leads to use and

dealing... this crossing over now seems to include a new step. Those involved in the informal economy can easily gain access to illegal activities; through such activities the worker-delinquent will eventually come across the heroin market and will very often end up using the drug. (Ruggiero, 1992, p. 101)

In the marginalized strata of the population the consumption of pro-hibited commodities and illicit activities often interact with legal activities:

some areas live almost wholly off the petty criminal economy. Trading of all kinds, shops completely stocked with stolen commodities. ... Whole com-munities, including very law-abiding and reserved people use the received stolen commodities market and live side by side with the quasi illegal. (Ruggiero, 1992, p. 78)

What is generally so striking is the variety of commodities and service produced, and this variety goes far beyond illegal substances. Even the use of cash is superseded in a return to forms of barter in which commodities are inter-exchanged and exchanged for drugs.

The tenuous line between the legal and the illegal resembles the thin divide between dealer and consumer. Even the 'runner' is also usually a consumer: 'runners are recruited from dealers to make deliveries or seek out customers. Runners ... collect the commodities, go to the appointment and bring back the money. They only receive some petty cash reward and their personal daily dose' (Ruggiero, 1992, p. 63). Thus the consumption of illegal substances (which is not necessarily drug addiction) does not conform with the model of the consumer as final market user; on the contrary, consumption often becomes an organizing activity – a job.[23]

The 'industrious bazaar' leaves us with a very different image of the consumer from that put forward by standard economics. The drug con-sumer is effectively a market agent who, using various strategies, creates new organizational forms and new transactions in response to regu-lation.

In the organization of drug traffic, the case of the final consumer is instructive: consumers, whose sovereignty in market economies is so often emphasized, are assigned the most wretched position in an illegal market, since the market serving them is a prohibited market. To what institutions can illegal consumers appeal in carrying out their trans-actions? They may seek solidarity with those in a similar position, by trying to ensure continuous information and some form of protection of their supplies, or they may try to integrate upstream, that is, they may try to control the production of the commodities destined to satisfy their needs; they may try to avoid being disciplined by those operating at the level immediately above their own.

But who protects the sovereignty of the consumer? The usual answer is competition, through market forces. But if the market forces are undermined, who will protect competition? Here the answer is, no one. The only solution is do-it-yourself:[24] work back through the division of labour, become a producer–consumer, exercise direct control over the satisfaction of needs, changing role and the division of labour.

5 Conclusion

In this chapter it has been shown that the activities and relationship that characterize both organized and unorganized crime can be explained to a considerable extent by the very fact that activities are illegal. For example, because courts cannot be used to enforce agreements, alternative enforcement institutions arise. And because smaller-scale operations are easier to conceal, criminal activity is forced to forgo opportunities for scale economies in the attempt to control transaction costs. Consumers may eventually integrate backwards in production and distribution, becoming dealers. Thus, it is possible to deduce the nature of the institutional arrangements that will facilitate the transactions the agents want to carry out.

The proscription of behaviour imposed on individuals, for example the prohibition of drugs or alcohol, changes the forms and boundaries of privately accepted institutional arrangements and the ways of making them operative, that is, it changes the forms in which transactions are organized in order to complete them. This is perhaps another way of saying that transactions are entrusted to governance structures able to complete them in accordance with the associated costs (Williamson, 1985), but it is also a way of saying that the ideal market does not exist; actual markets are the product of rules and norms defined at a social level. Schelling rightly pointed out that illegal markets are created by politics, but he failed to understand that what holds for illegal situations is not a *ceteris paribus* transposition of what holds for legal situations. New institutional economics (North, 1990; Williamson, 1985) offers a much more useful approach to interpret a shift in institutional environment, yet caution is required in the exercise of comparative static.

The nexus between the institutional environment and the institutional arrangement is highly complex: studies of the illegal market organization and agents' behaviour within it reveal that not only are the transaction governance forms modified from those in standard markets, but the set of transactions is reshaped as a response to changes in the division of labour and in the roles of the various agents.

As we have seen, prohibition affects a consumer commodity (or service) and transforms all the activities associated with it into illegality. Anyone involved in prohibited transactions is subject to various sanctions. And all those involved reorganize their operations to carry out their transactions. The agents – entrepreneurs, employees, suppliers, creditors, regulators and consumers – change their way of interacting, that is, of organizing themselves with the purpose of making the transactions they are interested in continue to flow.

Transactions do not take place in a vacuum; they take place in an institutional environment and require various kinds of institutional arrangement to govern them. Prohibition cancels the possibility of referring to a higher, more formal level of institutional orders and sanctions (no court will defend property rights and enforce a contract); it does not cancel transactions. Transactions will take place, but they are now pushed back to another, more primitive institutional environment. A prohibited market is a black market: but the black market is not simply an illegal market, it is a market with a lower degree of institutionalization protecting agents and their transactions.

Notes

*   This work draws on a number of themes first developed with A. Becchi (Becchi and Turvani, 1993), whom I should like to thank here. The paper was first presented at the Colloque sur l'Economie des Coûts de Transaction, at the Sorbonne, 26 May 1994. The discussion was then very fruitful and I thank my discussant, F. Jenny, for his comments. I thank W. Baumol for carefully reading and commenting on the paper and R. Richter for his criticisms. I also benefited from discussion when the paper was presented at the Comparative Institutional Analysis Seminar at Stanford in November 1994, and in Williamson's workshop in Berkeley, in September 1994. Of course, responsibility of the final result is mine.

1.   For recent studies in Italy, see Becchi and Rey (1994); for the US, see Greenfield (1993).

2.   In this way we follow Schelling's (1980, p. 377 reprint of the 1967 edition) suggestion that: 'there are good policy reasons for encouraging a *strategic* analysis of the criminal underworld. Such an analysis, in contrast with *tactical* intelligence aimed at the apprehension of individual criminals, could help in identifying the incentives and disincentives to organize crime, in evaluating the costs and losses due to criminal enterprises, and in restructuring law and programs to minimize the costs, wastes, and injustices that crime entails'. Our analysis, however, makes use of the microeconomic tools offered by new institutional economics. The agents' organizational responses, in particular, should be included with other strategic behaviour.

3.   Debating drug policy is beyond the scope of this work. As will become clear in the rest of the chapter, however, prohibition cannot be the proper tool to deal with drug problems. Economists generally agree that drug legalization would reduce the price and increase the demand for drugs. Drug users would benefit, while illegal suppliers would suffer elimination of rents. At the social level the effect would be a reduction in social control costs, even though it is not clear what could be the effect

on social health. Cigarette smoking, however, has been substantially reduced by means of very soft prohibitions, education being the most effective tool. See Niskanen (1992), Kopp (1994), Trebach and Inciardi (1993).

4. Western societies have prohibited the use of narcotics for some time, although in the past psychoactive substances were valued for their properties and were socially accepted. In the United States the earliest legislative measure was the banning of San Francisco opium fumoirs in 1875. The first international commission met at The Hague in 1912. But it was only in the 1930s when the prohibition of alcohol was lifted that the drug market really began to be controlled. Prohibition has continually been extended and strengthened, culminating in the measures introduced by the most recent Republican administrations. European legislation is not uniform. In 1991, 55 countries signed a convention in favour of prohibition, including many with production areas. For a historical and economic analysis of alcohol and narcotic prohibition, see Becchi and Turvani (1993).

5. 'A good many economic and business principles that operate in the "upperworld" must, with suitable modification for change in environment, operate in the underworld as well' (Schelling, 1980, p. 377). Like Schelling we will try to apply to illegality the same conceptual categories of institutional economics used to analyse legal organization forms.

6. Bentham's concept of the sanction is more like a regulatory principle than a penalty: there are various levels or systems of sanctions: physical, political, moral and religious. The existence of various systems of sanctions may create problems of consistency. Bentham also considered physical sanctions to be very important, that is, the non-intentional automatic consequences of certain types of conduct: for example, disorder and the risks to survival in a state of nature dominated by violent behaviour.

7. Values play an important part in determining an individual's calculus. *Moral suasion* does not apply to the minority which does not share the values of the majority. If the rules imposed are not shared, the power of the sanction will not suffice. The rationality of the institutional order will not be accepted and rules will not necessarily result in an efficient order. As Schelling (1980, p. 386) points out: 'in the black markets it is especially hard to identify just what the evils are. In the first place, a law abiding citizen is not obliged to consider the procurement and consumption of illegal commodities inherently sinful. We have constitutional procedures for legislating prohibitions; the out-voted minority is bound to abide by the law but not necessarily to agree with it'. On this subject, see North's work and the importance he attaches to ideology and consensus.

8. Biological positivism, which flourished after Darwin, provided the basis for scientific criminology. Cesare Lombroso challenged the notion of a rational choice-making human being; by making humankind subject to the laws of evolution, physical and psychic characteristics of agents will determine their behaviour (including criminal behaviour).

9. North (1981, pp. 46–7) points out that: 'while we observe people disobeying the rules of society when the benefits exceed the cost, we also observe them obeying the rules when an individualistic calculus would have them do otherwise. . . . Their myopic vision has prevented neo-classical economists from seeing that even with a constant set of rules, detection procedures, and penalties there is an immense variation in the degree to which individual behaviour is constrained'. North claims that an ideology, that is the values surrounding an individual, plays an important role in calculating benefits and costs associated with a given action. Ideology, that is a set of values, may be the outcome of a process combining multiple systems of sanctions, corresponding to several orders in which individual behaviour is embedded. For a study of the interplay between formal and informal norms and orders see Ellickson (1994).

10. It is difficult to use the contractual paradigm for analysing forms of transactions

governance if the voluntary participation in the exchange is de facto invalidated. In this case we may speak of a return to status relationships.

11. Violence is always behind the corner and it is the *credible threat*. 'Fear of feud is the only deterrent to feud'; its existence 'serves to inhibit the unrestricted use of violence by individuals to their owner. Compensation does not hinder the development of feud, but, on the contrary, is a source of impetus propelling it from one killing to another' (Black-Minchaud, 1975, p. 118).

12. The essence of this type of economic reasoning is that virtuous behaviour is not virtuous but, rather, is advantageous, just as prohibited behaviour may be advantageous. Accordingly, a person will commit a crime when the expected utility is greater than what might have been obtained using his or her resources in other activities. For a well-informed individual the decision to commit a crime will depend on the chances of being caught, the severity of the sanctions, the earnings and all the other factors which the individual will rationally include in his or her cost–benefit analysis. Analogous results may be obtained by making crime comparable to work (Ehrlich, 1973). The decision to undertake a criminal activity can be reduced to a problem of allocating time among various activities on the basis of remuneration. It depends on rewards expected for alternative activities, the aptitude for taking risks and the probability of being captured and punished. Rational criminal behaviour implies that law enforcement is always possible if costs are not too great.

13. Organized crime is an industry effectively coordinating two elements: the criminal activity and the defence activity. The criminal group is a lasting structure of identified members who use criminal means, including violence, to obtain and maintain profits and power. Six features characterize the organization: continuity, structure, limited membership, criminal activities, violence and power as an end. The defence strategy implies the ability to corrupt politicians, public employees, private firms, and the police in particular, and so on. Clearly these features of an organized crime group are not enough – apart from a few exceptions – to distinguish it from a normal firm.

14. 'The decisive question is whether the goal of somewhat reducing the consumption of narcotics, gambling, prostitution or anything else that is forced by law into the black market, is or is not outweighed by the costs to society of creating a criminal industry' (Shelling, 1980, p. 393).

15. This study focused on effective enforcement strategies for the prohibition of heroin in the United States and was based on a detailed study of narco-traffic. See also Moore (1990), Reuter (1983) and Reuter et al. (1991).

16. The first strategy – concealing connections with the industry – entails avoidance of visible connections with production, distribution and consumption. It also means avoiding association with people known to be active in the sector and preventing others from coming across information about connections with the illegal transactions. The second strategy concerns the need to conceal traces, or cover up the evidence. These strategies basically tend to push up the cost of enforcement and the application of prohibition by mixing legal and illegal activities, hiding the goods and above all by developing greater geographical and organizational mobility in order to make information redundant. The third strategy is an offensive strategy, that is, corruption.

17. For more information see Lewis et al. (1992) for the British market. For Italy, see Becchi and Turvani (1994); for France, see Schiray (1994).

18. There would not appear to be any great constraints of a financial nature because although the construction of an illegal network requires availability of capital, the international market swarms with financial institutions in the grey area between the upper- and underworld.

19. According to the Anti-Mafia Parliamentary Commission report on the *camorra* (*L'Unità*, Supplement 7 February 1994, pp. 20–28), 'the *camorra* is composed of a set of bands which come together and break up very easily, at times peacefully, and at times with bloodshed. This highly elusive composite structure made up of tiny units has only been replaced by a hierarchical organization twice in the last few

decades. . . . At present a total of 111 families and 6,700 affiliates appear to operate in the Campania region'. Historically the *camorra* has an urban structure and grew up within commerce and institutional transformations. 'Its mercenary characteristics, along with the lack of a lasting hierarchical structure, make the *camorra* organizations flexible, able to adapt since they have no pre-established rules. . . . The *camorra* has always been enterprising and has sought to fit into economic processes and take advantage of them. . . . Unlike the Sicilian Mafia, the *camorra* does not establish an alternative order to that of the state, but seeks to govern social disorder'.

20. Georgescu-Roegen asks why a science interested in means, ends and economic distribution patterns should dogmatically refuse to study the process whereby new means, ends and economic relations are created (1971, p. 318).

21. In analysing the behaviour of consumers of psychoactive substances, Becker and Murphy (1988) discuss the rationality of the addict. For a critical study of their model, see Becchi and Turvani (1993).

22. I do not justify those involved in illicit traffic, but I propose an interpretation of its terminal segment, where consumption and distribution are interwoven and where consumption is associated with minor delinquent activities. See also Reuter et al. (1991). This should not lead to an underestimation of the connection between illicit consumption and criminal activities or their harmfulness to society. Dealing may be considered as the opportunity for unscrupulous consumers to increase their own earnings; it could be so because there is a diffuse market power in the distribution structure of prohibited substances and large profit margins even in the terminal phase. Because of their close relationship with customers, dealers could discriminate according to the individual consumer's willingness to pay. The ranks of consumer–distributors would increase, gradually extending the market, and dealers would exploit consumers.

23. 'Today's consumers of heavy drugs are a far cry from the vaguely Bohemian picture conjured up by certain literary works. . . . The everyday reality is made up of hyperactivity, hustling, and an assiduous presence on the market and continuous relations of a productive and commercial nature' (Ruggiero, 1992, p. 97).

24. For some rather picturesque accounts of the functioning of drug markets, see Dorn, Murji and South (1992).

References

Anderson, A. (1994), 'Organized Crime, Mafia, and Governments', mimeo, Stanford University: Hoover Institution.

Arlacchi, P. and R. Lewis (1990), *Imprenditorialità illecita e droga. Il mercato dell'eroina a Verona*, Bologna: Il Mulino.

Beccaria, C. (1764), *Dei delitti e delle pene* (1987 printing), Milano: Garzanti.

Becchi, A. and G. Rey (1994), *L'economia criminale*, Bari: Laterza.

Becchi, A. and M. Turvani (1993), *Proibito? Il mercato mondiale della droga*, Roma: Donzelli Editore.

Becchi, A. and M. Turvani (1994), 'Domanda ed offerta nel mercato internazionale dei narcotici: effetti della proibizione', in S. Zamagni (ed.), *Mercati illegali e Mafie*, Bologna: Il Mulino, pp. 297–346.

Becker, G.S. (1968), 'Crime and Punishment: An Economic Approach', *Journal of Political Economy*, **76** (April), 169–217.

Becker, G.S. and K. Murphy (1988), 'A Theory of Rational Addiction', *Journal of Political Economy*, **96** (April), 675–700.

Black-Minchaud, J. (1975), *Cohesive Force – Feud in the Mediterranean and the Middle East*, Oxford: Basil Blackwell.

Buchanan, J. (1980), 'A Defense of Organized Crime?', in R. Andreano and J.J. Siegfried (eds), *The Economics of Crime*, New York: Wiley & Sons, pp. 395–403.

Catanzaro, R. (1989), *Il delitto come impresa: storia sociale della mafia*, Padova: Liviana Editore.

Choiseul Praslin de, C.H. (1991), *La drogue. Une économie dynamisée par la repression*, Paris: Presses du CNRS.
Dorn, N., K. Murji and N. South (1992), *Traffickers: Drug Markets and Law Enforcement*, London: Routledge.
Ehrlich, J. (1973), 'Participation in Illegitimate Activities: A Theoretical and Empirical Investigation', *Journal of Political Economy*, **81** (3), 521–67.
Ellickson, R. (1994), *Order Without Law*, Cambridge, MA: Harvard University Press.
Falcone, G. and M. Padovani (1992), *Cose di cosa nostra*, Milano: Rizzoli.
Gambetta, D. (1992), *La mafia siciliana. Un'industria della protezione privata*, Torino: Einaudi.
Georgescu-Roegen, N. (1971), *The Entropy Law and the Economic Process*, Cambridge, MA: Harvard University Press.
Greenfield, H. (1993), *Invisible, Outlawed, and Untaxed*, London: Praeger.
Heineke, J. (1978), 'Economic Models of Criminal Behavior: An Overview', in J. Heineke (ed.), *Economic Models of Criminal Behavior*, Amsterdam: North-Holland, pp. 1–32.
Kopp, P. (1992), 'La structuration de l'offre de drogues en réseaux', *Revue Tiers Monde*, juillet–septembre, 517–36.
Kopp, P. (1994), 'Consommation de drogue et efficacité des politiques publiques', *Revue Economique*, **45** (6), 1333–55.
Lewis, R. (1992), 'Flexible Hierarchies and Dynamic Disorder: The Trading and Distribution of Illicit Heroin in Britain and Europe, 1970–1990', in R. Lewis et al. (eds), *Strange Gossip. Drugs Problems*, Oxford: Oxford University Press, pp. 99–115.
Ministero degli interni (1990–1992), *Attività antidroga delle forze di polizia nel 1989–1991*, Roma.
Moore, M.H. (1977), *Buy and Bust. The Effective Regulation of an Illicit Market in Heroin*, Lexington: Lexington Books.
Moore, M.H. (1990), *An Analytical View of Drug Control Policies*, Cambridge: Kennedy School of Government.
Niskanen, W. (1992), 'Economists and drug policy', *Carnegie-Rochester Conference Series on Public Policy*, **36**, 223–48.
North, D. (1981), *Structure and Change in Economic History*, New York: Norton & Co.
North, D. (1990), *Institutions, Institutional Change and Economic Performance*, Cambridge: Cambridge University Press.
President's Commission on Organized Crime (1986a), *Report to the President and the Attorney General, The Impact: Organized Crime Today*, Washington DC: US Government Printing Office.
President's Commission on Organized Crime (1986b), *Report to the President and the Attorney General, America's Habit: Drug Abuse, Drug Trafficking, and Organized Crime*, Washington DC: US Government Printing Office.
Reuter, P. (1983), *Disorganized Crime: The Economics of the Visible Hand*, Cambridge, MA: MIT Press.
Reuter, P. et al. (1991), *Money from Crime: A Study of the Economics of Drug Dealing in Washington DC*, Santa Monica: Rand Corporation.
Ruggiero, V. (1992), *La roba. Economie e culture dell'eroina*, Parma: Pratiche Editrice.
Santino, U. and G. La Fiura (1990), *L'Impresa Mafiosa*, Milano: Franco Angeli.
Schelling, T.C. (1980), 'Economics and Criminal Enterprise', in R. Andreano and J.J. Siegfried (eds), *The Economics of Crime*, New York: Wiley & Sons, pp. 377–94 (first edition 1967).
Schelling, T.C. (1984), 'What is the Business of Organized Crime?', in *Choice and Consequence*, Cambridge, MA: Harvard University Press, pp. 179–94.
Schiray, M. (1994), 'Les filières-stupéfiants: trois niveaux, cinq logiques. Les stratégies de survie et le monde des criminalités', *Futuribles*, **185**, 23–43.
Stigler, G.J. (1970), 'The Optimal Enforcement of Laws', *Journal of Political Economy*, **78** (3), 526–36.
Thornton, M. (1991), *The Economics of Prohibition*, Salt Lake City: University of Utah Press.

Trebach, A. and J. Inciardi (1993), *Legalize it?*, Washington: American University Press.
Williamson, O.E. (1985), *The Economic Institutions of Capitalism*, New York: Macmillan.
Williamson, O.E. (1993), 'Calculativeness, Trust, and Economic Organisation', *Journal of Law and Economics*, **XXXVI** (April), 221–70.

6 Transaction costs through time*
Douglass C. North

1 Introduction

An economic definition of transaction costs is the costs of measuring what is being exchanged and enforcing agreements. In the larger context of societal evolution they are all the costs involved in human interaction over time. It is this larger context that I wish to explore in this chapter. The concept is a close kin to the notion of social capital advanced by James Coleman (1990) and applied imaginatively to studying the differential patterns of Italian regional development by Robert Putnam in *Making Democracy Work* (1993). This chapter, therefore, is a study in economic history which focuses on the costs of human coordination and cooperation through time which I regard as the key dilemma of societies past, present and future.

The evolution of societies is a function of the quantity and quality of human beings, the human command over nature, and the structure humans impose on their interaction. An understanding of the inter-action between demographic, technological and institutional factors would provide fundamental insights into societal evolution. This chapter is a very preliminary step in exploring the transaction costs involved in the interaction of two of these three basic determinants of societal evolution, institutions and technology.

Three landmarks in the historical reduction of transaction costs were the institutions that made possible impersonal exchange, the assumption by the state of the protection and enforcement of property rights and realization of the gains from the modern revolution in science. In what follows I shall begin by posing the dilemma of human coordination and cooperation in terms of standard transaction cost analysis (Section 2), explore the way the dimension of time affects the costs of transacting (Section 3) and examine some of the major changes in economic insti-tutions that laid the foundations of impersonal exchange (Section 4). Section 5 explores the conditions that underlay the assumption by the state of the protection and enforcement of property rights. I then analyse the complex interplay between technological and institutional change in the past century and a half that arose from the revolutionary changes in scientific knowledge (Section 6).

2   Transaction costs and social coordination

Ronald Coase forced economists to think about the costs involved in human interaction. He was concerned to explain the reason for the existence of firms (1937) or the conditions under which the allocative implications of microeconomic theory held (1960). But the study of transaction costs in addition to giving us insights into static economic analysis also holds the key to unlocking the doors to an improved understanding of economic and societal performance through time.

In the ten millennia since the first economic revolution, humans have haltingly evolved institutions to structure human interaction which have permitted and encouraged increasing productivity and economic growth. Broadly speaking, the economic institutions have been those that have permitted the growth of markets or improvements in, or the introduction of, new technology. The political institutions have been those that improved the security of property rights and the enforcement of contracts. In fact the two institutional sources have been inextricably intertwined. The historical decline in transaction costs has reflected both voluntaristic and coercive solutions to problems of exchange. Since I have outlined this evolution elsewhere I shall not repeat it here.[1] What I wish to explore here is innovations that permitted such significant reductions of transaction costs that they made possible production and exchange that had not existed before. I wish to do this in order to explore the specific conditions in time that led to these breakthroughs. But first I must look at the way learning through time determined these changes.

3   Social learning

In economic analysis change is primarily a consequence of changes in relative prices. And indeed that has been a powerful tool to explore historical change.[2] Here I seek to understand the underlying sources of changes in relative prices. Many of them arise from exogenous shocks or the gradual accumulation or diminution of one supply factor more rapidly than another. It has been technological change, however, that has been the primary explanatory variable of economists and economic historians. But clearly that explanation is incomplete. We are not only left with the question of what has determined the varying rate of technological change through history but also with the question of what has determined the differing ability of economies to take advantage of the technology that exists. Surely if technology was the whole answer all the world should be rich since most of the technology is openly available. The inability of economies to make use of the existing technology efficiently suggests that it is the (dis)incentives embodied in economic and political organization that is at issue. That in turn leads us to the belief systems that humans hold which shape the institutions that they create.

Neoclassical theory assumes that people know what is in their self-interest and act accordingly. This rationality tenet of faith is simply incorrect as a guide to the perceptions of humans throughout history which have shaped the institutions that they have created to structure human interaction. Instead, the learning process that has shaped the belief systems of humans throughout history has produced widely diverse perceptions about how the world is and should be ordered.[3] Most have led to poor economic performance or stagnation; a few have led to economic growth.

Human learning is a product of the accumulated experience of past generations carried over intergenerationally as culture and the 'local' experiences of the members of a society.[4] As societies evolved from tribal beginnings they developed different languages and, with different experiences, different mental models to explain the world around them. With growing specialization and division of labour they evolved polities and economies but the diversity of experiences and learning produced increasingly different societies with different degrees of success in solving the fundamental problems of scarcity. The reason is that as the complexity of the environment increased with increasing interdependence, institutions were required to permit anonymous, impersonal exchange and to structure polities to provide protection and enforcement of property rights, but the likelihood of creating the necessary institutions to capture the gains from trade of more complex contracting varied. In fact most societies throughout history got stuck in an institutional matrix that did not solve the institutional requirements involved in the three major transaction cost-reducing innovations described at the beginning of this chapter.

4   Institutional change and economic exchange

Between the eleventh and fourteenth centuries in Europe a commercial revolution led to the revival of trade and an era of substantial economic growth. The key to this expansion was the development of a set of institutions that permitted anonymous exchange to take place across space and time. Intercommunity credit markets, insurance markets, contracts for future delivery, and the bill of exchange were all institutional features of this commercial revolution.

The evolution of the Law Merchant was characteristic of the institutions that undergirded this expansion. Merchants gradually evolved codes of conduct in different parts of Western Europe to define exchange relationships among themselves. In the absence of a coercive enforcement mechanism by states, reputation and ostracism served as the basis of enforcement. But as the size of the markets grew a reputation mechanism, alone, was an insufficient guarantee of performance and a legal code administered by private judges drawn from commercial ranks enhanced the effectiveness of the reputation mechanism by providing incentives for information dissemination, imposition of sanctions on violators, and payment of judgements levied against an individual merchant.[5] A critical feature of the Law Merchant is that it evolved into and was integrated with formal legal codes downstream, thus providing a path-dependent evolution from informal codes of conduct to formal coercive enforcement by the state.

This last point deserves special emphasis. Developing institutions to structure impersonal exchange occurred in many economies during the era of the commercial revolution. But many such innovations did not, in contradistinction to the Law Merchant, lead downstream to further institutional development. Some ended with no further development. Avner Greif in a forthcoming study compares Genoese traders with traders who had adopted the cultural and social attributes of Islamic society in the Mediterranean trade of the eleventh and twelfth centuries. He detects systematic differences in their organizational structure traceable to contrasting individualistic versus collectivist behavioural beliefs. Traders from the Islamic world developed ingroup social communications networks to enforce collective action which, while effective in relatively small, homogeneous ethnic groups, do not lend themselves to the impersonal exchange that arises from the growing size of markets and diverse ethnic traders. In contrast, the Genoese developed bilateral enforcement mechanisms which entailed the creation of formal legal and political organizations for monitoring and enforcing agreements – an institutional/organizational path that permitted and led to more complex trade and exchange. Greif suggests the generality of these different belief structures for the Latin and Muslim worlds and then makes the connection between such belief systems and the subsequent institutional development of the Western world that led to modern economic growth.[6]

5   The role of the State
It was in Western Europe in general and the Netherlands and England specifically where polities emerged that took over the protection and enforcement of property rights. It was the lack of large-scale political and economic order that created the essential environment conducive to political/economic development. In that competitive decentralized

environment many alternatives were pursued as each society confronted its own unique external environment. Some worked, as in the case of the Netherlands and England; some failed, as in the case of Spain and Portugal. But the key to the story is the variety of options pursued and the likelihood that some would turn out to produce political/economic development. Even the relative failures in Western Europe played an essential role in European development and were more successful than other parts of the world because of competitive pressures.

The last point deserves special emphasis. It was the dynamic consequences of the competition among fragmented political bodies that resulted in an especially creative environment. Europe was politically fragmented; but it was integrated in having both a common belief structure derived from Christendom, and information and transportation connections that resulted in scientific, technological, and artistic developments in one part spreading rapidly throughout Europe. To treat the Netherlands and England as success stories in isolation from the stimulus received from the rest of Europe (and to a lesser degree Islam and China) is to miss a vital part of the explanation. Italian city states, Portugal, and Germanic states all fell behind the Netherlands and England; but banking, artistic development, improvements in navigation, and printing were just a few of the obvious contributions that the former states made to European advancement.

The Netherlands and England pursued different paths to political/ economic success, but in each case the external environment was conducive to the evolution of a belief structure that induced political and economic institutions that lowered transaction costs. In both polities, competition among the evolving nation states was a deep underlying source of change and equally a constraint on the options available to rulers within states. It was competition that forced the crown to trade rights and privileges for revenue, including most fundamentally the granting to representative bodies – variously parliament, the States General, the Cortes – control over tax rates and/or certain privileges in return for revenue. But it was the evolving bargaining strength of rulers *vis-à-vis* constituents that was the decisive feature of their subsequent development. Three considerations were at stake:

1. the size of the potential gains the constituents could realize by the state taking over protection of property;
2. the closeness of substitutes for the existing ruler – that is, the ability of rivals (both within and outside the political unit) to the existing ruler to take over and provide the same, or more, services;

3. the structure of the economy which determined the benefits and costs to the ruler of various sources of revenue.

Let me briefly describe the background conditions of the two polities – the Netherlands and England – that led up to the contrasting external environments that shaped the belief systems.

To understand the success of the Netherlands one must cast a backward glance at the evolution of the prosperous towns of the Low Countries, such as Bruges, Ghent and Liège; their internal conflicts; and their relationship to Burgundian and Habsburg rule. The prosperity of the towns, whether based on the wool cloth trade or metals trade, early on made for an urban-centred, market-oriented area unique at a time of overwhelmingly rural societies. Their internal conflicts reflected ongoing tensions between patrician and crafts and persistent conflicts over ongoing efforts to create local monopolies which, when successful, led to a drying up of the very sources of productivity which had been the mainspring of their growth. Burgundian (and later Habsburg) rule discouraged restrictive practices, such as those that developed in the cloth towns of Bruges and Ghent, and encouraged the growth of new centres of industry that sprang up in response to the favourable incentives embodied in the rules and property rights. In 1463, Philip the Good created a representative body, the States General, which enacted laws and had the authority to vote taxes for the ruler. The Burgundians and Habsburgs were rewarded by a level of prosperity which generated tax revenues that made the low countries the jewel in the Habsburg Empire.

England evolved along a route different from that of continental polities. Being an island made it less vulnerable to conquest and eliminated the need for a standing army and undoubtedly contributed to the different initial belief structure that Macfarlane (1978) describes. The Norman conquest, the exception to British invulnerability to external conquest, produced a more centralized feudal structure than on the continent. The political institutions, in consequence, differed in several important respects from those of the continent. There was a single parliament for the entire country; no regional estates as in France, Spain and the Netherlands. There was also no division into towns, clergy and nobility. But the more centralized feudal structure did not gainsay that the crown could not overstep the traditional liberties of the barons, as the Magna Carta attests.

We can now turn to examining the evolving bargaining strength (and the three underlying determinants) of ruler versus constituent, which shaped the belief structure and the path of each polity. Take the Netherlands. The productive town economies stood to gain substantially by the political order and protection of property rights provided by the Burgundians and then by Charles V. The structure of the economy built around export trades provided the means for easy-to-collect taxes on trade, but not at a level to adversely affect the comparative advantage of those export trades. The liberty to come and go, buy and sell as they saw fit, led to the evolution of efficient economic markets. But when Philip II altered the 'contractual agreement', the Seven Provinces became convinced that they could only prosper with independence. The resistance was initiated by the States General, which in 1581 issued the Act of Abjuration of allegiance to Philip II and claimed sovereignty for the Provinces themselves. The powers of the newly independent country resided with each province (which voted as a unit) and a unanimity rule meant that the States General could only act with the unanimous approval of the Seven Provinces. Cumbersome as that process was, this political structure survived. The polity not only evolved the elements of political representation and democratic decision rules but equally supported religious toleration. The belief structure that had evolved to shape the independent polity was more pragmatic than 'intellectual', a consequence of the incremental evolution of the bargaining strength of constituents and rulers.

As with the Netherlands it was England's external trade that provided an increasing share of crown revenue with taxes on wine, general merchandise and wool cloth; but it was the wool export trade that was the backbone of augmented crown revenue. Eileen Power's classic story of the wool trade (1941) describes the exchange between the three groups involved in that trade: the wool growers as represented in parliament, the merchants of the staple, and the crown. The merchants achieved a monopoly of the export trade and a depot in Calais, parliament received the right to set the tax, and the crown received the revenue. Stubbs (1896, 3, p. 599) summarized the exchange as follows: 'The admission of the right of parliament to legislate, to enquire into abuses, and to share in the guidance of national policy, was practically purchased by the money granted to Edward I and Edward III'.

With the Tudors, the English crown was at the zenith of its power but it never achieved the unilateral control over taxing power that the crowns of France and Spain achieved. The confiscation of monastery lands and possessions by Henry VIII alienated many peers and much of the clergy and as a consequence 'Henry had need of the House of Commons and he cultivated it with sedulous care' (Elton, 1953, p. 4). The Stuarts inherited what the Tudors had sown and the evolving controversy between the crown and parliament is a well-known tale.

Two aspects of this controversy are noteworthy for this analysis. One was the evolving perception of the common law as the supreme law of the land – a position notably championed by Sir Edward Coke – and the other was the connection made between monopoly and a denial of liberty as embodied in the crown grants of monopoly privileges.

6. Technological and institutional change

A fundamental revolution occurred in the second half of the nineteenth century, which I have termed the second economic revolution.[7] This revolution was a consequence of a change in the stock of knowledge arising from the development and implementation of scientific disciplines. It resulted in the systematic marriage of science and technology and a basic transformation in the organization and structure of production and distribution (see Chandler, 1977). The overall implications for economies that could take advantage of this technology were increasing returns and consequent high rates of economic growth – characteristics of the Western economies for the past century and a half. But taking advantage of this technology entailed a wholesale reorganization of economies to realize that potential. In those Western economies that have, at least partially, realized this potential the result has been stresses and strains that have threatened and do threaten their continued adaptive efficiency. For the rest of the world the inability to reorganize has prevented them from realizing this productive potential and produced 'underdevelopment' and political instability. It is an extraordinary irony that Karl Marx, who first pointed out the necessity of restructuring societies in order to realize the potential of a new technology, should have been responsible for the creation of economies that have foundered on this precise issue. Let me first examine the micro-level characteristics of the organizational requirements before turning to the macro-level societal implications.

Realizing the gains from a world of specialization requires occupational and territorial specialization on an unprecedented scale, and in consequence the number of exchanges grows exponentially. In order to realize the gains from the productive potential associated with a technology of increasing returns one has to invest enormous resources in transacting. In the United States, for example, the labour force grew from 29 million to 80 million between 1900 and 1970; during that period production workers grew from 10 million to 29 million, while white-collar workers (the great majority of whom are engaged in transacting) increased from 5 million to 38 million. The transaction sector (that part of transaction costs that goes through the market and therefore can be measured) in the United States in 1970 made up 45 per cent of GNP (Wallis and North, 1986).

Let me briefly elaborate some of the measurement and enforcement problems that account for the size of the transaction sector. Necessary to be able to realize the gains of a world of specialization, are control over quality in the lengthening production chain and a solution to the problems of increasingly costly principal–agent relationships. Much technology, indeed, is designed to reduce transaction costs by substituting capital for labour or by reducing the degrees of freedom of the worker in the production process and by automatically measuring the quality of intermediate goods. An underlying problem is that of measuring inputs and outputs so that one can ascertain the contribution of individual factors and the output at successive stages of production. For inputs there is no agreed-upon measure of the contribution of an individual input. Equally there is room for conflict over the consequent payment to factors of production. For output, not only is there residual unpriced output, that is, waste and pollutants, but also there are complicated costs of specifying the desired properties of the goods and services produced at each stage in the production process.

Another characteristic of this new technology is that firms have large fixed capital investments with a long life and (frequently) low alternative scrap value. As a result the exchange process embodied in contracts has to be extended over long periods of time, which entails uncertainty about prices and costs and the possibility of opportunistic behaviour on the part of one of the parties to the exchange. A number of organizational problems emerge from these characteristics associated with this technology.

First, increased resources are necessary to measure the quality of output. Sorting, grading, labelling, trade marks, warranties and licensing are all, albeit costly and imperfect, devices to measure the characteristics of goods and services. Despite the existence of such devices, the dissipation of income is evident all around us in the difficulty of measuring the quality of automobile repairs, in evaluating the safety characteristics of products and the quality of medical services, or in measuring educational output.

Second, while team production permits economies of scale to be realized, it does so at the cost of worker alienation and shirking. The 'discipline' of the factory is no more than a response to the control problem of shirking in team production. From the perspective of the employer the discipline consists of rules, regulations, incentives and punishments essential to effective performance. Innovations such as time-and-motion studies are methods of measuring individual performance. From the viewpoint of the worker they are inhuman devices to foster speedups and exploitation. Since there is no agreed-upon measure of output that constitutes contract performance, both are right.

Third, the potential gains from opportunistic behaviour increase and lead to strategic behaviour both within the firm (labour–employer relations, for example) and in contractual behaviour between firms. Everywhere in factor and product markets the gains from withholding services or altering the terms of agreement at strategic points offer large potential gains.

Fourth, the development of large-scale hierarchies produces the familiar problems of bureaucracy. The multiplication of rules and regulations inside large organizations to control shirking and principal–agent problems results in rigidities, income dissipation and the loss of flexibility essential to adaptive efficiency.

Finally there are external effects: the unpriced costs reflected in the modern environmental crisis. The interdependence of a world of specialization and division of labour increases exponentially the imposition of costs on third parties.

The institutional and organizational restructuring necessary to take advantage of this technology is, however, much more fundamental than restructuring economic organization – although that task, the creation of efficient markets, is complicated enough. The entire structure of society must be transformed. This technology and accompanying scale economies entails specialization, minute division of labour, impersonal exchange and urban societies. Uprooted are all the old informal constraints built around the family, personal relationships and repetitive individual exchanges. Indeed, the basic traditional functions of the family – education, employment (the family enterprise) and insurance – are either eliminated or severely circumscribed. New formal rules and organizations and an increased role of government replace them.

The contention of Marxists was that these problems were a consequence of capitalism and that the inherent contradictions between the new technology and the consequent organization of capitalism would lead to its demise. The Marxists were wrong that the problems were a consequence of capitalism: they are ubiquitous to any society that attempts to adopt the technology of the second economic revolution. However, as the foregoing paragraphs have attempted to make clear, Marxists were right in viewing the tension arising between the new technology and organization as a fundamental dilemma. These tensions have only partially been resolved in the market economies of the Western world. The growth of government, the disintegration of the family, and the incentive incompatibility of many modern political and economic hierarchical organizations are all symptoms of the consequent problems besetting Western economies.

However, it has been the relative flexibility of the institutions of the Western world – both economic and political – that has been the mitigating factor in dealing with these problems. Adaptive efficiency, while far from perfect in the Western world, accounts for the degree of success that such institutions have experienced. The basic institutional framework has encouraged the development of political and economic organizations that have replaced (however imperfectly) the traditional functions of the family; mitigated the insecurity associated with a world of specialization; evolved flexible economic organization that has induced low-cost transacting; resolved some of the incentive incompatibilities of hierarchies and encouraged creative entrepreneurial talent; and tackled (again very imperfectly) the external effects that are not only environmental but also social in an urban world.

Notes

* Section 5 of this chapter is drawn from Douglass C. North (1995) and an earlier version of Section 6 was part of an essay entitled 'Institutions, Transaction Costs and Productivity in the Long Run' (North, 1993) prepared for the Eighth World Productivity Congress.
1. See North (1991).
2. See North and Thomas (1973) and North (1981).
3. For a discussion of cognitive science and the foundations of human learning see Denzau and North (1994) and North (1994).
4. See Denzau and North (1994) for an elaboration of this argument.
5. For an analysis of the institution and a game-theoretic model of the way it worked see Milgrom, North and Weingast (1990).
6. Avner Greif, (1994).
7. The first economic revolution was the development of agriculture in the eighth millennium BC in the Fertile Crescent.

References

Chandler, Alfred D. Jr (1977) *The Visible Hand: The Managerial Revolution in American Business*, Cambridge, MA: Harvard University Press.

Coase, Ronald (1937) 'The Nature of the Firm', *Economica*, **4**, 386–405.

Coase, Ronald (1960) 'The Problem of Social Cost', *Journal of Law and Economics*, **3**, 1–44.

Coleman, James (1990) *Foundations of Social Theory*, Cambridge, MA: Harvard University Press.

Denzau, Arthur T. and Douglass C. North (1994) 'Shared Mental Models: Ideologies and Institutions', *Kyklos*, **47**, 3–31.

Elton, G.R. (1953) *The Tudor Revolution in Government*, Cambridge: Cambridge University Press.

Greif, Avner (1994) 'Cultural Belief's and the Organization of Society: A Historical and Theoretical Reflection on Collectivist and Individualist Societies', *Journal of Political Economy*, **102** (5), 912–50.

Macfarlane, Alan (1978) *The Origins of English Individualism: The Family Property and Social Transition*, Oxford: Blackwell.

Milgrom, Paul, R.: Douglass C. North and Barry R. Weingast, Barry R. (1990) 'The Role of Institutions in the Revival of Trade: The Medieval Law Merchant, Private Judges, and the Champagne Fairs', *Economics and Politics*, **2**, 1–23.

North, Douglass C. (1981) *Structure and Change in Economic History*, New York: Norton.

North, Douglass C. (1991) 'Institutions', *Journal of Economic Perspectives*, **5** (Winter), 97–112.

North, Douglass C. (1993) 'Institutions, Transaction Costs and Productivity in the Long Run', Prepared for the Eighth World Productivity Congress in Stockholm, Sweden.

North, Douglass C. (1994) 'Economic Performance Through Time', *American Economic Review*, **84** (3), 359–68.

North, Douglass C. (1995) 'The Paradox of the West', in Richard Davis (ed.) *The Origins of Modern Freedom*, Stanford: Stanford University Press.

North, Douglass C. and Robert P. Thomas (1973) *The Rise of the Western World: A New Economic History*, Cambridge: Cambridge University Press.

Power, Eileen (1941) *The Wool Trade in English Medieval History*, London: The Clarendon Press.

Putnam, Robert (1993) *Making Democracy Work*, Princeton: Princeton University Press.

Stubbs, William (1896) *The Constitutional History of England*, **III**, Oxford: The Clarendon Press.

Wallis John J. and Douglass C. North (1986) 'Measuring the Transaction Sector in the American Economy', in S.L. Engerman and R.E. Gallman (eds) *Long Term Factors in American Economic Growth*, Chicago: University of Chicago Press.

Index

adaptation 30, 31, 47, 77, 80, 81, 103
  see also bilateral adaptation;
    maladaptation
adhocracy 34
adverse selection 65, 66
agency relationship 63, 65, 66, 73, 133,
  157, 158
agency theory 1, 31, 50
Akerlof, G. A. 5
Alchian, A. A. 3, 11, 21, 23, 31, 32,
  35, 41, 52,
Alford, R. 14
Allam, D. 39
antimonopoly *see* monopoly
Aoki, M. 11, 19, 31, 43, 45, 46, 47,
  48
Armour, H. O. 43, 44, 48
Arrow, K. J. 1, 3, 4, 6, 18, 23
Aspremont, C. D' 65, 83
asset specificity xiii, xv, 6, 10, 14, 15,
  19, 33, 36, 37, 38, 39, 40, 41, 42,
  44, 45, 46, 47, 48, 49, 50, 51, 61,
  62, 69, 70, 102, 113, 114, 129
  see also human specificity;
    investments; physical
    specificity; site specificity
authority 21–3, 35, 79, 96, 97, 101, 105,
  129, 131
autonomous groups 39, 40

Bain, J. 12
bargaining 41, 68, 114, 115, 154, 155
Barnard, C. I. 22, 31
Barnett, W. 3, 12
Baron, J. 14
barriers to entry 12
Beccaria, C. 127, 130
Becker, G. S. 127, 133
behavioural assumptions 7, 8, 36, 45,
  129
  see also bounded rationality;
    opportunism
behavioural theory 1
beliefs 151, 152, 153, 154, 155

Ben-Ner, A. 19
Berle, A. E. 45
Biggart, N. 7
bilateral adaptation 22, 152
bilateral bargaining 52
bilateral dependency 10, 37, 39, 99
bilateral monopoly 60, 64, 65, 69, 114
black market *see* illegal market
Board of Directors 18, 43, 49, 50–52
  see also executive committee
Bonin, J. 17
Bounded Rationality 7, 36, 45, 60, 61,
  69, 78, 79, 81, 129, 131, 132
Bouttes, J. P xiii, xiv, 35.
Bowen, D. E. 48
Bowles, S. 17
Boycko, M. 86, 106, 107, 108, 116
Brown, A. N. 93
Buchanan, J. 127, 135
bureaucracy 10, 86, 89, 90, 96, 97, 98,
  101, 103, 158

Cable, J. 43
Caldwell, M. 20
capital market 3, 13, 14, 16, 17–18,
  120
capitalism 88, 158
Carroll, G. 3, 12
central planning 86, 88, 89, 90, 93, 96,
  99, 100, 101, 103
centrally planned economy *see*
  central planning
Chandler, A. D. 43, 47, 156
Cheung, S. 31, 35
classical contract 10
coalition 40, 41, 52, 60
Coase, R. H. 3, 4, 5, 8, 11, 13, 22, 30,
  35, 45, 150
Coase theorem 3
Coleman, J. 5, 149
command 36
command economy 89–101
commitments 99
Commons, J. R. 13, 24

competition 3, 10, 23, 41, 42, 46, 64,
    71, 87, 88, 103, 104, 109, 110,
    111, 113, 118, 119, 122, 128, 131,
    135, 142, 153
complete contract *see* contract
contract xiv, 9, 10, 12, 15, 18, 19, 22,
    23, 31, 32, 34, 35, 37, 38, 40, 41,
    50, 51, 59, 60, 61, 63, 65, 66, 67,
    69–82, 98–101, 102, 104, 105,
    111, 113, 116, 128, 131, 150, 156,
    157
    complete contract 59, 61, 62, 66,
        68, 69–75, 76, 77, 78, 80, 81, 82,
        83
    duration (of . . .) 33, 34
    failures 36
    incomplete 9, 14, 31–3, 41, 62, 66
    labour . . . 22, 31, 32, 33–5, 40, 41
contract law 6, 21, 22, 86, 88
contract theory 59, 61–9, 70, 105
contracting 3, 4, 14, 15, 17, 19, 23, 151
contractual arrangement *see* contract
contractual hazards 17, 158
control xv, 10, 18, 30, 36, 42, 45, 48–9,
    59, 68, 69, 74, 75, 76, 79, 80, 86,
    87, 93, 96, 98, 105, 109, 117, 118,
    119, 132, 133, 136, 142, 155, 157,
    158
Cooper, J. 95
cooperation 19, 32, 33, 40, 41, 45, 59,
    63, 67, 78, 149
coordination 10, 30, 35, 37, 41, 44, 47,
    48, 50, 59, 60, 61, 64, 67, 68, 69,
    71, 72, 73, 75, 77, 78, 79, 81, 82,
    92, 93, 94, 97, 103, 149
Coriat, B. 45
corporate control 120
corporate culture *see* organizational
    culture
corporate governance xiv, 2, 108, 119
Crawford, R. G. 32, 41
credibility 16, 23, 60, 99, 102
credible commitments 8, 9, 15, 33
criminal market *see* illegal market
Cyert, R. 45

Davis, L. E. 30, 89, 128
Debreu, G. 3
debt 17, 18, 48, 49, 90
demography 149

Demsetz, H. A. 35, 44
discrete structural analysis 6, 9
discretionary power *see* power
disintegration 103–4 116
    see also vertical integration
division 2, 40, 43, 44, 45, 46, 51,
    101, 102, 110, 113, 114, 115, 116,
    118
divisionalization *see* division
Dixit, A. 12
Dosi, G. 12
Dow, G. 35, 42
Dugger, W. 44

Eccles, R. 3
economies of scale 92, 93, 95, 115,
    127, 134, 135, 142, 157, 158,
economies of scope 113, 114
efficiency xiii, 3, 4, 6, 14, 15, 17, 18,
    19, 21, 23, 24, 32, 35, 43, 44, 45,
    48, 50, 86, 88, 93, 102, 103, 104,
    105, 109, 110, 111, 112, 113, 114,
    117, 118, 119, 120, 121, 122, 135,
    150, 155, 156, 158, 159
Elton, G. R. 155
employment contract *see* labour
    contract
employment relationship xiii, 2, 31,
    32, 41, 42
enterprise xiv, 17, 90, 91, 92–6, 97, 98,
    99, 101, 102, 105, 106, 107, 109,
    110, 111, 112, 113, 114, 116, 117,
    118, 119, 120, 121, 122, 158
equity 17, 18, 49, 51, 107, 109, 110,
    112
evolutionary theory 1
executive committee 79–80
    see also Board of Directors
exit 41
exploitation 158
externalities 116

Fama, E.
fiat 23, 35–6, 40, 45
financial assets 46
financial market 46, 48, 120
firm xiii, 2, 10, 11, 18, 19, 21, 22, 23,
    30, 34, 39, 45, 50, 52, 59, 60, 61,
    62, 65, 66, 67, 69–72, 73, 74, 76,
    77, 81, 82, 83, 86, 87, 88, 89, 93,

94, 101, 104, 105, 107, 108, 109,
    111, 112, 115, 117, 120, 122, 132,
    134, 135, 138, 158
  as nexus of contracts 22, 31
Fisher, S 13.
forebearance 22
franchising 48, 96
free rider 18
Freeman, J. 3
frequency (of transactions) 6, 36, 37,
    38, 39, 44, 75, 129
Freris, A. 92
Friedland, R. 14
Friedman, M. 3
fundamental transformation 9, 60, 61,
    64, 67
Furubotn, E. 2

game theory 1
general equilibrium 3
Gérard-varet, L. A. 65, 83
Gintis, H. 17
governance *see* governance structure
governance structure 6, 7, 15, 18, 19,
    30, 31, 34, 35, 36, 42, 43, 46, 52,
    69, 87, 101, 132, 142
government bureaucracy *see*
    bureaucracy
Greif, A. 97, 99, 152
Grossman, S. 62, 67, 68, 73, 82

Hamamdjan, P. xiii, xiv, 35
Hamilton, G. 7
Hannan, M. 3, 14
Hansmann, H. 18
Hart, O. 6, 62, 67, 68, 73, 82
Hatchuel, A. 70, 73, 74
Hewett, A. 92
H-form 11
hierarchy (ies) xiii, xiv, 1, 7, 11–12, 22,
    30, 32, 35–42, 46, 48, 49, 50, 68,
    69, 71, 75, 76, 77, 79, 91, 92, 101,
    102, 103, 110, 158, 159
  industrial hierarchy 87, 89, 90–93,
    95, 102, 103, 104, 105, 106,
    109, 110, 111, 112, 117, 118,
    119, 122
hierarchical intensity 37–8
hierarchical relationship 31, 35–42,
    68, 73, 74

Hirschman, A. 41
Holmstrom, B. 83
Homans, G. 1
horizontal aggregation 102, 111, 113,
    122
horizontal integration *see* horizontal
    aggregation
hostages xv, 132
human assets xiii, xiv, 19, 31–42, 45,
    46, 102, 104
hybrid forms xiv, 2, 6, 7, 30, 35, 45,
    46, 48, 49

implementation 34, 37, 62, 73, 76, 79
  implementation theory 63–5
incentive 10, 16, 30, 31, 33, 34, 37, 44,
    45, 46, 48, 50, 51, 59, 61, 62,
    64–6, 70, 75, 77, 80, 81, 82, 105,
    130, 131, 133, 136, 150, 152, 157,
    158, 159
incentive scheme *see* incentive
incomplete contract *see* contract
increasing returns 156
industrial associations 86, 92–3, 101,
    104, 117
inefficiency *see* efficiency
information 3, 37, 43, 44, 46, 51, 63,
    64, 65, 66, 67–8, 73, 74, 76, 80,
    81, 88, 90, 92, 102, 104, 105, 112,
    114, 115, 118, 122, 133, 136, 137,
    138, 140, 141, 152, 153
innovation 11, 52, 61, 68, 69, 70, 71,
    76, 79, 80, 81, 82, 150, 151, 152,
    157
institution 61, 64, 66, 69, 72, 86, 87,
    88, 89, 90, 105, 117, 122, 127,
    130, 133, 139, 142, 149, 150, 151,
    152, 153, 154, 156–9
institutional arrangement xiii, xiv,
    30, 31, 35, 89, 128, 130, 131, 142,
    143
institutional economics 23, 128, 139
    see also new institutional
    economics
institutional environment xiii, xiv, xv,
    7, 36, 47, 88, 89, 103, 104, 118,
    120, 121, 127, 128, 129, 139, 142,
    143
integration 71–2

see also horizontal aggregation and
vertical integration
interest groups 20, 86
intermediate goods 3, 15, 63, 64, 73,
75, 78, 157
intermediate product market *see*
intermediate goods
internal spot market 34, 40, 62
investment 9, 10, 17, 18, 49, 62, 63,
67, 68, 100, 102, 108, 109, 120,
157
specific investment 63, 64, 65, 66,
68, 71, 72, 73, 81, 82, 104, 116,
132, 137,
Invisible Hand 1

Jensen, M. 31, 45
J-form xiv, 11, 43, 44, 45, 46, 47
joint ventures 11, 12
Jones, G. E. 48
Joskow, P. xiv, xv, 7, 15, 37, 104

Kahneman, D. 14
Kandel, E. 97, 99
Kenney, R. 15
Klein, B. 15, 32, 41
knowledge 20, 22, 60, 71, 73, 74, 75,
76, 79, 149, 156
Koopmans, T. 3
Kopp, P. 138
Kreps, D. 5, 16,
Kroll, H. 93
Krueger, A. 8
Kuhn, T. 5
Kunreuther, H. R. 14

labour market 3, 14, 18–19, 41, 103
see also contract (labour contract)
Laffont, J. J. 62, 64, 65, 66, 75
Landes, W. 21
Law Merchant xv, 151–2
learning 61, 70, 139, 150, 151
Llewellyn, K. N. 10
lock-in 41, 44, 60, 64

Macfarlane, A. 154
Machiavelli 9
macroeconomics 118, 122
maladaptation 46, 47
see also adaptation

management theory 59, 72, 73
managerial discretion 45, 46, 50
March, J. 5, 9, 31, 45, 52
market economy xv, 35, 86, 87, 88, 89,
93, 94, 95, 98, 99, 101, 102, 103,
104, 105, 109, 110, 113, 114, 117,
118, 121, 122, 141, 158
market failure 23
market power 115, 116, 122, 134
markets 1, 2, 6, 7, 10, 11, 12, 16, 21,
22, 35, 37, 45, 46, 48, 49, 52, 59,
62, 63, 67, 75, 79, 86, 87, 88, 89,
101, 102, 112, 113, 115, 119, 120,
129, 130, 131, 134, 135, 136, 138,
139, 140, 141, 142, 150, 152, 154,
155, 156, 158
illegal markets xv, 101, 127, 128,
131, 132, 133–5, 138, 139, 140,
141, 142, 143
informal markets 101, 140
Marx, K. 23, 156
marxism 96, 158
Masten, S. 7, 22, 31, 32, 36, 48
maximization (principle of . . .) 2
McManus, J. C. 31
Means, G. C. 45
Meckling, W. H. 31, 45
Menard, C. xiii, xiv, 32, 35, 37, 47, 48
M-form xiv, 43, 44, 45, 46, 47, 51
Michels, R. 8
microanalytics xiv, 23, 24, 128, 129
microeconomics 122, 150
Milgrom, P. 89, 121
Miller, M. H. 17, 48
Mintzberg, H. 34, 73
Mitchell, W. C. 24
Modigliani, F. 17, 48
Modigliani-Miller theorem 17, 48
Moe, T. 3, 20
monopoly 15, 17, 87, 93, 94, 100, 102,
103, 106, 107, 109, 112, 113, 114,
115, 116, 119, 121, 122, 128, 132,
134, 135, 137, 154, 155, 156
Moore, M. H. 135, 136
moral hazard 65
multidivisionalization *see*
divisionalization
Muramatsu, K. 41

natural selection 2, 3, 101

Nelson, R. R. 3, 12
neoclassical economics 1, 151
network 39, 48, 51, 59, 111, 114, 115, 116, 138, 139, 152
new institutional economics 5, 24, 35, 127, 128–133, 137, 142
nonseparability (of tasks) *see* separability
North, D. C. xiii, xiv, xv, 7, 30, 89, 128, 142

obligational market 34, 40, 62, 64
oligopoly 11, 94
opportunism xiv, xv, 7, 8, 9, 32, 34, 36, 39, 41, 42, 44, 45, 46, 49, 50, 51, 60, 61, 64, 69, 70, 77, 78, 80, 102, 114, 116, 129, 131–3, 136, 157, 158
optimality 24, 32, 33, 67, 68
second best 65
optimum *see* optimality
organization xiii, 1, 2, 4, 5, 6, 9–10, 13, 17, 19, 21, 22, 23, 30, 31, 32, 33, 34, 35, 36, 37, 40, 41, 42, 43, 45, 46, 47, 48, 49, 51, 52, 59, 60, 61, 67, 70, 76, 80, 81, 82, 86, 88, 93–6, 99, 104, 105, 107, 109, 120, 122, 127, 128, 129, 132, 133, 135, 136, 137–9, 140, 141, 142, 151, 152, 156, 158, 159
organization theory 9, 10, 11, 23, 24, 31, 45, 48, 52
organizational culture 10, 42
organizational design 4, 44, 45, 47
organizational forms 11, 59
ownership 87, 106, 108, 112
see also property rights

Pareto, V. 24
Pfeffer, J. 12, 14
physical assets 18, 33, 42, 46, 60, 102, 103, 104
politics 3, 13, 19–21, 127, 131, 142, 152–6
population ecology 14
Posner, R. 21
power 1, 12–21, 23, 32, 35, 36, 39, 42, 45, 46, 49, 50, 51, 52, 68, 72, 76, 77, 80, 81, 130
Power, E. 155

price 2, 16, 22, 30, 75, 78, 90, 93, 97, 98–101, 115, 135, 136, 140, 150, 157
price control 88, 100
price mechanism *see* price
pricing *see* price
primitive teams 34, 40, 62
principal-agent *see* agency; agency theory
private ordering xv, 99, 131, 132, 151, 152
privatization xv, 86, 87, 88, 89, 94, 96, 98, 102, 103, 104, 105, 106–12, 115, 116, 117, 118, 119, 121, 122
product market 3, 13, 14, 15, 18–19, 63, 94, 158
production association 92–4, 96, 99, 101, 102, 105
professional bureaucracy 34
profit 74, 92, 96, 100, 101, 120, 134
profit maximization 3, 4, 8, 101
profitability 44, 101
project contract 59, 60, 66, 68, 71, 72, 74, 76, 78–80, 81, 82
property rights xv, 4, 6, 20, 50, 86, 87, 88, 128, 143, 149, 150, 151, 152, 153, 154, 155
public ordering xv, 19, 99, 131
public ownership 107
public policy 17
Putnam, R. 149
Putterman, L. 17

quasimarket relationship 39, 40

rational choices 127, 129
rationality 1, 2, 24, 65, 70, 127, 128, 130, 151
Rebitzer, J. 23
redeployability *see* redeployable
redeployable 6, 17, 18, 41, 46, 49, 51, 103
regulation 19, 42, 47, 107, 111, 115, 116, 122, 130, 134, 136, 141, 157
relational team 34, 40, 62, 67
remediableness 7, 20, 21, 23, 24
rent 23, 32, 42, 65, 70
reputation 10, 16, 18, 41, 152
residual claimants *see* residual rights

residual rights 18, 49, 59, 61, 66–8, 69,
71, 72, 74, 75, 76, 77, 78, 79, 80,
81, 82,
see also property rights
resource dependency 14
revelation principle 66
Richter, R. 2
Roberts, J. 89, 121
routines 10, 33, 35, 70, 74, 75
and routinization 37, 39, 44, 70, 71
Ruggiero, V. 140, 141
rules xiv, 16, 18, 20, 36, 50, 61, 70, 127,
128, 130, 131, 137, 139, 142, 154,
155, 157, 158

safeguard 14, 15, 46
salary *see* wages
satisficing 2
Schanze, E. 48
Schelling, T. 127, 134, 135, 139, 142
Schmalensee, R. xiv, xvi
science xv, 149, 156
selective intervention 9, 10
separability (of tasks) 33, 34, 40, 41,
62, 64, 69
Shelanski, H. 7, 15
Simon, H. 1, 2, 8, 9, 22, 24, 31, 35
simple hierarchy 39, 40
site specificity xiv, 42, 112
Smith, A. 1, 23
social capital 149
social choice function 63
specific assets *see* asset specificity
Speidel, R. 10
Spulber, N. 92, 93
state (role of) 152–6
state-owned enterprise 86, 87, 97, 103,
105, 116, 121
Stigler, G. 3, 12, 20, 21, 127, 130, 133
Stone, K. 19
strategic behavior 12, 116, 134
strategy 37, 41, 43, 49, 59, 66, 76, 79,
80, 104–5, 129
Stubbs, W. 155
supervision 74
system analysis 1, 4–5

taylorian enterprise 59
team production 157
technology xv, 11, 34, 39, 42, 45, 52,

62, 63, 67, 137, 139, 149, 150,
153, 156–9
Teece, D. J. 12, 43, 44, 48
T-form 11, 12
Thorelli, H 48
Tirole, J. 5, 62, 64, 65, 66, 75, 87
trade association 97–8, 102, 103, 104,
105, 109, 117, 118, 119, 121
trade-off 30, 33, 39, 43, 44, 49, 65, 75
transaction 6, 9, 10, 13, 18, 30, 35, 36,
41, 43, 44, 45, 47, 48, 50, 104,
109, 111, 127, 128, 129, 130, 131,
132, 133, 134, 135, 136, 137, 138,
139, 142, 143, 151, 157
attributes of . . . xiii, 6, 36–7, 40, 42,
43, 52, 129
transaction costs xiii, xv, 3, 4, 5, 6, 7,
13, 17, 30, 40, 41, 42, 43, 49, 51,
69, 87, 92, 113, 128, 129, 130, 134,
137, 140, 141, 142, 150, 153, 156,
157, 159,
transaction cost economics xiii, xv, 1,
5–7, 9, 10, 11, 13, 14, 15, 17, 19,
21, 23, 24, 30, 31, 33, 35, 36, 37,
42, 43, 44, 45, 47, 48, 50, 51, 52,
59, 60, 82, 87, 129, 149
transactional *see* transaction
Turvani, M. xiv, xv
Tversky, A. 14

U-form xiv, 43, 44, 45, 46, 47
uncertainty 6, 9, 33, 36, 38, 41, 42, 43,
44, 46, 47, 50, 62, 66, 68, 71, 82,
88, 102, 109, 118, 122, 129, 131,
133, 136, 137–9,
unions 19, 40–42
utilitarianism 129, 130, 133, 139
utility 128, 129, 133, 136
and utility function 63, 64, 65, 82

Van Hoomissen, T. 19
Veblen, T. 24
vertical aggregation *see* vertical
integration
vertical integration xv, 15, 18, 47, 52,
95, 96, 102–3, 111, 113, 114, 115,
116, 122, 132, 133, 137, 140, 142
voice 41, 42
vouchers 107, 108, 120, 121

wages 41, 69, 92, 120
Wallis, J. 157
Weber, M. 70
Weitzmann, M. 75
White, H. 3
Williamson, O. E. xiii, xiv, 4, 6, 7, 8,
  10, 11, 12, 17, 19, 21, 22, 30, 31,
  32, 33, 35, 36, 37, 38, 41, 42, 43,
  45, 46, 47, 48, 51, 60, 61, 62, 64,
  67, 68, 69, 87, 80, 128, 131, 142

Winter, S. G. 3, 12,
Woodward, J. 52
work (organization of) 30, 31, 34,
  42, 76
worker-managed enterprises 17, 18,
  120
worker-management enterprises 97,
  120

zone of acceptance 23